A History of Wales
1815–1906

WELSH HISTORY TEXT BOOKS

WELSH HISTORY TEXT BOOKS—VOLUME 3

A History of Wales
1815–1906

D. GARETH EVANS

UNIVERSITY OF WALES PRESS
CARDIFF
1989

British Library Cataloguing in Publication Data
Evans, D. Gareth, *1948–*
  A history of Wales, 1985–1906
   1. Wales, 1837–190–1
   I. Title
  942.9081

ISBN 0–7083–1027–3
    0–7083–1028–1 Pbk

Typeset in Wales by Megaron, Cardiff
Printed in England by Richard Clay Ltd., Bungay

I GOFIO NHAD A MAM

DAVID JOSEPH A GWEN EVANS

Preface

This is the third volume of a trilogy on the history of modern Wales. During the last two decades numerous scholars have focused their attention on the nineteenth century, and the debt which this work owes to those historians is immeasurable. It is hoped that they will accept this volume as a token of my gratitude.

A number of colleagues and friends have encouraged and helped me during the preparation of this book. Emeritus Professor Ieuan Gwynedd Jones offered invaluable and stimulating advice. Mr Richard Carter of the Welsh Joint Education Committee initially encouraged me to tackle this project and I owe him a special word of gratitude. The Principal and staff of Trinity College, Carmarthen, and my colleagues in the history department, are to be commended for their support and comfort during one particularly difficult period.

The University of Wales Press, and Susan Jenkins, in particular, have guided me safely through the various stages of publication, and I am enormously grateful to them for their many kindnesses.

The final acknowledgement is probably the most profound of all. Emeritus Professor Glanmor Williams read the whole manuscript and made many valuable suggestions. Whatever defects remain are my own. I am deeply grateful to him for his advice, encouragement, and kind support over the years.

Finally, I must mention my late parents. My father died a few years before this work started; but my mother lived to see its commencement. I sincerely hope that they would have liked this book, for it is dedicated to them.

St David's Day, 1989   D. GARETH EVANS

Contents

Maps

The Publishers wish to thank the following for permission to use material whose copyright is in their possession:

Oxford University Press for the map of Wales published in *Rebirth of a Nation: Wales, 1880–1980* by Kenneth O. Morgan in 1981. Also for the map entitled 'The March on Newport' published in *The Last Rising* by D.J.V. Jones in 1985.

Mrs Mair Wynne Evans for the map entitled 'Distribution of Works' Schools' published in *Education in Industrial Wales 1700–1900* (Avalon Books, Cardiff, 1971).

Abbreviations

MAP 1. The Counties of Wales (to 1973)

1. Agriculture and People 1815–1850

Introduction

IT is estimated that the population of Wales grew from *c*.489,000 in 1750 to *c*.530,000 in 1780. Certainly by the time of the first census in 1801, growth was well advanced, with some 587,000 people living in Wales. The most significant rises in population occurred in those areas where economic activity was most marked, and the counties of Denbigh, Flint, Monmouth, and Glamorgan experienced a rapid expansion as birth-rates grew and as migrants were increasingly attracted to new industrial communities. Even famines and epidemics were unable to check the general upward turn in population patterns after 1750.

Demographic changes put considerable pressure on the propertied classes in Welsh society and, following the Restoration, there was a gradual concentration of property into fewer hands. Rising rentals, mineral profits, and an expanding trade provided substantial returns for enterprising landowners. Demographic changes of another kind, which had commenced in the late Stuart period, were also having a profound effect on the gentry class; in many county families the male line had failed and long-established dynasties were simply disappearing from the social scene. Indeed, around 40 per cent of the estates of Montgomeryshire vanished in the seventy years before 1760 and, by the middle of the eighteenth century, many Welsh estates had fallen into the hands of absentee English or Scottish landowners.

From around 1750 an increase in prices brought fresh opportunities for the more substantial farmers, who could invest their surplus capital in agricultural improvements in order to meet the growing demands for food. For the agricultural labourers, however, it was a different picture altogether. They experienced a fall in living standards and became increasingly vulnerable to the effects of demographic growth, increases in food prices, and fluctuations in employment. Many were forced to seek alternative sources of employment, and growing numbers encroached on the commons. As landlords enclosed these lands, hundreds of labouring people were deprived of the right to enjoy the benefits of the commons, and many were compelled to leave their native districts. Some simply roamed the countryside in search of employment, while others were attracted to the new industrial centres. The pressures of rising population, land hunger and soaring prices, especially in the years after 1760, swelled the numbers of paupers, squatters, and vagrants.

From the mid eighteenth century onwards there was a growing indication of improvement in agriculture, and the general trend was towards stock-raising and meat production. As London's population increased, the demand for Welsh beef grew accordingly and, by the middle years of the eighteenth century, over 30,000 cattle and sheep were moved annually by the drovers across the Welsh border to the English markets. Agricultural improvement also led to the land being cultivated more efficiently, and enterprising landlords took a greater interest in new scientific methods of cultivation and crop rotation. Agricultural societies were also set up — the first being the Breconshire County Society in 1755 — to promote sound practice and encourage a more enterprising attitude among farmers. Farmers in the more fertile lowland valleys and coastal plains benefited considerably from these new methods. The small farmers, however, found it difficult to survive and were forced to seek alternative ways of subsidizing their paltry incomes. Many in north and mid Wales turned to the woollen industry in an effort to improve their economic and social plight.

General Features and Trends

In the nineteenth century, agriculture occupied a declining position in the Welsh economy, and yet it still played an important role in the public mind, at least until the third quarter of the century. There were probably two reasons for this: first, it provided the growing population of Wales with the bulk of its food; and second, in the period up to the 1870s, the ownership of land had conferred a political and social position in the community. Population grew in all the Welsh counties up to

1841, in both industrial and rural districts. Thereafter, the pace slackened, markedly in the rural counties, while the population in the industrial counties of Glamorgan and Monmouth continued to surge ahead. It has been widely recognized that, of the net migration of 388,000 people from rural Wales in the period 1851–1911, there was a net inflow of 320,000 into the Glamorgan and Monmouthshire coalfields. The impact on population distribution in the Principality was quite astounding: the industrial settlements had acted as demographic magnets, attracting large numbers from the rural counties. Statistical evidence indicates that, whereas 80 per cent of the Welsh people lived in rural and non-urbanized areas at the beginning of the nineteenth century, by 1911 only 20 per cent lived in such areas. The pace of migration accelerated in the second half of the century, and the years between 1851 and 1911 saw a significant decrease of 45.8 per cent in the numbers involved in Welsh agriculture.

Throughout most of our period Welsh farming was mixed in character, with an emphasis on livestock and dairying. There were obvious regional variations, with the north Wales counties of Anglesey, Caernarfon and Merioneth concentrating on cattle-rearing, whereas Denbigh, Flint and Montgomery made butter and cheese. In the Vale of Glamorgan the emphasis was on arable for corn and roots for livestock farming and, elsewhere in south Wales, the breeding and rearing of store animals and the manufacture of butter and cheese prevailed. The farms were small, family concerns and, in the first half of the century, semi-subsistent farming predominated. The farmer could produce almost all his and his family's essential requirements in food and clothing. However, there was not much left over to sell and proceeds from the limited sales usually went to meet the financial demands of rent, tithes, land taxes, and labourers' wages.

The period after the Napoleonic wars was a prosperous one for Welsh corn farmers, with a number of circumstances combining to produce high prices. A series of bad harvests, an inflationary policy by the Government, and the difficulty of procuring cheap imports all played a part in securing favourable prices for the farmer. Although there were short crises in periods such as 1821–3 and 1832–6 caused by the good harvests, the general trend from 1815–46 was one of prosperity with domestic demand for wheat constant until the 1850s.

Those engaged in livestock and dairy farming were not as favoured during the period. After 1815 prices dropped substantially and farmers were forced to sell their stock in large quantities. In 1816 south Wales cattle were being sold at a third of their former price, and sheep at a half. In 1817 and 1818 the depression deepened and farmers were releasing stock at any price. Wet summers and poor harvests were producing a crisis situation and, although there was a brief respite in 1819–21, prices fell again in the period up to 1823. Prosperous conditions did return in the middle years of the 1830s.

The three summers from 1839 to 1841 were exceptionally bad and farmers everywhere had to buy corn at famine prices for their own use. Store-cattle prices were very low in 1839 and 1840, and in 1842–3 there was a general fall in prices. This has usually been attributed to the effects of Peel's tariff measures of 1842 and the slump in the iron trade. Farm prices in south-west Wales were also affected by the industrial areas, and a depression in the iron industry soon had harmful repercussions on the countryside. As we shall see in Chapter 9, agricultural conditions improved in the three decades following the repeal of the Corn Laws in 1846.

The Early Agricultural Societies

Most of the agricultural societies in the smaller counties of Wales seem to have reached their apogee in the latter part of the eighteenth century. However, some were revitalized during the peak years of the Napoleonic wars when agriculture experienced a period of unprecedented prosperity. Penry Williams of Penpont breathed some life into the Brecknock Society and, by 1817, a new set of rules had been formulated and the larger tenant farmers had been attracted as members. By the 1820s the Society was offering incentives to improve standards of livestock husbandry, and any gentleman wanting to impress county society felt that he had to join the Agricultural Society. J.B. Harford, the Bristol banker and aspiring parliamentary candidate, who became the owner of Peterwell and the force behind Lampeter's development, actually tried to upstage the

Cardiganshire County Society by offering a series of premiums to his own tenants. These premiums reflected a clear understanding of many of the needs of local farming.

Interest in the societies was, however, waning and, from 1821 to 1824, the Cardiganshire Society found its membership falling from 92 to 84. By the middle of the nineteenth century the old county agricultural societies were gradually giving way to local farming clubs and debating groups, in which practical tenant farmers played a major role. Radnorshire was particularly well served by such organizations — the Hay and Wyeside Agricultural Society first met in 1848, followed by the Knighton and Temeside associations in 1850, and the Knighton Farmers' Club in 1851.

Throughout most of the century the language barrier had been a formidable obstacle to the development of the agricultural society. The vast majority of the inhabitants of rural south-west Wales were monoglot Welsh-speakers, and yet there were hardly any books on Welsh agriculture written in the Welsh language. Thomas Johnes of Hafod did secure a Welsh translation of his *Cardiganshire Landlord's Advice to His Tenants*, thanks largely to the work of William Owen Pughe. But this was a rare instance and, even by the end of the nineteenth century, the Royal Commission on Land was compelled to conclude that language was still a major barrier to agricultural development.

Landowners and Agriculture

The amount of owner-occupier land in Wales was small throughout the century. Substantial estates were let out to tenant farmers, and the owners of smaller properties of under 1,000 acres often let their lands, while becoming tenants of other farms on neighbouring estates. The gentry and landowning classes derived their main source of income from their estates in the form of rents, and many drew the greater part of their incomes from royalties paid by the lessees of the mineral deposits. In Glamorgan and Monmouthshire this was very much true, particularly on an industrial estate such as that of the Marquis of Bute. In 1822 only £548 of the total estate revenue of £9,417 came from non-agricultural sources, such as minerals, royalties, manorial dues, and investments. However, by 1868 farm rents at £8,450 accounted for only 7.6 per cent of the total revenue of £109,659. One effect of this was that it enabled the estate to subsidize the shrinking agricultural sector and, in the mid nineteenth century, rents remained quite stable in the counties of Glamorgan and Monmouthshire, at a time when they were increasing considerably in other Welsh counties. In north Wales, also, the profits yielded by the slate quarries on Lord Penrhyn's extensive property were approximately double the revenue from his farm rents.

As most of their estates were let to tenants, most Welsh landlords were unimportant as agricultural producers. Their farming activities were largely confined to their home farms, which provided food for their household, and which became centres of experiments in farming techniques. C.R.M. Talbot of the Margam and Penrice estate introduced turnip husbandry on his farm at Penrice Castle, Gower, from 1844. Sir Hussey Vivian established a model farm in Gower in the same period. Landlords encouraged the agricultural societies and farming clubs and helped to found a number of them in the second half of the eighteenth and early part of the nineteenth centuries. Some, like Sir Watkin Williams Wynn of Wynnstay and Sir Charles Morgan of Tredegar, attempted to promote agriculture by setting up annual shows in the years after 1820.

Other landowners tried to promote agricultural improvement amongst their immediate tenantry. Lord Cawdor introduced superior horses on his south Wales estates for the use of his tenants at nominal prices. Many landlords decided that to enclose the commons and wastes was the surest way of promoting agricultural development. E.D. Evans has shown in his study of Wales in the eighteenth century that seventy-six Acts of Parliament were introduced in the period from 1801 to 1815, with the purpose of enclosing some 200,000 acres of land. Some of these, however, were never fully implemented. In the period after 1815 there was still some life in the enclosure movement, as the figures in Table 1.1 show. By the close of the 1860s enthusiasm was waning and there were no Inclosure Acts in the 1870s.

The coming of the railways, as we shall see, was a crucial development and many of the larger landowners became directors of the new companies. When the South Wales Railway

Table 1.1

Period	Number of Acts	Acres enclosed
1820s	3	360
Late 1830s	7	3,587
1840s	14	21,957
1850s	47	42,214
1860s	46	63,967

between Swansea and Carmarthen was constructed the company was supported by several enthusiastic landowners. In Glamorgan, John Nicholl Carne, Mr Homfray of Penllin, and Rowland Fothergill of Merthyr, became promoters of the Cowbridge to Merthyr Railway. In north Wales Lord Mostyn, the Merioneth landowner, was a strong advocate of the Aberystwyth and coastal railway. But there were some, even among the larger owners of land, who were apathetic and occasionally hostile to the introduction of railways. In 1845 Sir Richard Bulkeley Phillips of Picton Castle opposed the South Wales Railway project because it would cross some four miles of his property.

Landlords and Tenants

It is difficult to know to what extent all the landlords were involved in their estates, and the degree of participation varied from one estate to another. Estate management, so David Howell tells us, was a 'cooperative enterprise' between the landlords and their agents. Agents were usually local professional people, solicitors, auctioneers, and even retired army officers. Many often lacked a detailed knowledge of farming but, provided they were trustworthy and reasonably efficient in their business dealings, they could often be invaluable local servants for the landed interest. Agents were not always harsh in their relationships with tenants and, in many cases, displayed a keen and sensitive appreciation of the tenant's difficulties, as did the Wynnstay agent in 1826. It was the sub-agent who often upset the apple-cart and soured relations between landlord and tenant.

Absentee landlords were not as great a problem as was once thought, and the Welsh Land Commission at the end of the century acquitted them of this charge. It seems that absenteeism became less prominent as the century advanced, and evidence would suggest that most landowners did, in fact, devote some part of their annual incomes to improving their estates. Large landowners often invested sizeable amounts on their estates and David Howell and others have shown that it is important seriously to question the old Nonconformist and Radical allegations that the tenants were largely responsible for agricultural improvements. After the 1820s Welsh landowners undertook an increasing share of the repairs and improvements on their estates. The Bute and Ashburnham estate papers reveal a growing concern for estate improvements and repairs in the decades after 1820. There were substantial repairs on the Bute estate in the early 1840s and on the Ashburnham estate in the years 1830–2. C.R.M. Talbot of the Margam and Penrice estate insisted that his tenants, who farmed under annual agreements, bore the brunt of necessary repairs and, in return, he dutifully reduced rents by 10 per cent each year.

A sufficient body of evidence has been adduced to show that there was increased landlord investment on the large estates, particularly where there were incomes from mineral and urban property. The smaller estates, with restricted capital funds at their disposal, were more reluctant to spend on repairs. The larger owners, however, had the necessary capital and spent as much as 20–5 per cent of their gross incomes on estate improvements. For example, over a thirty-two year period, the 142,000 acre Wynnstay estate in north Wales could afford to spend just over 20 per cent of its gross annual rentals in this way. Many who carried out these substantial improvements received only a small return in rent increases on their outlay; and, on the Bute estate, returns from increased rents were negligible for most of the century.

Landowners often showed considerable sympathy for their tenants where rents were concerned. When times were difficult, tenants were permitted to accumulate arrears or to pay irregularly and at their own convenience. Rent allowances were organized on the Edwinsford and Court Derllys estate in Carmarthenshire in 1822. Even in the early 1840s when depression eroded the incomes of large and small estates, agents often had to persuade landowners to increase their rents. The smaller landowners naturally found it much more difficult to allow such compassionate rent schemes or to sustain reductions in income.

Agricultural Wage-earners

Welsh farms were usually small units and, because of the small-scale nature of farming, there was no pronounced class division between tenant farmers and the agricultural labourers and farm servants. The small, Welsh farmer usually worked the land alongside his labourers, and the scarcity of farms often meant that farmers' sons had to become labourers on neighbouring farms. The latter often achieved their ambition of becoming tenant farmers. This picture contrasts with that in most English districts where the distinction between farmers and labourers was usually clearly marked.

Wage-earners fell into two broad groups: the indoor farm servants, and the outdoor married labourers. The first category would include adults and children of both sexes. Children would often enter service at the age of nine, though it was customary for them to be accepted in the nine to thirteen age group. Those who were employed in this category were found board and lodging on the farm, and hired on an annual or half-yearly basis. These indoor farm servants played an important part in the household economy through to the end of the century. In the 1861 census, for example, we find that about a half of the hired labour force in Wales, and in the English counties of Cumberland and Westmorland, was of the indoor servant type. In other parts of England the ratio of indoor servants was far lower. The reasons for the survival of the indoor servant class in Wales would seem to be the following: in pastoral regions livestock needed close and constant supervision; restricted capital meant that the small-scale farmer was reluctant to part with money, and so he preferred to pay labourers in kind, by providing board and lodging; a shortage of good suitable homes for married labourers was a factor of some importance in tilting the balance in favour of the indoor servant; and finally there was the point already noted, namely, the absence of any class cleavage between farmer and labourer in Wales. The second category was the outdoor married labourer, a far more prominent figure in the English counties after the 1830s. He rented his cottage, either on the farms or in the nearby village, and he was usually hired on a weekly basis and, in many areas, provided with meals and light refreshment on the farms as part of his wage.

Working conditions and domestic circumstances were quite poor and there was little material improvement until the 1870s. Indoor servants worked from early morning until late into the night, and the married labourer's day could last from 5.0 a.m. to around 8.30 p.m. Although there were no fixed holidays or half-days before 1914, most farm servants were granted three or four days, or even a greater number of half-days a year for attending weddings, funerals, an eisteddfod, a local fair, or even a preaching festival. Wages in the early part of our period ranged from about 1*s*. a day in winter to 1*s*.6*d*. in spring and summer for the outdoor labourer. Areas in south-east Wales, closer to the ironworks, offered wages of 8*s*. to 10*s*. for a rural labourer in winter, and from 9*s*. to 12*s*. in summer. In the years from 1820 to the 1840s the drastic fall in farm prices produced a reduction in cash earnings. The Poor Law Commissioner for south Wales noted in 1837 that wages were generally low in the agricultural parts.

It would be misleading to assume that cash wages constituted the total earnings of the labourer. In the early part of the century the labourer had often been provided with a cottage and a garden at a low rent, a potato plot on the farmer's land, corn at a standard price, and fuel free of charge. These perquisites were widely granted in south-west Wales until the 1860s, and their cash value could be represented in the following way:

Fuel	26*s*. p.a.
Potato land	26*s*. p.a.
Rent-free cottage and garden	52*s*. p.a.

Or, to put it another way, where his cash wages were 9*s*. a week, they were raised to 11*s*. a week.

The real problem facing the outdoor farm labourer after 1815 was the want of regular employment, especially during the winter months. A few labourers were occasionally engaged on

farm improvements, but the vast majority, before the introduction of the New Poor Law system, were forced to rely on
parish relief. With the advent of a New Poor Law in 1834 able-
bodied labourers found it increasingly difficult to secure parish
assistance, and circumstances forced them into the workhouse.
Fortunately, the New Poor Law was not stringently applied in
all areas and unions would permit able-bodied workers to
receive outdoor rather than indoor relief. The more adventurous,
or perhaps the most desperate, went to Merthyr Tydfil in search
of work in the winter months, only to return to the farms as
conditions improved in summer.

Though the vast majority of agricultural wage-earners
existed in harsh and impoverished conditions, there is no
evidence to suggest that they were an extremely lawless or
violent group. Crimes of violence were virtually unknown
amongst rural inhabitants. Thefts of poultry, sheep, horses,
cattle, and barley were quite common in the countryside, and
the worst offenders seem to have been the cottagers and
squatters. Poaching was another common practice and, in the
period from 5 May 1846 to 1 April 1848, no fewer than 284
persons were convicted of offences against the Game Laws in the
Welsh Assizes and in the Quarter and Petty Sessions.

Wage-earners seemed completely uninterested in combining
to revolt or to riot against the authorities after the fashion of
their contemporaries in the southern and south-eastern counties
of England in the autumn and summer of 1830–1. The only
activities of any real significance in Wales occurred in east
Glamorgan and in Monmouthshire, where threatening 'Swing'
letters, disturbances, and burnings became transient features.
But there were no widespread disturbances in south-east Wales
in these pre-Reform years. One reason for this was that
labourers had regular employment, and wages tended to be
above the average rates. Another factor was that Wales was
predominantly a region of pastoral farming and of small-sized
farms, with a higher degree of family labour and, consequently,
with a lower incidence of conflict between employer and
labourer. Thirdly, the radical outpourings of the metropolitan
press had little influence on the monoglot Welsh-speaking wage-
earners. Finally, the scattered nature of farming militated
against the combination of agricultural workers.

The Impact of the Railways

In the early nineteenth century the marketing of agricultural produce in Wales was largely determined by three factors: climatic and physical conditions imposed restrictions on pastoral farming so that the major items of output comprised livestock, wool, butter, cheese, and eggs; the absence of large local markets meant that Wales had to export its products; and thirdly, land communications, linking Wales with the rest of Britain, were so poor and inadequate that coastal shipping was of the utmost importance to the rural economy.

Exports were usually of animals in store conditions to be fattened in more lush environments. They were taken on the long trek eastwards to markets in the Midlands and south-east England by the drovers, whose routes became the new arteries of communication. Much of the grain and dairy produce was sold to local purchasers, and the ascending industrial clusters of south-east Wales did little to change that traditional picture in the years preceding the advent of the railways. Agricultural products were often shipped along the coast to Bristol, as a marketing centre, and thence to the industrial towns of south Wales.

The inadequate communication links with south Wales imposed unbearable burdens on Welsh farmers and the resulting transport costs limited the influence of industrialization on Welsh farming in the pre-railway era. One good example of this problem would have been the marketing of butter, which was sent from south-west Wales over the hills to the industrial township of Merthyr. The two-way journey in one-horse carts usually took a week and accounted for a labourer's entire week's service. Communication difficulties also explain the purchasing policies of the Dowlais ironmasters, who preferred to feed their horses on grain imported from Ireland. Even after the South Wales Railway was constructed across the coastal plain, farmers in the Vale of Glamorgan found that transport links with the ironworks remained poor and they thus preferred to send their livestock to the ironworks by road.

The railways did, however, have a significant impact on farming in Wales. Transport costs were reduced as the droving system gradually faded out of existence. As the drovers disappeared so did the costs of toll payments, grass for animals, shoeing of livestock, and beer and lodgings. But the railways not only reduced transport costs, they also provided a faster and more effective system of marketing; and this enabled farmers to produce fat cattle. Shipments of animals, and mainly fat pigs, from north Wales ports to Liverpool ended, so that whereas 12,072 pigs were shipped from the combined ports of north Wales in 1847, a mere sixty-five were shipped in 1855.

The railway system remodelled the marketing of livestock by influencing the decline of the fairs. Those fairs which were held on or near the railways tended to flourish at the expense of those located at a distance. The railways also enabled dealers to travel directly to the farms and to purchase cattle and livestock by means of private sales at the farmsteads. Areas actually far removed from the centres of demand could now fatten their animals rather than send them as stores to be fattened near towns and cities.

Coastal traffic in butter, cheese, and corn declined as the railway network spread throughout Wales. The rural areas of south Wales could now send their produce directly to the industrial towns, and Bristol's role as an agricultural entrepot came to an end. The railways, therefore, opened up the industrial markets of south-east Wales and the Midlands for the Welsh farmer.

Farmers often complained that the railway companies also brought problems to the Welsh economy; especially as they enhanced the possibility of flooding the Welsh markets with cheaper foreign goods. While the railways also produced higher prices for farm produce in those years before foreign competition threatened the markets, as prices increased so the landlords raised the rents, and this was a predominant feature of the third quarter of the nineteenth century.

In the long run, the railways did not change the traditional system of Welsh farming. The majority of Welsh farmers shared conservative, unadventurous attitudes which effectively militated against any basic changes in the nature of farming. Welsh peasant-tenants preferred to farm as cheaply as possible and they equated successful farming with low expenditure. The climate and physical landscape were additional factors constraining agricultural development in the nineteenth century.

SUGGESTED READING

E.D. Evans, *A History of Wales, 1660–1815* (Cardiff, 1976).

D.W. Howell, *Land and People in Nineteenth-Century Wales* (London, 1978).

A.H. John and G. Williams (eds.), *Glamorgan County History*, 5 (Cardiff, 1980).

Articles:

R.J. Colyer, 'Early Agricultural Societies in South Wales', *W.H.R.*, 12 (1984–5).

R.J. Colyer, 'The Conditions of Employment amongst the Farm Labour Force in Nineteenth-Century Wales', *Llafur*, 3 (1984).

D.W. Howell, 'The Agricultural Labourer in Nineteenth-Century Wales', *W.H.R.*, 6 (1972–3).

D.W. Howell, 'The Impact of Railways on Agricultural Development in Nineteenth-Century Wales', *W.H.R.*, 7 (1974–5).

2. Industry and Communications 1815–1850

Introduction

DURING the eighteenth century the pace of industrial change accelerated for a number of reasons. The first was undoubtedly the widespread use of new technology. The use of steam-power brought efficiency and quickened the pace of production and, from 1775 onwards, more efficient methods of hauling and improvements in the techniques of blast employed in smelting followed the invention of Watt's steam-engine. The gradual use of coal to smelt pig-iron helped the iron industry expand considerably. A second factor of some importance was the inflow of capital from England. Merchants from Bristol, London, and the Midlands invested large sums of money in industrial ventures. The third factor which precipitated industrial production was the impact of war. The Seven Years' War (1756–63), the American War of Independence (1775–83) and the French Revolutionary and Napoleonic wars (1793–1815) stimulated new demands for iron, copper, lead, tin plate, and coal. Perhaps it was the iron industry which prospered most of all under the stimulus of war: in the 1740s the Pentyrch furnace and forge were rebuilt, as was the forge at Melingriffith; and in 1753 Isaac Wilkinson bought the Bersham Ironworks in north-east Wales and immediately expanded its productive capacity. In 1759 the Dowlais Iron Company was formed by a partnership of nine, the majority of whom were English investors. In 1763 John Guest and Isaac Wilkinson took out a lease on the Plymouth Ironworks. Two years later, a forge and furnace were set up at Cyfarthfa. In 1777 Richard Crawshay joined Anthony Bacon at Cyfarthfa, and a period of rapid expansion began.

War also stimulated the growth of the copper industry and from 1740 onwards English merchants developed non-ferrous smelting industries in west Glamorgan and south-east Carmarthenshire. By 1750 about a half of the copper produced in

Britain came from the Swansea area, and by 1800 west Glamorgan was the principal centre of copper smelting in the world. In Anglesey, also, an important copper industry developed; particularly after Thomas Williams had established the Parys Mine Company in 1778. By 1790 Williams had set up works in Flintshire, Lancashire, and south Wales had acquired a monopoly over British copper.

Coal production also expanded in the period. Output in north Wales increased from 80,000 tons in 1750 to 110,000 tons in 1775, while in the south there was a similar overall upward trend from 140,000 tons in 1750 to 650,000 tons in 1775. A combination of factors stimulated the coal industry: the adoption of Newcomen's steam-pump for pumping and winding; the use of coal as a substitute for charcoal in the smelting of pig-iron; the invention of Cort's puddling process in 1783–4; the expansion of the non-ferrous industries in the Swansea area produced an increased demand for fuel; and, finally, the expansion of the iron industry after 1760 provided an additional fillip.

Most industries were affected by these changes and, although a few experienced only modest advances, the vast majority expanded steadily. As industries developed, so transport facilities progressed in response to the industrial challenge. The turnpike system was extended into Wales after 1750, and by 1770 a reasonably efficient road network had been created. Maritime trade also helped to promote prosperity, as hundreds of small vessels traded along the Welsh coast. Shipping tonnage increased at Swansea from 30,631 in 1768 to 120,582 in 1793. In the north-east, Chester and Deeside exported 92,000 tons of lead and lead ore in the period from 1758 to 1777.

In the early and mid eighteenth century, therefore, the ground had been carefully prepared for major industrial and economic changes in Wales, and a variety of developments had promoted economic growth: population growth had set the pace; agricultural changes and expanding trade had contributed; urban life had become more vigorous; outside investors were pumping money and entrepreneurial skills into the Principality; and improved communications oiled the economic machinery and hastened the exchange of goods and services.

The Copper Industry

From the late eighteenth century until the early twentieth century the county of Glamorgan alone produced 70 per cent of the British output of copper. If the areas of Llanelli and Burry Port in Carmarthenshire are included, then the proportion would be nearer to 90 per cent. In the early nineteenth century the south Wales region was the main world centre of copper smelting. Though small in terms of the number of people employed, the non-ferrous industries did make substantial contributions to the local and national economies: they provided employment in the smelting works; they helped to diversify the regional economy and to provide resistance against depression; they promoted the area's coal industry; and, lastly, these industries forged international links through the export trade.

The copper and non-ferrous metal industries were largely confined to the areas of west Glamorgan and south-east Carmarthenshire. A number of very important reasons accounted for this: coal deposits were readily available and, in the coastal patch between Port Talbot and Llanelli, they outcropped; coal could, therefore, be purchased cheaply and this point was noted by the copper magnate, Pascoe Grenfell, in 1812; south Wales had the further advantage of relative proximity to the major early sources of ores, Cornwall and Devon; the area also had good ports to which ores could later be brought from much farther afield, and from which the processed metal could be sent to Bristol, Birmingham, Liverpool, London, and overseas; the navigable waters of the rivers Tawe, Nedd, and Llwchwr facilitated the movement of ores to the immediate vicinity of the coal-mines and provided water for processing and power; finally, it must be emphasized that the range and richness of the different types of coal — anthracite, coking and gas — produced in the western districts of the coalfield were important locational factors.

For much of the century it is often difficult to assess changes in output and employment. The figures relating to the supplies of copper ores sold at 'ticketing' in Cornwall and Swansea do indicate a continuous increase in output until the mid nineteenth century. Of the total purchases of 278,000 tons of copper ores in 1856, around 64,000 tons were bought for three smelting works in Carmarthenshire, and the remaining 214,000 tons by the smelters in Glamorgan. By the middle of the nineteenth century the production of copper ores in Britain was declining rapidly, and this was accompanied by an increase in the importation of foreign and colonial ores to Swansea. This increase continued until the 1880s, after which there was a steep fall until the virtual end of the trade in the 1920s. The copper trade was, however, of immense importance to the Swansea region and, in 1858, the value of the output of copper there was £3½ million.

The numbers employed in the non-ferrous metal industries grew threefold from 1770 to 1850, and fourfold by 1860. In the decade after 1860 there was, in fact, a sharp fall in the numbers employed in copper smelting. In 1851 the number of workers employed in the non-ferrous metal industries of south Wales was 2,000. Yet the important factor was the way in which the industry stimulated the employment prospects of the area. It was calculated in 1823 that the smelting establishments on the River Tawe alone, with the collieries and shipping dependent on them, supported a population of from 8,000 to 10,000 souls.

In north Wales the picture was much bleaker by the beginning of our period. Thomas Williams, one of the great copper entrepreneurs, had died in 1800. By 1815 the number of men employed in the copper mines had diminished to about 600. Between 1801 and 1811 the population of Amlwch had dwindled by more than 700. There was a brief respite in the period 1811–21, but before 1840 the mines had fallen on depressed days and this was really the beginning of the end. Thomas Williams's son, Owen, had co-operated briefly with Pascoe Grenfell, the Cornish mine-owner, until about 1825. In that year Williams left the firm, though Grenfell battled on and continued smelting at Holywell until 1842. There was a short-lived revival again in the 1860s but by 1871 it appears that mining had been abandoned in Anglesey. Not so in Caernarfonshire, however, where an annual output of copper of 8,000 tons was produced as late as 1860. The census returns do reveal, however, a considerable drop in the number of copper miners from 318 in 1851 to 14 in 1891, and the overall trend was one of decline.

Almost all the copper entrepreneurs and investors were Englishmen and, between 1750 and 1850, the groups responsible for the largest additions to smelting capacity in south Wales were drawn from copper mining in Anglesey and Cornwall. One of the more important dynasties was founded by John

Vivian of Truro. In 1809 he formed a partnership with his sons, Hussey and John Henry Vivian, initially with an investment of £50,000, to set up the Hafod Works in Swansea. Vivian and Sons expanded largely by reinvestment of profits, so that by the 1880s it had a capital value of over £1,200,000. In the period before the 1880s most of the firms were partnerships. It was from the 1880s that limited companies emerged and by 1895 nine out of every sixteen firms fell into this category.

From the very start there was a stong tendency to create monopolistic arrangements in the non-ferrous industries and, from 1737 to 1779, the smelting firms of Glamorgan and Bristol were closely in agreement. In the period from 1815 to the early 1820s there was much keener competition in the industry and a struggle took place between Grenfell and Co., Vivian and Sons, Freeman and Co., and Nevill and Co. of Llanelli. In 1824 a Copper Trade Association was formed which embraced most of the prominent Glamorgan firms. The Association fixed prices at which manufactured copper could be sold and it lasted until the 1870s when keener international competition from countries like the USA and Chile forced its abandonment.

The major reason for the decline in copper production in the late nineteenth century was the prohibitive cost of transporting poorer grade ores from distant countries. After about 1825 the output of British copper ores failed to keep pace with the rapidly growing demand. Another factor was also the growth of copper mining abroad as the 'new' countries developed their mining activities. Cuba, Chile, Australia, and the USA entered the competitive field, and by the end of the nineteenth century the USA was the largest producer of copper. It has also been claimed that the indifference of Welsh copper firms to the taking of orders and the industry's monopolistic practices contributed to its eventual decline.

The Lead Industry

The American War of Independence and the French wars had had serious effects on lead mining in Britain. The spread of Napoleon's influence, the Berlin decrees, and the suspension of cash payments had virtually put an end to British trade with central and western Europe and the Mediterranean countries.

Exports of lead had fallen from over 14,000 tons in 1792 to less than 8,000 tons in 1808. It took some years to overcome the effects of the war, partly because of the slow recovery of some of the European markets, and partly because of the price fluctuations in the two decades following the peace of 1815. It was not until the 1840s that the lead industry revived in Britain. From then on, the home industry prospered almost everywhere and the production of ore increased to a maximum of 102,000 tons in 1856.

Lead mining in Wales was largely confined to two main regions: one extended from north Flintshire through Holywell, Mold and over the Denbighshire border; the other spread from north Cardiganshire into south Merionethshire and south-west Montgomeryshire. Of all the mining regions in Wales, that in north-west Wales contributed most to the British output of lead and zinc ores. From 1845 to 1938 Flintshire produced 10 per cent and Denbighshire 3 per cent of Britain's lead ore. In 1833 the price of ore had begun to rise and there was increased activity in north-east Wales. By 1845 Flintshire alone produced 9,119 tons out of a total Welsh output of 16,412 and, two years later, its output of 11,424 tons was well over double that of Cardiganshire. By 1850 gradual decline had set in and the yield of 11,475 tons in that year had dropped substantially to 3,007 tons in 1857. In Flintshire, despite much activity, the industry actually went from bad to worse. In 1852 Merllyn was the only mine to pay a dividend. The price of lead was now well below what the industry in Flintshire could afford, and there was a further fall in the price of shares. There was a slight recovery for some ten years after 1858 when capital again flowed freely into the region. The reasons for the steady decline after 1850 are not hard to find. Firstly, there were complaints from the mineowners about the high royalties charged by the landowners, though, in fairness, it should be noted that many had made considerable concessions in times of hardship. Secondly, the main hindrance was the perennial problem and expense of keeping mines free of surplus water. In addition, there was an urgent need to search for new ore deposits in areas where drainage would not pose too many difficulties.

Mines in Cardiganshire and Montgomeryshire produced just under 10 per cent of the total British output of lead ore and 12 per cent of the zinc ore. In 1815 it was reported that there were no flourishing mines in the area. From 1802 to 1808 only 250 tons of lead ore had been extracted at Esgair-mwyn, and the best mine was the old Cwmystwyth. An interesting new period commenced in the history of the Cwmystwyth and Nanteos mines in 1822, when they were leased to Sir George Alderson, an alderman of the city of London, and his brother Thomas. Within a short time they discovered at Cwmystwyth a vein which was apparently capable of producing 5,000 tons a year. From November 1826 to the following March some 13,235 tons were raised. Yet, although Cwmystwyth continued to produce well, the Aldersons, and a later Williams company, failed — largely on account of the severe depression in the industry. The turning-point was the year 1834 when John Taylor, who had contributed so much to the success of lead mining in Flintshire, took over the unexpired part of the Williams lease. A company was formed in which Taylor and his sons had the controlling interest, and work began on the famous Lisburne mines. By August 1835 a dividend of £10 a share was paid, and the Taylors were well and truly launched on a long and successful venture in Cardiganshire.

Taylor was one of the ablest engineers of his time and at the Lisburne mines he drove long levels to drain the workings and to open new ground; he built new reservoirs and cut fresh water channels to provide the machinery with power. The results fully justified his adventurous policies and the Lisburne mines operated from 1834 to 1893, during which period they produced 107,174 tons of lead ore, over 50,000 tons of blende from Frongoch, and a little copper ore. The total value of the output has been calculated at £1,338,793. The Taylors' success had the effect of attracting prospectors and capital into the area. In south-west Montgomeryshire, as in Cardiganshire, recovery began in earnest with the rise in prices after 1834. In neither area were all the mining ventures successful. Even in 1857, when there were around sixty mines operating in the county, only ten produced more than 200 tons each. Though the total output of lead ore reached almost 10,000 tons, a little over 7,000 tons came from only five mines — and the three Lisburne mines yielded 4,749 tons. In Montgomeryshire, of the 2,389 tons produced, Dylife yielded 828, Dyfngwm 376 and Llanerch-yr-Aur 312.

Towards the end of the 1860s production in Cardiganshire began to tumble, even though there was still a significant demand for lead. The decline cannot be blamed entirely on low prices. The most probable reason was the partial exhaustion of existing deposits and the failure to allocate funds for further exploration. The majority of mining promoters were obsessed with quick returns and easy profits. An additional factor was the financial malpractice endemic in the industry after 1870. The industry in mid Wales had acquired a bad reputation among investors. There were often far too many speculators, and a tendency to over-capitalize and waste expenditure on surface buildings and equipment. The reactions of the Taylor family are a good indication of the feelings of the industry, for as early as 1878 they had begun to pull out from the area and by 1893 they had completely withdrawn from Cardiganshire.

The Slate Industry of North Wales

Slate quarrying had not existed as an organized concern until the second half of the eighteenth century, and it was not until the nineteenth that slate became a universal roofing material in Wales. By 1815 the profits of the large Caernarfonshire concerns, Penrhyn and Dinorwic quarries, were rising steadily. The accounts of the Penrhyn quarry books for 1816–18 and 1820–27 manifest this:

Year	£.	s.	d.
1816	9,802	15	3
1817	12,570	5	2
1818	13,990	13	11
1820	14,910	11	$3\frac{1}{4}$
1821	16,398	3	$10\frac{1}{2}$
1822	25,850	19	$9\frac{1}{2}$
1823	30,026	0	$5\frac{3}{4}$
1824	32,057	9	4
1825	23,160	2	$5\frac{1}{2}$
1826	29,992	11	6
1827	34,303	10	10

The output of the slate quarries in Caernarfonshire increased from under 20,000 tons in 1786 to over 90,000 tons in 1831, and that of Merionethshire from about 500 tons to over 12,000 tons in the same period. This expansion was largely due to the increase in population and to the industrial revolution, both of which produced urgent demands for roofing materials for towns and factories. The French wars had checked the growth of the industry, and the imposition of heavy wartime taxes and the increasing costs of coastal shipment had depressed it. From 1816 to 1819 the building trade improved and, despite a brief lull between 1819 and 1822, trade recovered in the three years after 1822. From 1825 to 1830 stagnation again set in, with prices falling by nearly 30 per cent.

In the period after 1830 the slate industry continued to expand and actually had great difficulty in keeping pace with the demand for new factories and housing. By the 1830s the canals had reduced transport costs, but it was with the advent of the railways that really substantial savings were made. In the early 1840s Wales was still without railway communication, and it was not until the Cambrian and Central Wales lines reached Merionethshire, Montgomeryshire, and Radnorshire in the 1860s that these remote districts were brought into direct communication with their ports. The short local railways were of great importance to the industry, and the most successful of these was the Ffestiniog Railway completed in April 1836. The railway provided a quicker and cheaper method of transport, and the tonnage of slates transported from Ffestiniog quarries to Porthmadoc harbour grew from 4,275 tons in 1836 to a peak of 120,426 tons in 1882. In the Nantlle area, the Dorothea Quarry became the largest and most profitable concern — from 1849 to 1859 the total value of the slates sold rose from £5,427 to £16,630.

With the abolition in 1831 of the tax on slate carried coastwise, there was a substantial fall in the costs of production, and slates gradually began to replace tiles as a roofing material in London, Lancashire, the Midlands, and the large industrial conurbations. The onset of the 'Hungry Forties' affected the slate industry adversely, although this was to some extent counteracted by the railway boom of the 1840s which brought a marked improvement, stimulating new building programmes and so accelerating the demand for slates. There was also considerable expansion overseas and it was generally believed that the Hamburg fire of May 1842, which had effectively destroyed public buildings and over 2,000 houses, had given the Welsh slate industry its first real opportunity to export to Germany. In 1848, slates were sent to customers in Magdeburg. The Penrhyn Quarry mainly concentrated its export trade in America in the areas around Boston and New Orleans. The expansion of the Australian market provided a new opening, and from 1852 to 1856 large quantities of slates were sent from Porthmadoc to Liverpool, and thence to the Cape of Good Hope. The value of Welsh slates exported to western Europe actually trebled in the period from 1856 to 1880.

Wages in the north Wales industry were based on piece-work, and rates rose steadily in the second half of the nineteenth century. In 1843 'good quarrymen' were being paid 2s.6d. per day; by 1865 the rate had increased to an average of 3s.6d. The level of wages in the slate industry was usually higher than the prevailing agricultural rates in the area. Nevertheless, many of the quarrymen had smallholdings to supplement their industrial wages, and those who failed to make ends meet often emigrated from the quarrying areas. Emigration had begun in the eighteenth century and by the 1840s numbers had increased significantly. From 1795 to 1860, 1,146 persons left the Ffestiniog district for the USA. Emigrants usually settled in New York State; but there were other settlements in Pennsylvania, Wisconsin, and Ohio. In the early days of the industry the rate of immigration far outpaced that of emigration and the 1841 census returns show that the Bethesda district had the highest number of people born outside the area:

	Number of persons	*Those born outside the area*
Bethesda	7,967	1,030
Llanberis	6,986	685
Nantlle	6,281	423

In the parish of Ffestiniog immigration was considerable and, in the decade 1851–61, the increase in population was 1,093.

This represented a percentage increase of 31.59, of which 14.31 per cent could be attributed to natural increase, and 17.28 per cent to immigration. Population increase was in fact quite remarkable in the slate-mining areas. Between 1801 and 1881 population increased by 350 per cent in the Bethesda district, by 600 per cent in the Llanberis district, 300 per cent in the Nantlle district, and by 1,400 per cent in the parish of Ffestiniog.

The Woollen Industry

From the Middle Ages to the mid nineteenth century the woollen industry had been Wales's most important single industry, and textile manufacturing was as essential to the rural community as the blacksmith or the carpenter. By the middle of the eighteenth century Montgomeryshire had become the centre of flannel manufacture and, around 1800, once the carding engine was introduced, many mills developed into small factories. The next process to be affected by mechanization was spinning and, by the 1840s, the spinning-jenny had ousted the traditional spinning wheel.

The weaving process changed in a different way, and the weaver retained his status as an independent craftsman for almost as long as the industry flourished. By 1837 there were seventy-four weaving factories in Newtown, Montgomeryshire, and these accommodated 710 looms, and employed 425 men, 227 women and 35 children. Newtown's prosperity and enhanced status may be judged from the rapid rise in its population:

Year	*Number of persons*
1771	800
1801	990
1811	2,025
1821	3,486
1831	4,550

In 1821 a branch of the Shropshire Canal reached Newtown, and by 1825 there was a service between Newtown and Manchester. The opening of the Newtown–Builth road in 1825 facilitated the transportation of flannel by cart and wagon to south Wales. The period after 1840 saw the virtual extinction of the widely dispersed domestic woollen industry and its gradual concentration around Newtown and Llanidloes. This occurred largely as a result of the addition of steam-power, and gradually all the processes of woollen manufacture were amalgamated in simple factories.

By the early 1850s steam-power was already in use in Newtown. But, thereafter, the industry in mid Wales suffered increasing competition from Yorkshire and Lancashire. Indeed, it can be argued that possibly the greatest mistake made by the woollen manufacturers of mid Wales in mid century was to compete with the manufacturers of Yorkshire and Lancashire on their own terms, with the result that it was soon well-nigh impossible to distinguish the products of Montgomeryshire from those of Rochdale. In the second half of the nineteenth century the advantage passed to the villages of the middle Teifi Valley, as places like Llandysul, Drefach and Felindre became the new centres of woollen manufacturing in Wales. This is discussed at greater length in Chapter 8.

The Iron Industry

The iron industry in south Wales had become concentrated in two areas. The first was along the northern rim of the coalfield, where the major ironworks were located — Dowlais, Cyfarthfa, Penydarren, and Plymouth in Glamorgan, and Ebbw Vale and Blaenavon in Monmouthshire. The second area extended along the south-western part of the south Wales coalfield and into south-eastern Carmarthenshire. In this latter area, the iron-works were usually smaller and closely affiliated to the tin-plate works. By the late eighteenth century, and well into the early part of the new century, the first area predominated. Until the rise of the sale-coal industry, the iron industry was the major industrial employer of men and capital in south Wales. By the beginning of the nineteenth century, south Wales had become the main centre of the iron industry, and in the period 1800–50, the greater part of its production had come from Glamorgan.

In the period after 1815 the industry suffered a slump and low prices were prevalent until the early 1830s. There was, however, a gradual growth as the domestic demand for iron and the growing export trade made an impression on the industry. From 1823 to 1830 pig-iron output rose from 182,325 tons to 277,643 tons a year, which represented a 50 per cent growth. South Wales's share of the national output remained at a steady 40 per cent. The 50 per cent growth compared unfavourably with the 150 per cent increase in output from 1806 to 1823. Although prices remained low in the twenty years or so after 1815, there was expansion, and notably at the Dowlais complex. In 1817 Dowlais had produced 12,524 tons of pig-iron from seven furnaces, two of which had been erected in that year. From 1821 to 1823 an additional blast furnace was built in each succeeding year. By 1823 the ten blast furnaces produced 22,287 tons of pig-iron or approximately 10 per cent of the total for south Wales. There was very little further expansion at Dowlais until the construction of the Big Mill to roll rails in 1830. It was in that year that it probably overtook Cyfarthfa as the major producer in south Wales, and its owner, Josiah John Guest, seems to have been mainly responsible for this. Guest was always far more adventurous than his rivals and, when prices tumbled, he would often undercut his competitors in order to sell his iron. Guest would also take swift advantage of any price increases and break the quoted prices agreed at the quarterly meetings of the Welsh ironmasters.

Outside the Merthyr district there were promising signs of activity, and some small ironworks were completed in the decade or so after 1815. The Bute Works (1825), and the Rudry Ironworks (1828) were set up in the Rhymney area. While in west Glamorgan, works were established at Cwmafon (1815), Maesteg (1826), and Pontrhydyfen (late 1820s). Some of these, however, had short life-spans; the Rudry Works was closed in 1834, and the Bute Ironworks was soon absorbed into the larger Rhymney complex.

In north Wales the iron industry had enjoyed almost fifty years' unprecedented growth, culminating in the boom of 1824–5. The American and French wars had certainly revived the industry in these parts, and in east Denbighshire the opening of the Ellesmere canal system had provided a further stimulus. The peace of 1815 did bring a temporary lull as the price of pig-iron dropped from a wartime maximum of £7 a ton to less than £4 in

1816. It rose again to reach an unprecedented £7.10s.0d. in
1825. The great boom had erupted and east Denbighshire, with
its rich deposits of coal and ironstone, was well blessed. By 1827
it was estimated that the twelve furnaces in north-east Wales
were producing around 24,000 tons, or 3.5 per cent of the total
output for England and Wales. It seems that a plateau of success
had been reached for, thereafter, very few ironworks were built
in the north. Even the old firms found it difficult to keep afloat,
and by 1847 north Wales had more furnaces out of blast than in.
The advent of the railway had given the half-a-dozen bigger
works around Wrexham a stimulus in the 1840s. But the overall
trend was static as production merely kept stationary in the
period from 1830 to 1847. In 1839 there were twelve furnaces in
blast in north Wales, with an output of 28,000 tons. Nine years
later there were only five furnaces producing an output less than
that of 1827.

In south Wales the coming of the railways brought further
expansion and, by 1835, most of the large works were producing
rails. Because there was no comparable iron industry in the
southern part of Britain, south Wales was in the enviable
position of being able to corner more than a proportionate share
of the home market. It seems that the railway boom fell into two
distinct phases before 1850: that of 1835 to 1840, and that of
1844 to 1848. Dowlais, however, did not fit quite so neatly into
this chronology, for there was a rush of orders in 1835–6, an
order for the GWR in 1839, a spate of orders in 1842, and then
some tenders and orders for 1845–7. Dowlais also received some
international orders, in 1835 and 1836 from north American
railroads, and in the late 1830s from the Berlin–Leipzig railway
in Germany and from the St. Petersburg–Pauloffsky Railway
Company in Russia. The Cyfarthfa Ironworks in Merthyr
Tydfil was also capturing some of the international markets and
William Crawshay, its owner, often corresponded directly with
American and French buyers.

The growth of the railway network certainly created a
massive demand for iron. The Dowlais company responded by
building a second works, the Ifor Works, in 1839 to meet the
challenge, bringing the total number of furnaces there to
nineteen. In 1840 the Little Mill was added to increase the rail-
rolling capacity and by 1842 Dowlais was functioning at full

capacity. Profits often fluctuated with trade, from £77,413 in 1838 to £15,334 in 1843, to a celestial £172,746 in 1847. Dowlais was at its peak in the 1840s. Cyfarthfa profits likewise peaked at £100,507 in 1847. Both these iron complexes had dominated the industry in south Wales, and the figures for iron shipments along the Glamorgan Canal as given in Table 2.1 indicate the relative strength of Dowlais and Cyfarthfa.

Table 2.1   Iron sent down the Glamorganshire Canal, 1817–1840
(Figures in tons)

Works	1817	1820	1826	1830	1835	1840
Cyfarthfa and Hirwaun	14,191	19,010	20,206	19,892	35,090	35,507
Dowlais	9,936	11,115	16,601	27,647	39,145	45,218

In west Glamorgan there was considerable expansion at Ystradgynlais and Ystalyfera. The Ynyscedwyn Works at Ystradgynlais had actually started iron production in 1711 under a joint venture of Ambrose Crawley and John Hanbury. We are told that its output had increased to 800 tons per annum in 1796. By 1837 it was in George Crane's hands. But the largest single industrial unit in the upper Swansea Valley in the nineteenth century was the Ystalyfera Ironworks. The first blast furnace was created there in 1838, and in 1839 it was owned by J.P. Budd, who controlled the works through to the 1880s. In 1846 there were six furnaces in operation, and five years later there were eleven. The Ystalyfera Ironworks was actually of a similar size to the Plymouth and Penydarren Works in Merthyr and by the 1860s it was producing 30,000 tons of pig-iron and employing a total work-force of some 4,000.

The Coal Industry

From the middle of the eighteenth century through to the 1840s the coal industry had been expanding steadily, along predictable lines, in response to home demand. The major industrial sources of demand for coal from 1750 to 1840 were the smelting of copper and iron. The development of the copper

industry around Swansea led to an internal demand for coal in
the Swansea district for smelting purposes, and also to an
external demand for coal as fuel for the pumping engines of the
Cornish mines. Both these demands quickened after 1750 and,
in 1784, over 70 per cent of the Cornish ores were bought by
Glamorgan smelters and the coal required for smelting was
probably around 120,000 tons. By the late 1830s that figure was
closer to 300,000 tons. The iron industry also made increased
demands on the coal producers and, by 1840, the amount of coal
used for iron smelting was at least double that used for copper
smelting. It has been estimated that around 800,000 tons of coal
were consumed by the Glamorgan Ironworks alone in the
production of around 168,000 tons of iron.

The really spirited attempts to expand the coalfield markets
before 1840 came not so much from the Cardiff area as from the
coal proprietors around Swansea and Llanelli. In 1799 coal
shipments from Swansea alone are reported to have totalled
245,000 tons — over twice the shipments from all south Wales
harbours fifty years earlier. The demand emanated largely from
coastwise markets, and the Cornish mines remained important
customers. Yet from the 1820s, changes were gradually occurring
as steam-shipping started to overtake sail and, by the 1830s, the
East India Company was seeking supplies of coal for its shipping
fleet. There was some custom among foreign steamship companies and, in 1842, in response to an order from the Tagus
Steam Navigation Company, George Huxham, a Swansea
shipbroker, shipped nearly 800 tons of coal to Lisbon. R.J.
Nevill of Llanelli dispatched coal to the West Indies.

Coal-mining in the Swansea area, and on the western arm of
Glamorgan, remained particularly active. In 1841 the collieries
owned by the Smith family in Llansamlet employed 421 workers
and produced around 70,000 tons of coal per annum. By the mid
1820s the shipments of stone-coal and culm, which provided the
main canal traffic along the Swansea Canal, were averaging
131,000 tons per year. In the vale of Neath similar developments
were taking place after the canal was opened in 1794–5. In 1795
the Aberpergwm Colliery, just nine miles north of Neath, was
shipping its coal to Ireland and to the west of England. In 1824
the collieries of the Neath Valley acquired an outlet to Swansea
by means of Tennant's Canal. The growth of coal-mining in this

western region of the coalfield was largely a product of the canals.

In the eastern region the growth of coal-mining ante-dated the arrival of canals as collieries developed simply as adjuncts to the ironworks. An independent sale-coal trade was impossible, as coal could not stand the cost of transportation to distant Cardiff. With the opening of the Glamorgan Canal in 1794 a coal trade through Cardiff slowly developed, but Newport was still a force to be reckoned with largely because of its major exemptions from taxes. By the Acts of 1797 and 1802 Newport had secured exemptions from duty on coal sent coastwards. The trade figures for the main canal-supplied south Wales ports in 1833 are clear evidence of this: Newport (440,492 tons), Cardiff (171,978 tons), and Swansea (387,176 tons).

The ironmasters had rarely engaged in the coal trade for they shared William Crawshay's view that iron offered greater profits. As sale-coal collieries became more independent of the ironworks so new regions began to feel the impact of industrialization. In 1820 there were coal-mining pioneers in the lower Rhondda: Walter Coffin shipped around 10,500 tons, and Richard Griffiths 6,000 tons. In 1830 Coffin sent over 46,000 tons on the Glamorgan Canal for sale mainly in Ireland and, by 1841 his Dinas collieries employed 414 workers. The 1841 census returns reveal that there were 7,696 people employed in the coal-mines of Glamorgan, and by 1840 it is estimated that the coal produced amounted to around two million tons.

In north Wales the principal coalfield extended in a long, narrow strip, nine miles at its widest, from near Oswestry to the Point of Air. Beyond this the seams dipped under the Dee estuary. In Derbyshire, where the lack of good communications had largely hindered the development of coal-mining, the immigrant ironmasters had taken the initiative in promoting mining activities. By 1829 there were forty-one pits on the Brymbo Hall estate alone, employing up-to-date machinery, and competing with their counterparts in Flintshire in the Chester market. The Flintshire coalfield had benefited from a number of factors: first, there was increasing demand from the lead, copper, and brass industries; the rise of the Buckley potteries stimulated mining activities at Hawarden; agriculture also played its part, as farmers needed coal to burn the increasing amounts of lime being used on the land; coal was also used increasingly for domestic fuel; and finally, in the inland districts, it was the improvement in communications that promoted the extension of coal-mining, and colliery owners often figured prominently as pioneers of the canal network. Coal production accounted for the growth of many important centres at this time, including Wrexham and Holywell. The latter grew from a population base of 2,000 in 1778, to 5,000 in 1801, and to 10,000 in 1851. By 1834 some 75,000 tons of coal were exported from Chester alone.

What part did the landowners and coalowners play in the development of the industry, and who were they? The landowners were crucial, for they owned the lands and the property rights to the coal. Most were enthusiastic about the ventures and particularly eager to exploit the wealth-bearing capacity of their lands. Some actually participated directly in the industry, like the Mansels, Herberts and Prices in Glamorgan. Most, however, withdrew from direct involvement, largely because of their lack of interest, their restricted funds, and perhaps their reluctance to incur risks. The mineral lease made their with-drawal possible, for it safeguarded the landowner's interests and guaranteed him a reasonably safe income. Other benefits that accrued to the landowner were usually an increase in the value of his property as roads and bridges were built; and the ensuing industrialization often brought returns from subsidiary industries and ancillary concerns. In most areas, and even when they leased out their coal lands to others, the landowners played a far from passive role; their eagerness, for example, to find lessees for their coal property, was often shown by the numerous advertise-ments in local papers.

The industrialists, though not a homogeneous group, played a far more active role in the development of mining, especially those engaged in the copper and iron trades who had bought their collieries so as to control the supply of raw material. Part of the capital for the development of the Glamorgan coal industry, for example, emanated from local sources. Edward Martin of Swansea, mineral agent to the Duke of Beaufort, had a share in several collieries after 1800, at Abercrave, Cwmllynfell, and Cwm Clydach. Coal-owners were also attracted from merchants, tradesmen, and from the legal profession. At Cardiff, local names were largely associated with the early development of this trade: Walter Coffin was a tanner from Bridgend, and Thomas Powell, Monmouthshire, exercised a dominating influence on the Cardiff trade in these early years.

The pre-eminence of western parts in overseas coal shipments proved short-lived and soon the competitive possibilities of Cardiff were realized. In the 1820s Newport had actually dominated the eastern trade, and coal shipments from Newport were four times as large as those from Cardiff. But with the improved communication facilities as the Bute West Dock and the Taff Vale Railway were opened, and as the demand for steam coal increased, so the rise of Cardiff as a major port seemed assured. The figures in Table 2.2 demonstrate the changing picture more clearly.

Table 2.2   Coal shipments (tons)

	Coastwise		*Exports*	
	1840	1851	1840	1851
Cardiff	162,283	501,002	3,826	249,001
Newport	482,398	451,491	7,256	151,668
Swansea	460,201	352,247	33,089	41,502

In the decades after 1840 the north-eastern counties of England and south Wales would engage in a struggle to decide whose coal was the better. In 1840 the north-east accounted for 72 per cent of all coal shipped overseas from the United Kingdom. By 1870 the north-east's share had fallen to 49 per cent, largely because of the gradual encroachment of the south Wales trade which, in that year, accounted for 31.2 per cent of the country's coal exports.

Developments in Transport and Communications

Roads
Thomas Telford had been commissioned by Parliament in 1811 to survey the entire road way from London to Holyhead. In 1823 a new road across Anglesey was completed and by 1827

two suspension bridges were opened. The House of Commons had made a grant of £20,000 available in 1818 and, in 1819, an Act was passed to authorize the building of a suspension bridge across the Menai Straits. In 1821 it was decided to build a similar bridge at Conway. By 1830 the reconstruction of the Holyhead road was virtually complete and its contributions to the economic life of the north were considerable. It promoted inland trade in the counties of the north and influenced other turnpike trusts by giving them a model of road construction. The Royal Commission on the State of the Roads in 1840 commented favourably on almost all the turnpikes of north Wales, and the trusts covered a total mileage of around 1,200 by that year.

Coaching services had also started on the Holyhead road and were soon duplicated on the other important highways. It was 1823, however, before a daily Royal Mail began running between Shrewsbury, Welshpool, and Newtown, and 1840 before its circuit was enlarged to include Machynlleth and Aberystwyth. Once the Newtown–Builth road was completed in 1825, it was possible to transport goods through mid Wales from the manufacturing districts of northern England to the industrial quarters of south Wales.

In south Wales the turnpike trusts grew in importance from 1820 to the 1840s and their expenditure almost trebled. It was in this period that the renowned engineers Macadam and Telford appeared on the scene. Macadam was actually enlisted to advise many of the turnpike trusts in south Wales and supervised the construction of many roads with the Cardiff, Neath, and Merthyr Tydfil trusts. In 1823 the Postmaster-General instructed Telford to survey a mailcoach route in south Wales, and there were a number of proposals to amalgamate the trusts. But little was in fact achieved, for the trusts preferred to take individual decisions and were reluctant to heed Telford's advice.

Canals

The first authentic canals in south Wales were Kymer's Canal from his collieries and limeworks to Cydweli opened around 1769, and a short waterway from collieries at Llwynhendy, east of Llanelli, to Dafen. From 1794 to 1799 five great canal lines had been opened for industrial traffic down the Welsh valleys to

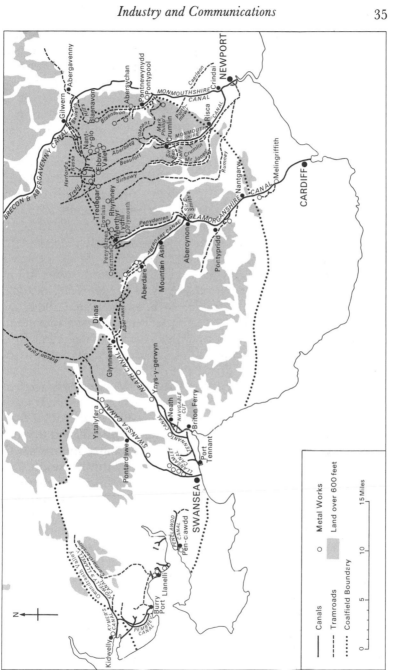

Swansea, Cardiff, and Newport. The principal Welsh canals had been built by the same group of engineers and they tended to be of the same dimensions. The first canal in north Wales had been dug in 1768 to convey Hawarden coals to the Dee. Eventually, the Ellesmere and Montgomeryshire canal systems opened up direct communication between the woollen and farming districts of Montgomeryshire, the coal and iron districts of Denbighshire, and the industrial north of England.

If the canals were the main arteries of communication, then the tramroads were the veins. Tramroads had a long history and they were usually constructed for use around the coal-mines and in conjunction with the canals. During the Napoleonic wars there was considerable expansion in their use, and two well-known tramroads in Glamorgan were constructed at Penydarren and Oystermouth. In the 1820s the mini-railway boom fostered a scheme to construct a line from London to south Wales. That never materialized, but another major scheme in 1824 to promote the Dyffryn, Llynvi and Porthcawl tramroad did come to fruition in 1828. By 1811 there were 150 miles of tramroad in south Wales, and by 1830, 350 miles.

The canals and their tramroads were of crucial importance in the economic developments of the first half of the nineteenth century. In 1804 it was estimated that the Swansea Canal carried 54,225 tons of coal, and the Neath Canal some 90,000 tons in 1810. By 1819 some 42,624 tons of iron were carried down the Glamorganshire Canal, and 37,709 tons along the Monmouthshire Canal. The rapid growth of the eastern valleys of Glamorgan after 1830 can be demonstrated by the vast increase in traffic along the Glamorganshire Canal to 294,750 tons. Despite growing competition from the Taff Vale Railway after 1841, the canal traffic had again doubled in the next few years to reach an apogee of 581,578 tons in 1851. Many of the canals paid more than satisfactory dividends after 1850: the Swansea Canal paid an average of 17.66 per cent in the second half of the 1850s, and an average of 9.24 per cent between 1861 and 1872; while the Neath Canal averaged 13.81 per cent from 1847 to 1871.

The main contribution of canals to the economic development of south Wales was that they released the iron-smelting industry from the constraints of its location. In 1847, 240,977 tons of iron were shipped along the Monmouthshire Canal, and 178,512 tons were transported by the Glamorganshire Canal and the Taff Vale Railway combined. Only a small proportion of the total iron was transported by the railways before the 1850s. All the four major canals of south Wales had been built to connect the northern parts of the coalfield with the coast, thus enabling the mineral resources of the upland districts to be effectively exploited. Such were the scale and pace of the iron industry's expansion that, between 1788 and 1830, it had increased production from 12,500 tons to 277,643 tons, or 41 per cent of the total British output. The canals facilitated this development.

The canals also initiated a vibrant coal trade. The western canals were promoted with this in mind. As early as 1804 the Swansea Canal carried 54,225 tons of coal for shipment, and in 1810 the Neath Canal transported 90,000 tons. It would certainly be feasible to assume that at least 75 per cent of the coal that left Swansea in the first half of the nineteenth century came down the Swansea Canal. The growth continued unabated in the early decades of the century so that in 1820 the Swansea Canal carried 150,000 tons, and in 1840 Swansea exported nearly 600,000 tons of coal and culm. The Glamorganshire Canal had limited coal trade until the 1830s largely because of Newport's exemption from coastwise duties. Before 1830, therefore, the Monmouthshire Canal had dominated the coal trade of the eastern half of the coalfield. After the 1830s coal-mining expanded in the valleys of Glamorgan, and the Aberdare Valley was the first district to experience the growth of steam-coal mining. From 1840 to 1853, 16 steam-coal pits were opened in the vicinity and during the 1840s the Aberdare Canal's tonnage more than trebled.

Canals had a developmental effect upon activity in their respective valleys, and a number of new enterprises set up along the canal banks. In 1816 the Brown Lennox Company came from Millwall to Pontypridd where it could ensure adequate supplies of iron from Merthyr to make chains. In 1839 the Vale of Neath Brewery built a short navigable cut to link up with George Tennant's Neath and Swansea Junction Canal. The canals also contributed to the expansion of those ports and towns at which they entered the sea. The ports of Swansea, Neath, Cardiff, and Newport rapidly developed as manu-facturing and commercial centres.

Canals had effectively cheapened the cost of transporting heavy bulk products, and it was this that ushered in the industrial revolution in south Wales. The industrial districts could now compete with areas more conveniently located, but without the strategic advantages of coal, ironstone and limestone in close proximity. It has been estimated that the costs of transporting were reduced on average by 65 per cent.

The canals did have a number of disadvantages: there were a large number of locks to negotiate — both the Swansea and the Glamorganshire had at least two per mile, and the Neath had three in every two miles; at times of heavy frost the ice brought traffic to a halt, so that food supplies were blocked, and there were severe hardships in the valley communities; thirdly, canals were an inflexible system of transport so that when traffic expanded there was little that could be achieved to increase the volume of traffic. Sometimes improvements were made, as when night working was adopted on the Glamorganshire Canal, or when the canal was improved in the 1820s to enable the use of large barges. But by the 1830s and 1840s traffic congestion was becoming a problem and many believed that the railways could offer an even cheaper mode of communication. The canals had, however, achieved a great deal, as the figures in Table 2.3 show.

Table 2.3   (a) Growth of the Canal System in South Wales; (b) Tonnage Carried by the South Wales Canals in 1845

(a)

1760	$75\frac{3}{4}$ miles of canals
1790	$92\frac{3}{8}$ miles of canals
1800	$224\frac{7}{8}$ miles of canals
1850	$273\frac{1}{2}$ miles of canals

(b)

	Tonnes
Monmouthshire Canal plus the Brecknock and Abergavenny	1,000,000
Glamorganshire Canal	410,000
Swansea Canal	300,000
Neath and Tennant Canal	300,000

The Railways

Numerous iron tramways had appeared in the late eighteenth and early nineteenth centuries. Lord Penrhyn had built a horse tramway in 1800 to carry the produce of his quarries to the newly-constructed Port Penrhyn. During the mineral boom of 1824–5 a seven-mile line was erected by Mr Assheton-Smith from his Llanberis quarries to Port Dinorwic. One of the first experiments in steam locomotion had been tried near Merthyr Tydfil in February 1804, when Richard Trevethick, a Cornishman who had first come to Merthyr in 1800, constructed a steam locomotive on the Penydarren tramroad. The outward journey from Merthyr, with loaded wagons of about ten tons of iron and seventy adventurous individuals, was a success. On the return journey, however, the locomotive failed and had to be hauled back by horses. The locomotive never ran again and was converted for use in the Penydarren Works. At least two decades were to pass before the possibilities of steam transport were to be exploited.

From the mid 1830s there were some significant developments in rail transport. In 1836, the Ffestiniog Railway, possibly the most famous of all Welsh narrow gauge railways, was opened. It was fourteen miles in length and, like most of the narrow-gauge lines, served the slate industry. In 1840 steam locomotives were introduced on Lord Penrhyn's railway; and, in autumn 1834, Lady Charlotte Guest, wife of the Merthyr ironmaster, Josiah John Guest, had noted in her diary that a Mr Brunel had visited their home to discuss the survey of a railroad from Merthyr to Cardiff. The first section of that Taff Vale Railway from Cardiff to Navigation House, Abercynon, was opened on 8 October, 1840. The Taff Vale line was completed in 1841.

Once the Liverpool and Manchester Railway was opened in 1830 a number of schemes were suggested. But of all those discussed in Glamorgan in the 1830s, only the Taff Vale was completed. This railway was promoted by three of the Merthyr ironmasters so as to reduce the traffic congestion on the canals. It was twenty-six miles long and became of vital importance to Cardiff. Many would argue that it was the great turning-point in Cardiff's modern history.

One of the great questions confronting railway enthusiasts and entrepreneurs in the late 1830s was that of communication with Ireland. Telford had already improved the Holyhead road, and the Menai and Conway bridges had been opened. The Irish interest in Parliament clamoured for the benefits of the new communication system. The problem was which port should be used as the terminus — Holyhead, or two rival claimants, St George's Bay, Llandudno, or Porth Dinllaen on the Nevin peninsula? All three were examined by a committee of two, Sir Frederick Smith and Professor Peter Barlow, who were appointed by the Treasury in 1839–40. Their verdict was for Holyhead. The Chester to Holyhead Railway was commenced in November 1845, with an initial work-force of 5,000 men. Within a year there were 12,000 navvies at work on the line which was completed in 1849. A very large part of the Welsh railway system was opened in the period from 1858–68 and this will be discussed in Chapter 8.

SUGGESTED READING

C. Baber and L.J. Williams (eds.), *Modern South Wales, Essays in Economic History* (Cardiff, 1986).

A.H. Dodd, *The Industrial Revolution in North Wales* (Cardiff, 1951).

E.D. Evans, *A History of Wales, 1660–1815* (Cardiff, 1976).

C. Hadfield, *The Canals of South Wales and the Border* (Cardiff, 1967).

J.G. Jenkins, *The Welsh Woollen Industry*, (Cardiff, 1969).

J.G. Jenkins, *Life and Tradition in Rural Wales* (London, 1976).

A.H. John, *The Industrial Development of South Wales, 1850–1950* (Cardiff, 1950).

W.J. Lewis, *Lead Mining in Wales* (Cardiff, 1967).

J. Lindsay, *A History of the North Wales Slate Industry* (Newton Abbot, 1974).

W.E. Minchinton (ed.), *Industrial South Wales 1750–1914* (London, 1969).

J. Simmons, *The Railway in England and Wales, (1830–1914)*, I (Leicester, 1978).

A.H. John and G. Williams (eds.), *Glamorgan County History*, 5 (Cardiff, 1980).

3. The Social Scene

The People's Health

PUBLIC health constituted a gigantic problem in Victorian Wales. Examination of its nature brings into clearer focus a whole spectrum of social issues which confronted people in the nineteenth century.

Patterns of Health

The Victorians thought that the mortality rate was the most reliable index to the health and sanitation of a locality, and a death-rate of 23 per 1,000 was the average for England and Wales in mid-Victorian times. The average index for Wales for the period 1840–60 was 22 per 1,000, but the variations from place to place were often quite considerable, with 17 per 1,000 being the rate for Builth and 29 per 1,000 being a peak for Merthyr Tydfil. The Registrar-General's Reports for 1841–50 indicate a pattern of mortality similar to that found in England, with eight out of forty-eight registration districts being above the national average. Some examples were Neath (22 per 1,000), Cardiff (22 per 1,000), Pontypool (23 per 1,000), Newport (24 per 1,000), and Merthyr Tydfil (28 per 1,000). There was one common factor to all these places — they were all mining or manufacturing centres: and Merthyr not only topped the Welsh league, but it had the unenviable position of ranking not much lower than the ten worst districts in England and Wales.

One of the worst features was the exceptionally high infantile death-rate and, for the period from 1837 to 1850, the ratio of deaths to 1,000 live births for England and Wales was 150. In the decade from 1850 to 1860 this rose to 156 per 1,000 live births. The ratio for Wales for most of the century remained fairly constant at 120. But if we consider the registration districts of south Wales, we find that, in 1861, more than one-third of all deaths were of children. In the town centres and slum areas in towns, the infantile death-rate was well above the average. In the period 1851–60 the average death-rate of persons of all ages per 1,000 living in Merthyr was 28.62, and of infants below the age of one year, 184.4. It tended to be true that the infantile death-rate was highest where the general mortality was highest, and this was usually the case in the urban areas and in manufacturing districts. It is interesting to note that infants in Welsh industrial towns died not through neglect but through attachment to their mothers for, in south Wales, Welsh mothers would carry their children around in shawls and hence expose them to all kinds of sudden temperature vicissitudes.

Until 1874 medical staff were not required to register precise diagnoses of the cause of death, and neither were relatives required to obtain a death certificate. It was the 1875 Public Health Act that ensured that medical officers were registered doctors and, in the decades preceding this Act, medical men were not particularly well qualified: in 1861 there were 523 medical practitioners in Wales of whom sixty-nine were qualified as MD, fifty-two had qualifications as physicians, and the others were apothecaries. The Poor Law Unions were obliged to employ medical men, but they were part-time appointments and they were poorly remunerated for the enormous districts they covered.

Causes of the Public Health Problems

In mid century, from 1847 to 1872, the problem of the health of the people was seen as an urban one, and all the important legislation of this period focused on the facts of urban disease. The Town Improvement Clauses Act of 1847 enabled local authorities to organize water supplies and drainage schemes. These culminated in the Public Health Act of 1848 which created a General Board of Health and empowered local authorities, when they existed, to set up local boards of health by democratic procedures. It was not until the Sanitary Act of 1866 that compulsory clauses were added to the legislation.

The 1848 Public Health Act and all subsequent legislation instituted a system of inspection. From 1848 to 1872, seventy

Welsh places came under the Health Act, and thirty-one of these were inspected in the period from 1849 to 1858. People could apply for the adoption of the 1848 Health Act either by petition of one-tenth of the owners of property and the ratepayers or if the death-rate were over the norm of 23 per 1,000. Once the work of building sewers, drains and water channels was undertaken, the costs could be prohibitive and the capital expended on sewerage, drainage and water supply from 1848 to 1871 was £1,194,750. Lampeter borrowed £550 in 1866 for a waterworks and slaughterhouse; Bangor raised £7,800 for drainage and other works in a matter of seventeen years; Cardiff borrowed £94,000 in the same period; Merthyr Tydfil borrowed £172,600 from 1857 to 1871; and Swansea raised £204,599 from 1853 to 1868.

In the industrial districts the twin evils of poor, inadequate housing and overcrowding had surfaced as major causes for concern and when Dr Julian Hunter produced his first report on the colliery districts of Monmouthshire, he discovered that in several places there were dwellings of extreme wretchedness and overcrowding. In some places where there was a rising population, the natural accommodation available was decreasing. For example, in Monmouthshire during the decade 1851–1861, there had been a decrease of 3,118 houses and an increase in population of 16,497. Almost twenty years later, the Medical Officer of Health for Merthyr was underlining the same pattern of problems. In north Wales, in the expanding slate-quarrying districts and in lead- and coal-mining villages, the situation was no better. Newport and Swansea had similar, endemic problems of overcrowding.

The quality of food eaten was an additional problem in both the rural and industrial areas. Inquiries into the diet of the labouring population were conducted in the 1860s by Dr Edward Smith, assistant to Dr Simon at the Medical Office of the Privy Council. In 1863 he visited parts of Anglesey, Denbigh and Conway, and areas from Dolgellau to Machynlleth. In the south he travelled from Aberystwyth to Lampeter, thence to Newcastle Emlyn, Milford Haven, Carmarthen and Swansea. He discovered that the labourers of south Wales and their families were obliged to endure inferior accommodation, furniture, comfort, and health. The houses of the poor people were characterized by mud-covered stone walls, bare ground, thatched roofs, and small windows. Their diet consisted of bread, made of wheaten flour, and oatmeal. They ate few vegetables, very small quantities of butter, cheese in moderate quantities, and meat as a very exceptional foodstuff. On the whole, Dr Smith concluded that the labourers in south Wales had a poorer standard of living in all respects than all the labourers examined in England and Wales. Even the labourers of north Wales were better fed than those in the south, where he observed a general deficiency of food.

Case Studies

In this section, case studies of health problems and social conditions are outlined: first, the condition of Merthyr Tydfil; then Swansea and its smoke problems; a composite examination of cholera epidemics; and finally, a cursory glance at some of the problems in the south Wales coalfield in the last quarter of the century.

Merthyr Tydfil at Mid Century

Anyone visiting the town in 1850 would find that no hospital had been built and that there were no public sewers nor drains in any part of the town. Only tradesmen's dwellings and the most recently built terraced houses were provided with privies. House refuse of all kinds was thrown on to the streets or along the banks of the Taff and, in one place during the epidemic of 1849, the parish authorities had to remove 500 cubic yards of rubbish which had accumulated beside the tramroad. There was no board of health in the town to deal with these problems, and the ironmasters denied any responsibility for them. In 1850 it seems that there were only three pumps and one shallow draw-well in Merthyr.

Alongside this picture of sanitary destitution, there was an air of prosperity and an estimated one in fifteen of all the premises in the town were retail shops or workshops. The High Street was the main shopping centre with twenty-three grocers, six butchers, three confectioners, and three wine and spirit merchants. It seems that cheese came high on the shopping list of all classes of workmen, and the Caerphilly and Gloucester

varieties were the favourites. The lowest paid workers —
labourers on 10*s*. a week, and girls earning 4*s*. to 6*s*. a week —
lived almost exclusively on cheese, and the cheapest kind
available. The High Street also had six or seven furniture
dealers or cabinet makers, four ironmongers, three china and
glassware shops and five clockmakers. All but the poorest homes
were crammed with furniture, pictures, ornaments and knick-
knacks.

In the homes of the highest paid workmen, those renting their
homes at 10*s*. or 12*s*. a month, there were five rooms and a small,
square garden. The kitchen would usually be furnished with a
mahogany chest of drawers, with an 8-day clock, a looking-glass
and various articles for display. The parlour would normally
contain a four-poster bed, another chest of drawers, and a glass-
fronted cupboard with articles of importance. We should also
remember that there were four pawnbrokers in the High Street,
and a total of eight in the town. As most of the workers were paid
on a monthly or six-weekly basis, these shops were of some
importance in the local economy.

No one walking through the town in 1850 would fail to have
noticed the paupers and those who were the victims of industrial
injuries. There were those who had suffered the loss of limbs, the
loss of sight, and the effects of blasts and explosions.

Swansea and the Copper Smoke Nuisance

In 1845 Sir Henry Thomas de la Beche wrote a report on the
health problems in Swansea and he noted that only eight men
and four carts were used to clean the five miles of streets.
Swansea's population had grown from 6,099 in 1801 to 20,152
in 1841 and the town's administrative machinery had been
completely swamped by the gargantuan sanitary tasks confronting it. The water supply, for example, had been so
neglected that by 1845 the Swansea Waterworks Company was
only connected to some 470 out of a total of 3,369 houses. Almost
3,000 householders relied on wells and streams or on the services
of water-vendors who sold it at a penny a pailful. After the
Report of 1845 there was considerable pressure to petition
Parliament for public health legislation and a progressive party
emerged within the Town Council. This party pushed for a
second inquiry into the sanitary condition of the borough, which

was undertaken by G.T. Clark. He noted that only 3,180 yards out of a total of 15,000 yards of highway had been sewered, and in Morriston the sewage was left to flow in the open gutters. He noted that the mortality rate in Swansea was 23 per 1,000 as compared with 15 per 1,000 in the nearby rural Gower peninsula. The worst districts in Swansea were those inhabited by the poorer classes: there was the Irish ghetto in the Greenhill district; in Back Street only 64 out of 117 houses had privies; and in Mariner Street 13 out of the 43 houses were without toilets. All refuse and household waste were thrown on to the streets. The outbreak of cholera in 1849 finally led to the adoption of the Public Health Act in 1850.

Swansea and its hinterland were the centre of the copper industry and presented additional health hazards. It was widely recognized that the men employed in the large copper works were generally well fed, well clothed and well housed, but their appearance and countenance was sallow. They breathed air which was largely impregnated with arsenic and sulphur, but the most formidable health hazard was the copper smoke. In the early years of the century attempts were made to solve the problem and, in 1820, a fund amounting to £1,065 was collected to reward anyone who could suggest ways of combating the smoke nuisance. J.H. Vivian himself produced a plan, but none was really effective. In the 1830s local farmers agitated against the copper owners and brought lawsuits against them. They argued that the copper smoke was affecting the animals' joints and their teeth. The lawsuits failed, largely because the industry was so central to Swansea's development. But the smoke nuisance was real enough and the prevailing south-westerly winds usually carried smoke in the direction of Kilvey Hill, Llansamlet, Foxhole, and Bon-y-maen for about 230 days a year. On bad days, sermons were short, appetites were small, and sickness was widespread.

Copper smoke remained a serious problem through to the 1860s when, at last, the Vivians introduced a new German method which was largely successful in controlling it. In the late 1840s the Vivians had erected a large number of houses for their workmen above the Hafod Works, at Tre-Vivian. In 1850 a complete sewerage system was added to the large houses.

Cholera Morbus, 1830–1866

Some historians have argued that the visitations of the cholera morbus acted as a far more important catalyst for the removal of uncivilized physical barriers to working-class improvement than did the influence of political revolutions in Europe in this period. The visitations of the cholera certainly quickened the social apprehensions of the British people in mid century. There were four great cholera outbreaks in Wales: in 1832, 1849, 1854, and 1866. The first epidemic spread from India in 1832, swept across Europe, via Moscow, and appeared in Sunderland in October 1831. It reached Flint in May 1832 and, before the end of July, 49 deaths had been recorded in Holywell. Revd John Elias soon reaped the fruits of the visitation and a religious revival erupted in the area. The chapels in Holywell were soon crammed with worshippers as early as 5.0 a.m. in the morning. At St Asaph the Bishop took an active role in establishing a local board of health. But the local papers in north Wales were reticent about reporting the cases of cholera, and this may have been a studied oversight on the part of editors in view of the impending visit of the Princess Charlotte and her daughter, the future Queen Victoria, to Anglesey in August to visit the Royal Eisteddfod at Beaumaris.

In south Wales the industrial centres of the coalfield experienced some of the most severe outbreaks of cholera. It appeared in Newport in July 1832, but caused only thirteen deaths. It spread to Swansea and, by 2 August, there were twenty-two deaths, a figure which rose to fifty-six a week later. The disease then moved to Llanelli, Briton Ferry, Neath, and Carmarthen. Two boards of health were set up in the latter town in anticipation of the disease. Over 600 were infected in Merthyr, and 160 died of the disease. It is difficult to be accurate in statistical terms at this early date, for the Registrar-General's office was not established until after 1832. But there are sources, such as Creighton's *History of Epidemics in Britain*, which give some figures for the period (Table 3.1).

One effect of the cholera was an increased pressure on central government to investigate the towns of the Principality and, in 1844, the Health of the Large Towns Commission proceeded to examine Merthyr Tydfil. Sir Henry de la Beche reported on the drainage and sanitation of the town and showed that most of the

Table 3.1   Deaths from the cholera morbus in 1832

Place	Deaths
Abergavenny	2
Caernarfon	30
Denbigh	47
Flint	18
Haverfordwest	16
Merthyr	160
Newport	13
Newtown	17
Swansea	152

surface water was contaminated by household refuse. The sordid social conditions at Merthyr stimulated a further inquiry by the General Board of Health and, in May 1849, T.W. Rammell, a superintending inspector, commenced his inquiries. Rammell's report did not appear until 1850, and in the meantime Merthyr had suffered another calamity with the visitation of Asiatic cholera, only six days after the public meeting was held in the town to provide evidence for Rammell's inquiries.

The 1849 cholera epidemic again spread from the east and reached Edinburgh in October 1848. In the following summer, 1849, 53,292 deaths were recorded for the whole of England and Wales. The first case in Wales occurred in Cardiff on 13 May 1849 and by 23 June, 138 deaths had occurred in the town. By November the disease had claimed 396 victims in Cardiff alone. It soon swept to Newport and Merthyr, where J.J. Guest, the ironmaster, insisted that the General Board of Health send a

Table 3.2   Cholera deaths in some Welsh towns in 1849

Places	Deaths	Places	Deaths	Places	Deaths
Caernarfon	16	Holyhead	42	Newport	209
Cardiff	396	Holywell	46	Swansea	262
Carmarthen	102	Merthyr	1,682	Tredegar	203
Flint	35	Neath	245	Welshpool	34

doctor to the area. Merthyr was divided into nine districts, each with a supervising medical officer. In July 1849, the cholera killed 539 in the town. The disease also ravaged Swansea, Carmarthen and Llanelli. In Swansea, where the disease broke out in the prison, there were 262 deaths. The recorded figures for some Welsh towns are shown in Table 3.2.

In 1854 a further wave swept the country; London being the worst hit centre, with 10,738 deaths. It spread to Wales and killed over 1,000 people; the worst-affected area being south Wales. Again the figures in Table 3.3 help to provide a clearer picture:

Table 3.3 Deaths from cholera in some Welsh towns in 1854

Places	Deaths	Places	Deaths
Bangor	3	Holywell	2
Cardiff	225	Merthyr	455
Cardigan	4	Neath	54
Haverfordwest	40	Newtown	19

Twelve years later, a fresh wave of the cholera morbus, emanating from the Middle East, appeared. It broke out in Southampton in the autumn of 1865, reaching Bristol in 1866. It soon spread to a number of seaports, and Swansea and Llanelli were quite severely affected. In Llanelli there were 150 deaths in one month, and other towns were making serious preparations in anticipation of the arrival of cholera. At Merthyr, T.J. Dyke, the MOH, began preparing the town in August, but to no avail and by 8 September, forty-four deaths had been recorded. At Dowlais, the Iron Company had opened a temporary hospital to contend with the problem. But the proposal to gather some of the victims in one place actually created a feeling of hostility among the workers and, soon after the first patient was admitted, they rioted, burst into the make-shift hospital, and insulted those in attendance. The workers further threatened strike action if the hospital continued, and the Dowlais Iron Comany was forced to withdraw the scheme.

The disease also spread to Aberdare, Pontypridd and the Ystradgynlais area. The Ystradgynlais–Ystalyfera industrial complex was the only township to arise in the Swansea Valley in this period and it displayed some of the worst features of rapid population growth. Dr James Rogers, the resident surgeon at the Ystalyfera Ironworks, was the only medical man of some standing in the area, and he had struggled for many years to improve the sanitary condition of the township. In the summer months of 1866 Dr Rogers's worst fears were realized and, in a two-month period, he attended 1,000 cases of cholera. There were ninety-five fatalities and he visited these 570 times. Rogers sent a detailed report to the Registrar-General and laid particular emphasis on the evils of unregulated house-building.

The disease abated in the south Wales coalfield in October 1866. It was during that month, however, that it spread to north Wales and coincided with a severe outbreak of scarlet fever. It reached the poorer parts of Caernarfon early in November. At least 471 had contracted the disease before Christmas, and 60 had died. The continuance of the infection there had induced John Simon of the Medical Department of the Privy Council to send Dr Seaton to investigate the sanitary conditions and to advise the local authority. The doctor was well acquainted with the slums of the East End of London, but he assured the town's mayor that he had, ' . . . never in all his experience witnessed anything so bad as the undrained portions of the town'. Robert Ellis (Cynddelw) was a Baptist minister in the town of Caernarfon from 1862 to 1875, and he co-operated with the vicar in visiting the homes of the cholera victims; but he would not support the local demand for public prayers to allay the

Table 3.4 Cholera deaths in some Welsh registration districts in 1866

Places	Deaths	Places	Deaths
Bangor	14	Merthyr	229
Caernarfon	75	Narberth	18
Cardiff	76	Neath	520
Carmarthen	143	Newcastle Emlyn	42
Haverfordwest	40	Newport	61
Holyhead	27	Pembroke	42
Holywell	88	Swansea	521
Llanelli	232	Wrexham	23

wrath of the supposedly Divine visitation. Cynddelw argued firmly that the disease was the result of pollutions and stenches in the town.

Accidents in the South Wales Coalfield, 1870–1906

Our final case study looks at the problems associated with mining, and it is possible to give a fairly accurate picture of the hazards involved in the years after 1850. The systematic recording of colliery deaths in the United Kingdom began in 1850 with the setting up of the Mines Inspectorate. The figures show us that coal-mines became safer places in which to work from mid-century onwards, and the death-rate per 1,000 persons employed and per million tons produced declined rapidly. The average annual underground death-rate per 1,000 persons employed declined from 5.15 for the period 1851–5 to 2.57 for the years 1873–82, and thence to 1.46 for 1903–12 for the industry as a whole. For south Wales the figures dropped from 2.8 in 1874–7 to 1.6 in 1909–12.

From the 1850s onwards the major causes of colliery deaths had been explosions, roof and side falls, shaft-winding accidents and accidents concerned with underground haulage of coal. Explosions in the south Wales coalfield, accounting for 21.7 per cent of its total death-toll over the period 1874–1914, were far more important than in other coalfields. Explosions could slaughter hundreds and some accidents are still deeply ingrained in the consciousness of south Wales communities. At the Albion Colliery, Cilfynydd, 290 men died in 1894, and, at the Universal Colliery, Senghennydd, 439 miners were killed in 1913.

Recent research in the field has shown that, although the death-rates in Wales improved in the period from 1874 to the First World War, the improvement seemed to be that much greater because of the higher death-rates which had prevailed in the south Wales coalfield in the 1870s. After 1899 the underground death-rate per 1,000 employees in south Wales failed to register any significant improvement, and this is in marked contrast with the rest of the industry. The death-toll in the industry actually mounted, and especially in the early years of the twentieth century. From 1900 onwards the number of recorded deaths never fell below 1,000, and exceeded 1,700 in

1910 and 1913, largely as a result of some ferocious explosions. The expansion of the coal industry in the years up to 1900 was achieved without any noticeable increase in the number of deaths, but the continued expansion in output after 1900 was only secured at the expense of a rising death-toll.

Attitudes of the People

The unavoidable risks to life and limb by violent accidents at work and a consciousness that they were prey to killing diseases and epidemics were the universal experiences of the working classes in this period. In fact, one could argue that an awareness of mortality rates and the distribution of certain diseases came to be regarded as the most important indicator of the essential differences between social classes. Public opinion on the health question was gradually being created by the diffusion of the printed word, by magazines, denominational journals, and by the voluminous literary output of the eisteddfodau. By the 1860s the enlightened views of the new social scientists and the advanced opinions of social reformers were gradually permeating the working-class cultures. The working classes were producing literature on topics related to health and they were often making independent attempts to understand the nature of their world. But the new knowledge and scientific opinions had to exist alongside the old practices and super- stitions, which were often the prerogative of the ministers of religion. For example, the Revd Rhys Pryse, Cwmllynfell, had become an expert on herbal medicines and produced a family book on herbs. He was also renowned for his astronomical knowledge, which he related to everyday affairs. A great deal of working-class education was being developed, but the working classes could only be effective in public health when they had learned the lessons of political organization and the politics of pressure groupings.

It was almost unavoidable that the middle classes would play a crucial part in the public health movement. The local government franchise was certainly not universal, and the qualification for election to a board of health was the possession of real or personal property. These qualifications were not abolished until 1882; and a survey in 1886 of representation on local boards discovered that, in the country as a whole, 30.8 per cent of their members were shopkeepers, 17.5 per cent manufacturers, 11.8 per cent gentlemen, 8.6 per cent merchants, 7.7 per cent farmers, 7.6 per cent builders, 3.2 per cent lawyers, and 2.2 per cent estate agents. The condition of the working classes rested on the shoulders of these people; and their attitudes can be clearly gleaned from their activities in the towns of Wales. In Llanelli the ancient landowners and the corrupt *ancien régime* of shopkeepers opposed the raising of a rate to clean the town. In Bridgend, where a local board of health was formed in 1849, there was a systematic opposition to reforms. The ironmasters were just as obdurate in their resistance to reforms: the Tredegar Iron Company owned the water company and effectively blocked any developments in their area; and in Merthyr Tydfil, also, the ironmasters delayed the supply of clean water for a decade.

It was only in those places where there was an enlightened middle-class leadership that there was any hope of achieving significant reforms. Cardiff was a model of reforming zeal, and so was Swansea. There was considerable political conflict in all these areas, but the working classes could take no effective part until the extension of the franchise and the accumulation of political experience through the growth of trade union activity. The working classes were dependent upon the co-operation of the enlightened members of the middle and professional classes for the adoption and extension of the public health movement. This enabled the working and middle classes to share the same moral concerns, to support similar religious and cultural institutions, and to accept the same kind of market economic values. In effect, it created an atmosphere of class co-operation in the decades from 1848 to 1870.

* * * * * *

Poverty and the Poor Law

The 1834 Poor Law Amendment Act met with a mixed reception in Wales. *The Cambrian* newspaper in Swansea saw no reason to join the detractors of the measure; while in north Wales *The Chronicle* attacked it as a violation of rights. No sooner was the measure enacted than the various districts were compelled to form unions of parishes. In the county of Glamorgan, such unions were formed at Neath, Swansea, Bridgend, Merthyr, and Cardiff in 1836. The Swansea Union, with a population in 1831 of 31,211 and an average Poor Law expenditure of £6,859 during 1834–6, consisted of twenty-seven parishes represented by forty guardians. The nearby Neath Union, with a population of 23,678 and an average expenditure of £7,510, had twenty-nine parishes and thirty-three guardians.

The administrative structure of the new law was imposed on the inhabitants of the parishes and, in general, they accepted the change without demur. The whole of Wales, with the exception of Monmouthshire, became the responsibility of Assistant Commissioner William Day from January 1836. By 1840 Day had made 655 visits to Wales. From March 1836, he was assisted by Sir Edmund Head, and by 1840 Head had made 602 visits. The Commissioners ensured that the unions were formed and the guardians appointed.

Every parish within a union was represented at a central board by one or more guardians, the number being determined by the population. The normal qualification for election was that a person should be assessed for the poor rate of the union. Guardians were entrusted with extensive powers: they were required to supervise registration and vaccination, to act as inspectors of nuisances, to assess rateable values, in addition to their primary function of administering poor relief. They were subject only to the direction of the central authority (Poor Law Commissioners until 1847, Poor Law Board from 1847 to 1871, and the Local Government Board from 1871 to 1919). The elections to choose guardians attracted considerable attention and there was often keen competition for places on the boards. In 1850 there were no fewer than twenty-three candidates for ten vacancies in the Swansea Union. The method of election was regularly censured and, as late as 1883, there were reports of confusion resulting from the different systems of electing local representatives. The guardians were usually elected in the following way — the number of votes given to each voter depended upon the amount at which he was assessed. In 1890 both the Swansea and Neath guardians supported the Merthyr board in urging the adoption of the ballot system in all local elections. The 1894 Local Government Act eventually resolved these problems by abolishing the property qualification for the office of guardian and introducing voting by ballot.

After the formation of unions and the appointment of boards of guardians, the Assistant Commissioners sought to persuade the guardians to approve the building of workhouses. Workhouses had been in existence before 1834. Of nineteen workhouses returned for Wales in 1776, two were in Glamorgan, one in Cardiff and the other in Neath. The latter seems to have had a fairly continuous history from the late seventeenth century. In 1837 the guardians of Neath were authorized to build a single workhouse for 150 inmates, at a cost of £3,900 and by 1839 it was ready. In Cardiganshire the Aberaeron Union was the first to build a workhouse, also in 1839. The Cardigan Union workhouse was also erected in 1839. In the same county, the Lampeter Board of Guardians was most reluctant to build a workhouse, and in 1848 they were still discussing the question. In 1867 the Lampeter Union was still without a workhouse. Tregaron likewise prevaricated and there was no workhouse there in 1850. The Poor Law Commissioner and the Board in fact lacked the power to compel any area to adopt the new policies and, as late as 1876, Tregaron had still not decided to build a workhouse.

In some counties the very evils and abuses that had prompted the central authorities to change to the New Poor Law system still persisted after 1834. Able-bodied pauperism prevailed in many forms and, many of the abuses, such as occasional or usual relief, persisted after 1850. There was certainly considerable opposition to the New Poor Law system and much lampooning in the press. *The Carmarthen Journal* was openly hostile to the new Act in the period. There were also a number of petitions against the Law. In 1838, 263 petitions signed by 225,000 persons were sent to Parliament asking for repeal of the Act. One of these came from Lampeter, and another from Llandysul, as late as 1842. Many guardians adopted evasive tactics over the workhouse question, as at Tregaron and Lampeter. The Commissioners regarded the workhouse as the essential element in the system, and the refusal of these two unions to build workhouses meant that they were working against the core of the new administration. In Pembrokeshire and Carmarthenshire hostility to the New Poor Law erupted into violent attacks against the workhouses, as the evidence to the 1844 Commissioners of Inquiry for south Wales reveals. By 1840, of a total of 1,430 able-bodied paupers in the county of Cardiganshire, only thirteen were relieved in the workhouses, the remaining 1,417 having received outdoor relief. In 1846, 6,292 paupers were relieved in Cardiganshire — 204 as indoor paupers, and 6,088 as outdoor paupers. The Commissioners had failed to end the system of outdoor relief and to abolish the practice of granting allowances in aid of small wages.

Those who were admitted into a workhouse arrived either by written order of the guardians or by a provisional order of a relieving officer, or by the workhouse master. Conditions in the workhouses varied considerably. Early observers at Neath commented on the overcrowding, while at Pontardawe and Gower, it was noted that the workhouses were, 'clean and in good order'. At Neath a series of unsuitable masters had marred efficient administration — in 1851 one master was dismissed as a result of misconduct against some female paupers, while in 1861 another was dismissed after being found guilty of misconduct against the cook.

Internal discipline seems to have relaxed slightly after 1847 and, although it was intended that the able-bodied should do some work, in many workhouses little seems to have been accomplished. From the 1860s, Bibles and periodicals were provided in the workhouses of west Glamorgan, and in 1868 J.T.D. Llewelyn of Penllergaer, who later chaired the Swansea Board, began the annual event of inviting the inmates to visit his estate. Concerts were often arranged in the workhouses, and from 1892 guardians were allowed to give tobacco or snuff to those who were not able-bodied. The dietary table for Swansea in 1862 provides us with a fair picture of life in a workhouse:

> able-bodied inmates received 7 ozs. of bread and a pint of gruel for breakfast; dinner on 3 days consisted of 4 ozs. of meat and either ¾ lbs. of potatoes or ½ ozs. of rice with 4 ozs. of vegetables. One lbs. of pudding was given on 2 days, and 4 ozs. of bread and 1½ pints of pea-soup on the other two. Supper was 7 ozs. of bread and 1½ pints of broth, with 2 ozs. of cheese and bread on 2 nights.

The 1844 Commission of Inquiry for south Wales had reported that the old and infirm were treated with kindness and consideration, and that the provisions supplied to the inmates of the union workhouses of south Wales were, 'equal both in quantity and kind to those which the better class of labourers, or even a large proportion of the poorer families, were able to obtain for themselves'. An examination of both the Aberystwyth and Cardigan workhouses bore this out.

Regulations also required each union to appoint a chaplain of the Anglican Church, and by 1843 there were chaplains at Neath and Swansea. There was also some progress in the hospital branch of the Poor Law administration. At Swansea, for example, a building known as 'the Garden' had been erected in 1836 as a fever hospital, and by 1843 some nurses had been appointed at a quarterly salary of £5.4s.0d. each. At Neath also, a fever ward was added to the workhouse in 1851. Although there were paid nurses at first, the guardians appear to have reverted to the old practice of using inmates.

The workhouses often made elaborate provisions for the children who were inmates. Most of these were either orphans or had been deserted by their parents. There were also those whose parents were inmates. In many workhouses schoolteachers were appointed as, for example, at Swansea and Neath in 1843. Many workhouses sent the children to local National or British schools, if they were available; and the Gower and Pontardawe Boards of Guardians decided on this policy until the 1880s. Thereafter, the Pontardawe guardians experimented with a workhouse school from 1881 to 1889. Poor Law inspectors were, however, beginning to criticize the workhouse accommodation for children in the 1860s and 1870s, and there was a gradual move towards the establishment of cottage homes for them. Three cottage homes were set up in the Cockett area of Swansea in 1877, and three in the Bryncoch area of Neath in the same year.

Although the structure of Poor Law administration was radically altered by the Poor Law Amendment Act of 1834, poor relief policy remained very much the same in most areas. In Cardiganshire, although three workhouses were erected in the county, there seems to have been little change in the nature of relief policy. The number of workhouse inmates was small, consisting mainly of children, vagrants, and chronic paupers. Where employment was often not available, the workhouse test was quite meaningless, and the Poor Law Commissioners seemed to have no answer to the problem of providing work for those willing to take it. The guardians preferred to grant outdoor relief rather than fill the so-called 'bastilles'. The real problem facing the new as well as the old Poor Law systems was not really pauperism, but poverty, to which neither the old nor the New Poor Law seemed to have an answer. In the Swansea area the cost of outdoor relief rose in the 1860s and the Swansea Board began supplying the local press with a weekly list of recipients of poor relief. By 1872 the inspectors were complaining that too much outdoor relief was provided in Swansea, and that the workhouse test was simply not being used often enough.

In the absence of other authorities, the treatment of the destitute unemployed fell to the guardians, and there was a marked increase in the 'able-bodied out of work' after 1840. Adverse trade conditions resulted in an increase, in one year, of 865 to a total of 8,140 on the outdoor lists of the Glamorgan unions alone. The general practice in south Wales was to provide outdoor relief to the unemployed. Yet the situation could often stretch to crisis proportions and, in the period 1876–7, there were 15,000 men out of work in the Swansea area. The year 1886 was exceptionally bad, but the cost of pauperism did not increase in south Wales, largely because of the support of charitable organizations and the stringent application of the rules by the guardians. With the imposition of the McKinley tariff in the early 1890s there was a sharp decline in the tin-plate industry and widespread unemployment in south Wales. Task-work was often provided by the guardians, and the charities were well organized during this particular crisis. Work was found for some of the unemployed by the 'distress committee' of Swansea Corporation in 1892–3 and 1894–5. With the Unemployed Workmen's Act of 1905 distress committees were set up in many major towns outside London, and this signalled the changing attitudes to the problem of unemployment as it became obvious that this was no longer entirely a matter for the guardians.

* * * * * *

The Friendly Societies

Friendly societies were of two types: the autonomous locally-organized society; and the affiliated orders whose lodges or branches were linked together in a single organization. There were a number of affiliated orders, embracing the Independent Order of Oddfellows, the Foresters, and the Philanthropic Order of True Ivorites. The True Ivorites were a Welsh-language order, and they were founded in 1836 at Wrexham. The Independent Order of Oddfellows was one of the earliest orders to establish itself in south Wales and, by 1835, it had thirty-five branches in Wales. Affiliated orders had arrived rather late in south Wales, although once established the Manchester-based Oddfellows soon became the outright leader of the movement in Glamorgan as elsewhere.

Looking at industrial Glamorgan in the nineteenth century we find that its population multiplied 15-fold between 1801 and 1911, to reach 1,130,818, and this was three times the rate of growth in England and Wales as a whole. In this heavily industrialized and populous county the number of people joining friendly societies increased until the last quarter of the century. The official returns of members of enrolled societies, that is, the ones which actually registered (and this clearly underestimates the impact of the friendly society movement, for there were numerous unregistered societies), gives us the minimum possible membership figure, and for Glamorgan it reads, as follows:

in 1802 — the figure was less than 10 per cent of the population of the county;

in 1850s — the figure was 15 per cent of the population of the county;

in 1876 — the figure was 20 per cent of the population of the county;

in 1910 — the figure was 15 per cent of the population of the county.

So even this minimal figure is an impressive one, for by the third quarter of the century one in five of the total population was a paid-up member of a friendly society. If the adult male membership is counted as a proportion of adult males in the population, we discover that at least half of the adult men in

Glamorgan contributed to friendly societies during the nineteenth century.

The societies appealed to workers at all social levels in every kind of occupation. The titles of various lodges manifested this — there were societies of Yeomen, Tradesmen, Gentlemen Farmers, Mason and Bricklayer. In 1910, at least forty separate colliery clubs were registered as friendly societies. The miners, in such a high-risk occupation, were well represented in the movement.

The regulations of the societies varied but, as a rule, members were allowed to claim benefit after paying an admission fee of up to £1 and weekly contributions of 6d for a period of a year. Sick benefit of between 6s. and 12s. was paid weekly, and there were reductions after six months and one year's continuous benefit to around 3s. a week. There were also funeral allowances of about £10 per member and £5 for a member's first wife. There were also other kinds of benefit, such as assistance for members in distressed circumstances or for travelling expenses incurred in the search for alternative employement. After 1850 friendly societies paid the equivalent of at least ten days' sick-pay to members each year, and by 1910 this figure was more like twenty days. In 1910, from receipts totalling £230,806, the 1,432 registered friendly societies in Glamorgan paid out £137,377 in sickness benefit, £33,495 for death benefit, and £12,301 for 'other' benefits.

From the printed literature available, it is possible to see that the friendly societies were well organized, issuing a constant output of sickness returns, printed rule books and membership totals. They tried their hand at producing journals and, in 1831, John Davies (Brychan, 1784–1864), a vigorous campaigner for the Oddfellows in Glamorgan, commenced *Yr Odydd Cymreig*. Despite his apparent abilities as a poet and an editor, the journal soon failed. Many of the societies might prove unreliable in difficult circumstances and there were frequent complaints of a lack of seriousness in society dealings, especially when funds were squandered on social or cultural jollification. Solvency was a perennial problem for the societies, particularly in those areas where there were constant demands on the funds. In Glamorgan the large number of coal-miners served to compound the problems, and in 1910 a total of 39 per cent of Glamorgan's registered friendly society members had received full sick-pay at some time during the year. Many colliery clubs were short-lived — the Glynneath and Rheola Colliery Friendly Society ended in 1899 after only three years, with no funds left in the kitty. The weight of society evidence indicates that, in the period 1855–75, some 15–20 per cent of members 'discontinued' during each five-year period in the registered societies.

Yet the societies were extremely popular and attracted a significant proportion of the population. They provided help when it was usually most desperately needed. There was no reasonable alternative source of help available for most people, and certainly no state welfare benefits. The Poor Law Act of 1834 and the harshness of the new structure drove large numbers of people into the arms of the societies. Furthermore, the sudden and sharp increase in society membership in the early 1870s can be attributed to the Local Government Board's desire to reduce the numbers of people seeking outdoor relief. This purge cleared at least half of the temporarily sick able-bodied men off the outdoor lists nationwide. Another important reason for the appeal of the societies was the range of their social and cultural attractions. The Ivorites were a Welsh-language society and they made every effort to promote the language and the culture of Wales after 1836. Most of the societies indulged in cultural activities and staged eisteddfodau or music halls in their localities. Some organized sports and day-trips for their members, and the majority enjoyed the decorative and processional paraphernalia of society life. Women's branches and young people's sections were formed so that there could be a complete family appeal.

Towards the last quarter of the century the old affiliated orders began to lose their appeal and the friendly societies steadily weakened. In the usual areas of south-west Wales it seemed that the Rebecca Riots, as early as the 1840s, had affected society membership. The Ivorites and Oddfellows had tried to dissuade their members from participating in the riots, and such actions gave the societies a semblance of reaction at a time of emergent radicalism. The temperance movement was an important influence and the Rechabite societies gradually ousted the Oddfellows from their prominent positions in places like Glamorgan. The temperance orders were almost exclusively responsible for the sharp rise in the number of friendly societies established in the 1880s and 1890s, and this masked the underlying trend of decline.

* * * * * *

Emigration

Emigration was one possible avenue of escape for those rural and industrial workers who wished to break out of the poverty traps and quit the social and economic afflictions of the period. The routes to America, Patagonia, Australia, New Zealand and other colonies presented themselves as ideal opportunities for those in search of a new world and a fresh start.

United States of America

After the middle of the eighteenth century emigration from Wales slackened, especially during the period of the American War of Independence and the long struggle against revolutionary France and Napoleon. There were, however, many who sought an escape route from the poverty, distress, and pressures of rural and nascent industrial society. In 1795, as many as seventy emigrants left Caernarfonshire for New York, and from 1794 to 1801 well over 1,000 people left Wales for the USA. Yet, of the 35 million who settled in the USA in the century after 1815, very few had actually emanated from Wales. In the official American census figures of 1890 it was estimated that 100,079 people born in Wales were then living in America. It is possible that two or three times as many had emigrated during the century, but large numbers of emigrants probably returned.

Official figures for immigration into the USA were available after 1820, and they indicate that, in the decade 1820–30, only 170 Welsh were recorded as immigrants. By 1850 the figure had reached 1,261, and in the following decade, as many as 6,319 Welsh people had entered as immigrants. Industrial immigrants in the early part of the century would seem to have been miners. They were often helped by the Welsh Society to settle in familiar Welsh settings. The Welsh tended to cling together and skilled iron-workers clustered in industrial towns such as Scranton and Wilkes-Barre. Before the end of the nineteenth century it was estimated that there were 5,000 native Welshmen settled in Scranton alone. Others, like the inhabitants of Llŷn and Llanuwchlyn, went to Oneidon County, while the 'Cardis' went to Jackson and Gallia in Ohio. In the later nineteenth century Welsh emigration came mainly from the industrial areas of south Wales. By the 1860s the iron and coal towns peppered along the coalfield often had their own emigration societies to help those members who wanted to leave for the USA. In the 1870s the North Wales Quarrymen's Union also helped workers prepare for the long and hazardous journey across the Atlantic.

Those who decided to leave their homeland often went in search of economic and material advancement. The economic attractions for those who had suffered the worst aspects of poverty in rural Wales and for those industrial workers who had experienced the harsh realities of iron, copper or coal production, are easy enough to understand. The farmers and inhabitants of rural areas ventured out first, followed after the 1830s by armies of industrial workers. After the imposition of the McKinley tariff in 1890 another wave of thousands of tin-plate workers followed in the rear. Once in the USA, the Welsh-American settlements soon scattered over a wide area. Most of the settlements were small, with less than 2,000 inhabitants. They were almost all located in the northern states, and the favourites were Pennsylvania, New York, Ohio and Wisconsin. As late as 1880 four-fifths of the Welsh lived in these states, and in 1900 one-third still lived in Pennsylvania.

The Welsh transplanted their institutions and their cultural activities to America, and religion was of paramount importance, as it had been in the homeland. By the 1830s the Welsh churches were numerous enough to justify the establishment of regional or national organizations. The Calvanistic Methodists had distinct presbyteries and state synods, with a national convention, while the Baptists and Congregationalists organized only regional associations. The Congregationalists were more numerous than the Baptists, with over 228 churches at the end of the century; and the Calvinistic Methodists were the proud possessors of 236 churches. It is estimated that over 600 Welsh chapels were founded in the USA, and these became the focus of the social and cultural life of Welsh people. As in Wales, the press, the eisteddfod and the patriotic societies were spawned by the chapels.

Patagonia

Michael D. Jones and many others who had spent some time in the USA recognized the rapid deculturation of the Welsh in America. He and these other enthusiasts sought a solution to this process whereby the Welsh emigrants to the USA were fast losing their Welshness. One way of solving the problem was to find a location where an integrated and autonomous Welsh settlement could be established. In 1861 a society to establish a Welsh settlement — Y Gymdeithas Wladfaol — was formed by a group of Welshmen resident in Liverpool. It was a committee of this society that was eventually responsible for promoting and organizing a settlement in Patagonia. The link between the settlement in Patagonia and the promotion and organization of emigration from Wales to Patagonia was the leadership of Michael D. Jones.

The initial group of 162 sailed from Liverpool aboard the *Mimosa* on 28 May 1865. When they disembarked at Puerto Madryn their numbers had depleted to 159 — five had died on the voyage, and two children had been born. Most of the passengers were from south Wales and, in particular, from the Aberdare and Rhondda valleys. At least sixty-five of the adults had been born in rural Wales, and so the passengers were a mixed group of rural and industrial workers. Most were young people, single and in their twenties, or were married couples in their thirties with young children. The Welsh Emigration Society discovered, as soon as it advertized for passengers, that the only people who were prepared to go were those attracted by the ideological nature of the venture, but who lacked the money, and those who were in a desperate economic plight. Anyone wishing to sail was accepted as a passenger, even those unable to pay their passage.

The first four years in Patagonia were a tale of woeful disaster. A complete lack of planning and organization resulted in the most extreme hardship. Irrigation was not introduced until 1868, and the absence of enclosures led to the loss of animals. There was considerable criticism of the venture in Wales, England and Argentina. The British Government issued a warning to all settlers, and there was a strong feeling in the Argentine that the scheme should be relocated or even abandoned. From 1865 to 1874 only twenty-five newcomers joined the settlement, and these came from America, Australia, and from the defunct Welsh settlement in Rio Grande de Sol in Brazil. In subsequent years there were three peak periods of emigration to the settlement: 1874–6, 1880–7, and 1904–12. These coincided with the equivalent peaks for British emigration to the Argentine: 1868–70, 1879–91, and 1900–12.

In 1874, after a particularly successful wheat harvest, settlers were encouraged to voyage once more to Patagonia. The initial group of thirty-two on board the *Electric Spark* from New York encountered disaster when the ship ran aground off Brazil. Another forty-nine settlers had left Wales and later linked up with the surviving passengers of the *Electric Spark*. In all, eighty new settlers sailed to the Chubut Valley. From 1874 to 1876 over 500 newcomers joined the settlement. Of these, around 70 per cent were from industrial areas, and a substantial majority from the Rhondda valleys.

Success in wheat production continued so that by 1880 wheat exports realized £15,000, which amounted to the work of 150 men. Once economic prosperity improved, the Emigration Society expanded its efforts to secure additional emigrants. The Argentine Government of 1880 was also eager to offer incentives to prospective emigrants. Bountiful harvests in 1879 and 1880 ensured that the Emigration Society's efforts were not in vain and, in the years 1880 and 1881, over 200 new emigrants sailed from Wales, with another 100 following in 1882. The largest contingent sailed from Liverpool aboard the *Villarine* in August 1881. A series of poor harvests in 1882, 1883 and 1884 decelerated the pace of emigration. In 1885, funds were provided by the British Government to build a railway; in that year also the harvest improved and almost 240 acres of land were guaranteed for settlers. Advertisements were soon placed in the newspapers to attract a labour force to build the new railway. The economic conditions in Wales were not as buoyant and the rural areas, in particular, were not as opulent as they had been. Patagonia offered some exciting possibilites and, on 19 June 1886, 462 emigrants sailed aboard the *Vesta*. This was the largest single contingent of Welsh settlers ever to sail for Patagonia, and it consisted of eighty-two workers and their families, and 160 single workers. The places of origin of many of these workers are recorded: thirty were from Neath, twelve from

Ffestiniog, and considerable numbers from Merthyr, Pontypridd, Aberdare, Penydarren, and the Aberystwyth area. Other shiploads of emigrants followed, and a total of over 550 new settlers arrived in the Chubut Valley in 1886.

In the 1890s only a limited number of Welsh settlers left for Patagonia. Emigration was reduced to around fifty people annually for the whole of the decade and, from 1899 to 1904, there was no inflow of migrants. In fact, in 1902, 259 settlers left Patagonia for Canada. There were three principal factors responsible for this pattern: in the first place, there was growing tension between the Welsh settlers and the Argentinian authorities in Chubut and a failure to agree over their attitudes to the Sabbath day — the Welsh Protestant Nonconformists were strict Sabbatarians and they refused to comply with the Argentinian law relating to military training on Sundays; secondly, a series of bad floods in 1899, 1901 and 1902 devastated property, crops and irrigation channels in the Chubut; thirdly, to make matters worse, external market conditions affected the economy, and the price of Chubut wheat dropped by 40 per cent between 1892 and 1900.

In the remaining years before the outbreak of war, several attempts were made by Welshmen at home and in Patagonia to attract new Welsh settlers. The press carried frequent articles on life in the southern hemisphere, and the Emigration Society distributed publicity material far and wide. The combined effect was successful and, from 1907 to 1913, over 700 immigrants, the largest number of Welshmen in any five-year period, joined the settlers. Most of those who left at this time were single and aged between twenty and forty.

Wales and the Atlantic Economy

In the years 1851–1911 Wales, along with most other European countries, lost a portion of its natural increase in population through migration. From a peak in the 1860s, Wales's rate of loss by migration dropped steadily until, in the first decade of the new century, there was a substantial gain through immigration. The years from 1861 to 1911 were ones of rapid economic growth for Wales, and the contrast with other European countries is especially marked in the 1880s, when countries such as England, Scotland, Ireland and Sweden, reached their emigration peaks. In the same period, the rate of outflow from Wales was negligible. The contrast became even sharper and clearer in the years 1901–11 when Wales was unique in having an annual rate of immigration of 45 per 10,000 of population, whereas all other neighbouring countries experienced considerable losses through emigration. In this first decade of the twentieth century, Wales actually joined the ranks of those countries of new settlement, such as the USA, and absorbed population at a phenomenal rate.

Recent research has shown that Welsh workers did not rush to cross the Atlantic in the second half of the nineteenth century. In the 1880s, when the absorptive capacity of the USA was at a peak, the effect on Wales was insignificant. There were four times as many English emigrants to the USA as Welsh, and seven times as many Scots; and, again in proportion to population, the sharpest contrast is with Ireland, where the rate was 77 per 10,000 as opposed to three per 10,000 for Wales. The reason for this comparatively low rate of Welsh emigration is that, in the 1880s, the internal demand for labour in Wales was relatively stronger than in the rest of Britain.

In the half-century after 1851 Wales experienced a period of sustained and rapid economic growth. The industrial counties of Glamorgan and Monmouthshire expanded at a time when the industrial sector of England expanded least, i.e., in the 1850s, 1880s and from 1901 to 1911. In the 1860s and 1870s the south Wales coalfield expanded slowly and only a small portion of the Welsh rural migrants could be absorbed in Wales. Net emigration resulted in 115,000 Welsh people moving away, mainly to England. In the 1880s the net outflow from the Welsh rural counties reached 106,000, but most of these were absorbed into the south Wales coalfield. In the 1890s when England was undergoing a home investment boom, the absorptive capacity of south Wales industry was reduced. Finally, in the first decade of the twentieth century, when a net Welsh rural exodus of 38,000 was confronted by an absorptive factor of 129,000 in the Glamorgan and Monmouthshire coalfield, Wales actually became an immigrant country and settlers began pouring in from the neighbouring English counties.

In conclusion, in the years from 1861 to 1911 we can detect a clear inverse relation between the Welsh coalfields and their

English counterparts. In the 1860s and 1870s the real expansion in coal-mining occurred in England; in the 1880s Wales almost monopolized the growth in the industry; in the 1890s England again swept into the lead; whereas in the decade 1901–1911 Wales experienced a vigorous and vast development.

* * * * * *

Crime in the Nineteenth Century

In the last decade or so historians have turned their attention to crime patterns in England and Wales, endeavouring to relate these to underlying social and economic trends. The historian of nineteenth-century crime in Wales has contended with two contemporary views of crime patterns. One view surfaced in the government records, the official correspondence and select committees of the period, and this interpretation regarded criminal and violent outbursts as the work of the uncivilized 'gwerin'. Lord Melbourne regarded the Merthyr Insurrection of 1831 as probably the worst of its kind in the Reform crisis. Home Secretaries could point to the Scotch Cattle, the Newport Rising of 1839 and the Rebecca Riots as further conclusive proof of the lawlessness and disorder endemic in Welsh society. What worried the authorities was the secrecy behind these various upheavals, and one purpose of contemporary inquiries into Welsh life was to unravel this so-called, 'volcanic mystery'. The infamous 1847 Report concluded that standards of morality and decency were low; Sir Edmund Head, the Assistant Poor Law Commissioner for Wales, even compared the south Wales coalfield in 1839 to a penal colony.

A second view of crime in Wales emerged in the writings of people such as Thomas Phillips, the mayor of Newport during the Chartist rising, and in Henry Richard's comments. They defended Wales's honour and, in so doing, they were supported by a host of clergymen, magistrates, and newspapers and journals. Their arguments were based on three essential assumptions. First, they argued that Wales had been the most loyal and peaceful part of Britain since the Acts of Union of 1536–42. They pointed to the official criminal statistics published in mid century which showed that the rate of committals for serious offences in Wales was between one and two times lower than that of England. Secondly, they argued that, of those who disgraced Wales, nearly one half were not of Welsh native stock. Various chief constables in Wales also blamed specific crime increases on immigrants: and the navvies, vagrants, the Irish, gypsies, sailors, and immigrant miners bore the brunt of the charge. It was claimed that the Welsh were naturally quiet and deferential and easily led, agitated by outsiders. The troubles of 1831 and 1839 could be placed at the door of Englishmen, and the Newport Rising, so it was argued, had been planned in England by such fiery characters as Feargus O'Connor. In the countryside, the troubles could be attributed to alien landowners, foreign land agents and representatives of an alien Church. The third plank in their defence of national honour was that crime was committed by a small, deviant group — 'bad characters' and runaway criminals and vagrants. This 'criminal class' was a small group and its movements could be easily monitored by the police in fairly well-defined areas, such as the 'China' district, 'Bute Street' and the 'Strand'.

These views of Welsh society and the growth of crime in the nineteenth century are often perplexing. Figures gleaned from parliamentary papers do tend to confirm Lord Aberdare's analysis that Wales was less blameworthy, and the rate of people committed to the higher courts in Wales was to remain lower than that in England until the twentieth century. Yet there is sufficient statistical evidence to show that the level of recorded crime in Wales was much higher than most contemporaries suggested, and when police court figures became available after 1857 the gap between Welsh and English crime-rates had dropped to only 20 per cent. By 1881 the gap had disappeared. The worst areas of Wales with the highest rate of offences were the industrial districts of Glamorgan and Monmouthshire. In the early part of the nineteenth century, the latter had the fastest growing rate of indictable committals in Britain. By mid century one in forty residents in the coalfield counties appeared in court each year. In 1861 Cardiff was regarded as the criminal capital of Wales with at least one in fifteen inhabitants facing court proceedings in that year.

In the second half of the nineteenth century the number of serious court cases had fallen to a very low level, yet the statistics of indictable offences known to the police indicate that the pattern in Wales during the second half of the century was one of a fairly constant increase in recorded crime. This was partly because of new legislation, new licensing and educational laws and partly the result of more police and court activity. The character of crime is a revealing indication of Victorian society in Wales. One third to two-thirds of the arrests were for drunkenness, assaults, stealing, vagrancy and malicious destruction; and the committals for assault and drunkenness were quite significant. Some historians would claim that the typical Welsh criminal at the end of the century was an aggressive working-class male with too much beer in his stomach and too few of his children at school. Murder and manslaughter were quite rare features, but violent attacks on people were characteristic of rural life, of rapid urbanization, and of the seaports. Carmarthen was widely regarded as one of the most violent towns in Europe in the early nineteenth century. Merthyr shared the same reputation, as did Cardiff, Aberdare and Mountain Ash. In some areas there were often pitched battles between whole villages. But the most common forms of violence were family troubles, sexual assaults, clashes between neighbours, assaults on police and drunken revelries.

In the urban areas, stealing was the second most popular crime, with one in four recorded offences in this category. Food, clothing, coal, wood and metals were the main targets, and the stolen property usually amounted to less than £30,000 in value per annum. In the country areas, clothing and foodstuffs were regularly taken, ground game and fish disappeared in large quantities. In Caernarfonshire, Radnorshire and Montgomeryshire there was a strong element of community protest in the crime as people battled over commonland rights. In fact, many types of crime were regarded as acts of protest. The Scotch Cattle movement in the south Wales coalfield was still virulent in the disputes of the 1850s. In south Wales also there were several attempts by thousands of workmen to remove Irish and English families from the valleys, and anti-Irish riots were most pronounced in the years 1849, 1850, 1857, 1866 and 1882. Added to these were the all-too-frequent election disturbances of 1852, 1868 and 1874.

Merthyr Tydfil in Mid Century

This was the Welsh boom town par excellence. It had grown from a town of 7,705 in 1801 to an industrial township of 43,378 in 1851. Most of its inhabitants were young and four-fifths were Welsh. The Irish constituted 9 per cent of its population by 1851. The town was the focus of the iron industry and, when demand was high, as in the mid 1840s, tranquility reigned. When the depressions descended in 1847–52 and 1857–63, there was severe dislocation. In the years 1833, 1842 and 1847–8 wages were reduced by 30–60 per cent and thousands were laid off work. In 1850 it was estimated that 20,000 were unemployed in the ironworks.

Housing was another problem in the community. Overcrowding and inadequate habitation were common features of the new boom towns. With a continual influx of thousands of people and a high birth-rate, which disguised the appalling death-rate, survival was the real problem. Over half of all the deaths in this town were of children under five years of age and, at the weekends, the streets were often 'black with funerals'. Fear of dirt, disease and death was part of the psychological make-up of an industrial centre such as Merthyr.

It is difficult to measure the extent of crime in such a community, and for a number of reasons: the implementation of the Juvenile Offenders Act of 1847 and the Criminal Justice Act of 1855 had a marked effect on petty session larceny figures; there were periods when magistrates, ministers of religion and the middle-class community launched campaigns to reduce crime, and the crime statistics may well reflect these crusades rather than the true size of the problem; the unrecorded crime figure was probably quite high; the changes in the numbers and attitudes of the police force had a significant impact on the crime rate in certain parts of the town, for example, in 1841, when the county force was established, Merthyr had nine policemen and Dowlais two. By 1847 the Merthyr Police District had 19 men and by 1864 it employed a force of 37 men.

It has been estimated that as many as two to three in every 100 persons living in Merthyr and Aberdare were arrested annually, and that crime waves peaked in the early 1840s, in 1847–8 and in the early and late 1850s. The criminal acts themselves could be divided into four broad categories. In the first category were crimes caused by poverty. These were associated quite often with vagrants and beggars. In the years 1847 to 1851 and in the mid 1850s large numbers of beggars were attracted to the town and, as the poor relief was more stringently applied, so many turned to crime. Similarly, female stealing was very much a matter of necessity — the great majority of female thieves stole clothes, food and coal.

The second category contained crimes arising in the works and, in the years 1848, 1850, 1852 and 1854, almost 100 people from Merthyr and Aberdare were charged with stealing coal from the ironmasters. The great majority of the charges were brought by the Guests and the Dowlais Iron Company. Other forms of works' crimes were those associated with wages, contracts and works' discipline, the destruction of company property and illegal strike activity. One blackleg, John Thomas, was killed in the Aberdare Valley when a bomb exploded in his home.

Leisure crimes were the third category, and these included cases of drunkenness and disorderly behaviour. By the 1850s and 1860s one in five of the persons apprehended in the town were charged with this offence. Drunkenness was associated with particular areas and with young people. Males were the worst offenders, but Commissioners like Seymour Tremenheere were impressed by the sight of young women consuming large quantities of beer in south Wales coalfield pubs. Some of the worst drunks in Merthyr were women with such decorative names as, 'Brecon Jane' Powell, 'Snuffy Nell' Sullivan, and 'Saucy Stack' Edwards. Violence was a real problem, and common assault, particularly assault against the police, accounted for a quarter to one-third of all charges. Even as late as the 1860s common assault remained the largest entry in the criminal register.

The fourth major category of crimes were of a familial or sexual nature. Stealing from the person was associated with prostitution, especially in the infamous 'China' district of Merthyr. The history of China (also known as the 'empire') became, in many ways, the history of nineteenth-century prostitution. There were a minimum of sixty prostitutes in China in the period 1839–40 and around forty in the period 1859–60. In an area where overcrowding was the norm, where ignorance, filth, disease and vice surrounded the young from infancy, prostitution seemed to be an escape-route for many females in the new industrial world. Prostitution and its ancillary trades provided the basis for the criminal world of Merthyr, or the 'celestial empire'. The authorities were concerned with the problem of stealing from the person and, in the period from May 1846 to May 1847, fifty residents of the 'empire' were apprehended. The 'emperor' and 'empress' of China, Benjamin Richards and Anne Evans, were sentenced to transportation, but no sooner had they left than a new 'imperial' regime usurped power. The prostitutes, or the 'nymphs', were instructed to steal from their clients. Once inside the brothels, the 'nymphs' would wait for their customers to become drunk or to be in compromising states, and the rest was easy for the likes of 'Big Jane' (Thomas), 'Big Nell', and the 'Buffalo' (Margaret Evans). For the more delicate girls, the 'Bullies' were at hand to offer assistance. These were the protectors of the criminal class and the 'nymphs', and they often assisted the girls in robberies.

After the 1840s respectable society led an onslaught on the 'empire'. The police, after the formation of the new model constabulary in 1841, and under the command of Chief Constable Napier, led the attack. In the period 1840–60 there was growing awareness of the need for better working-class educational facilities, and politicians of the calibre of H.A. Bruce were recognizing the distinct connection between the environment and the growth of crime. In 1860 Anglican missionaries spearheaded a six-month campaign to turn girls away from prostitution and in 1862, a climax of evangelical effort was reached when a 'House of Refuge for Distressed Women' was opened in Llandaff. By 1860 China was in decline, and for a variety of reasons: first, police harassment and sterner sentences were beginning to bite; secondly, there had been considerable educational improvement in the industrial townships; economic factors really dealt the death-blow, for by the 1850s and 1860s Merthyr's industrial decline had set in, and a flood of people began emigrating. The unskilled single men, who had provided the greatest source of profits for nymphs, began leaving for the new coal centres in the Rhondda and Aberdare valleys. Finally, from mid century onwards the middle classes began developing a wide range of organizations and propaganda to militate against the criminal underworld. A dedicated and small group of people established a network of institutions to promote alternative leisure interests and organizations. The years 1845–7 and 1856–8 were especially productive, and the chapels and works organized mass tea parties, fêtes, excursions, new sports and musical events. In the years 1840–60 Young Men's Improvement Societies appeared, together with a Library Association and Temperance Recreation Associations. By the 1860s the *Merthyr Guardian* could claim that the habits of the people had improved.

SUGGESTED READING

D.J.V. Jones, *Crime, Protest, Community and Police in Nineteenth-Century Britain* (London, 1982).
B. Thomas, *The Welsh Economy* (Cardiff, 1962).
G. Williams, *Religion, Language and Nationality in Wales* (Cardiff 1979).

Articles:
E.R. Baker, 'The Beginnings of the Glamorgan County Police', *Glamorgan Historian*, II (1965).
D. Jones, 'Did Friendly Societies Matter? A Study of Friendly Societies in Glamorgan, 1794–1910', *W.H.R.*, 12 (1984–5).
G.P. Jones, 'Cholera in Wales', *N.L.W.J.*, X (1957–8).
I.G. Jones, 'The People's Health in Early Victorian Wales', *T.H.S.C.*, (1984).
I.G. Jones, 'Merthyr Tydfil in 1850', *Glamorgan Historian*, IV (1967).
W.R. Lambert, 'Some Impressions of Swansea and its Copperworks in 1850', *Glamorgan Historian*, V (1968).
K. Strange, 'In Search of the Celestial Empire. Crime in Merthyr, 1830–1860', *Llafur*, 3, no. 1 (1980).
J.E. Thomas, 'The Poor Law in West Glamorgan, 1834–1930', *Morgannwg*, XVIII (1974).

4. Religion and Society
1815–1851

Background

IN 1756 Merthyr Tydfil, the parish which was to become the focus of the iron industry in south Wales, had no better use for its iron-ore than the repair of the parochial road. In 1710 the number of baptisms in the parish was seven, and in 1750 it was still only twenty-seven. There had been some iron smelting and the mining of outcrop coal in the area, but the coal had been used locally and there was little contact with the adjacent counties. Edmund Jones, who served the Independent congregations in the Ebbw Fawr and Ebbw Fach valleys, published an account of the scene of his ministry, the parish of Aberystruth, in 1779. It depicted an area where the land was poor and barren, the population sparse, and the chief source of income derived from cattle and sheep. The descriptions in Jones's book could equally well be applied to the whole district from Hirwaun to Blaenavon, which was destined to become the industrial cockpit of south Wales.

Across the River Rhymney, in the parish of Merthyr Tydfil, the scene was beginning to change. The four great ironworks of Dowlais, Cyfarthfa, Plymouth and Penydarren had been established in the years after 1759 and, by 1801, were sustaining a community of 7,705 people. With the exception of Merthyr Tydfil, which expanded rapidly, the other industrial areas in north Glamorgan and Monmouthshire grew slowly at first, and they always managed to preserve their sense of separateness and distinctiveness as valley communities. The mountains and landscape were certainly an important factor in this process.

It was this area, from Hirwaun to Blaenavon in the north, and south to Pontypool, which witnessed an unprecedented growth in population during the first half of the nineteenth century. The population of Monmouthshire alone rose from 45,568 in 1801 to 157,418 in 1851, a massive growth of 245 per cent. In the

Aberystruth subdistrict the population grew from 805 in 1801 to 14,383 in 1851, an overall increase of 1,687 per cent. In Glamorgan, the parish of Merthyr Tydfil experienced a population increase from 7,705 in 1801 to 46,378 in 1851, an astounding growth of over 500 per cent. The nearby parish of Aberdare exhibited even greater growth of over 900 per cent within the same period. It is fairly clear that these massive population increases in the industrial regions were caused largely by immigration. The new industrial districts were like magnets drawing multitudes of people from the rural counties of south and west Wales, and from the contiguous counties of England.

In this chapter we shall endeavour to examine the growth and role of religion in this emergent, industrial and immigrant society. Those who settled in the new Klondike-like settlements had travelled from rural areas on foot and in carts. They came as Christians and pagans, thrifty and profligate, clean and dirty. Once they settled in their new surroundings, most fell back on their traditions and customs; and one important, stabilizing tradition was that of religious affiliation.

The Nonconformists

In the years from 1801 to 1851 Protestantism was the religion of the Welsh people, and Nonconformity strengthened its hold on Wales. An overwhelming weight of evidence suggests that the new industrial society was strongly Nonconformist in tone and an analysis of the 1851 census on religion, shows that the mass of people in Wales had rejected the Established Church and provided themselves with places of worship. Wales became a Nonconformist country, famous for its doctrinal orthodoxy, and the simplicity of its denominational structure. All the denominations, including the Established Church, were evangelical in their theology; and moderate Calvinism was the theological belief of almost all the religious groups. Indeed, what is so impressive about nineteenth-century religious beliefs in Wales is the universal consensus that existed among the denominations. Similarly, there evolved a comparatively simple pattern of denominationalism; the multiplicity of denominations found elsewhere was not prevalent in Wales. Among the old Dissenters, the Independents were the most numerous, followed by the Baptists, and the Unitarians. They shared common theological beliefs which created a socio-political consensus. Similarly, among the Welsh Methodists there was little of that division and fractionalism which had splintered the original Wesleyan Connexion from 1797 onwards in England. The Welsh Methodists retained their intense evangelicalism and revivalism and were less interested in internal bickering and internecine warfare. On the whole, the denominations presented a united front on those issues that were of supreme importance. As they faced a world that was fundamentally irreligious, they knew that the Gospel united them and enabled them to adapt to the increasingly urban and industrial society of the early decades of the nineteenth century.

One of the reasons for the growth and success of Nonconformity in Wales was the importance of the laity in its structure, and the lack of a central control. This was in marked contrast to the more formalized structure of the Established Church, with its inherent tendency to stifle change. Nonconformist growth in the century was largely due to the successive waves of immigrants who came to seek work in the mining districts, and who were able to establish their individual 'causes' without reference to a central body or an elaborate governmental structure. As individuals moved into the congested industrial villages they were free to set up their own congregation, perhaps consisting of a few members huddled together in the long room of a small public house. Successive immigrants would move into the district, join the small congregations, and soon the cottage would replace the long room, and, in time, the first Bethel or Zion would appear. The laity enjoyed a prominent place in chapel affairs, and there was no sharp distinction between the pastor and those whom he served. In fact there were few settled pastorates during the first half of the century and most preachers had to find supplementary sources of income, as carpenters, miners, shopkeepers, clothiers, or as farmers. The settled ministry arose gradually, and only after a system of itinerant ministers had predominated. With the ministers often working closely with their congregation, in the mines and on the land, there was a community of interests and beliefs between the ministers and their flocks.

The Sunday schools served to promote the interests of the laity and provided a democratic organization within which the lay members could hold a multiplicity of offices as teachers, treasurers, superintendents and secretaries. Often, the Sunday schools were indistinguishable from the actual 'causes', and they would meet in the members' farmsteads or in their homes. Generations of immigrants were instructed in these schools, where they were provided with a basic, elementary education, in the days before the 1847 Report. It cannot be doubted that the Sunday schools were an important factor in the success of Welsh Nonconformity in the last century.

The success of Nonconformity in Wales during the first half of the nineteenth century was not entirely the result of its own characteristics and structure. Much of its success can also be attributed to the weaknesses of the Established Church in Wales. The Church, which had served a rural community for many centuries, was now called upon to adapt itself to a different society; and it was legally, constitutionally, and perhaps spiritually, unable to take the necessary steps to serve the new industrial society. One of the greatest needs in the growing communities was the provision of church buildings nearer the centres of the rising population. It was a pressing problem and an urgent need in the Welsh valleys. But the Church was unable to subdivide its large upland parishes, which had hitherto served the rural centres of population, unless and until Parliament legally changed the parish boundaries. This was one of the meanings of the 'Established' Church: it was established by Parliament. Nonconformity had no such fetters: the Nonconformists built chapels wherever immigrants 'gathered', beginning their public worship in a cottage, barn, or the long room of a public house, and without requiring the approval of bishops or parliaments.

Equally as important, however, in guaranteeing the success of Dissent was powerful and efficient preaching. Its characteristics were said to be sound doctrine, perspicuous style, richness of thought, an animated delivery, an earnestness, a solemnity, and a directness of appeal. Such men as John Elias, Christmas Evans and William Williams (Y Wern) were fine representatives of that unique style. They were masters of assemblies and congregations, who could sway their listeners and command attention with their persuasive rhetorical and oratorical gifts. The day of the settled ministry came slowly, so that ministers were usually preachers who regularly went on tour. When the settled ministry became the rule, the ministers were poorly paid. Evan Jones (Ieuan Gwynedd), a well-known populist figure in Nonconformist circles, stated that he knew of no minister in the Principality whose salary exceeded £120 per annum, and that there were not twenty ministers who received £100. It would seem that, in 1847, when Evan Jones made these observations, £50 would have been considered a high average salary. Even in Merthyr Tydfil in 1852, the pastor of Zoar Independent Church was paid a mere £5 a year.

Notwithstanding these pecuniary rewards, the denominations were able to attract men of great, natural ability, even though most of the ministerial candidates had received few educational opportunities. Dr Thomas Rees was the author of a number of books, and co-author of the history of the independent churches. Evan Jones is still revered for his pungent attacks on the 1847 Education Report. But it was the Baptists who seemed to attract some of the most eminent men as pastors: R.H. Stephen, Aber-carn, co-operated with Augusta Hall in popularizing Welsh literature; Robert Ellis (Cynddelw), who was pastor of Carmel Church, Sirhowy, from 1847 to 1862, was a celebrated poet, author and eisteddfodwr; William Roberts (Nefydd), pastor of Salem Church, Blaina, from 1845 to 1872, was an enthusiastic educationalist and agent for the British and Foreign School Society in south Wales; John Jones (Mathetes) was the author of a Bible dictionary in Welsh; Dr Thomas Price, Aberdare, was certainly one of the civil and religious leaders of his community. These stars of the Nonconformist constellation were social and cultural leaders who converted their chapels into community and cultural centres.

The chapels grew in number, and Nonconformity largely succeeded as a movement, because its institutions were not wholly 'religious'. The growth-pattern of the Nonconformist chapels in the new, expanding communities was revealing of the nature of Dissenting religion, and goes a long way to explaining the success of these institutions. When the chapels sent out offshoots, they set up schoolrooms, and then chapels. These schoolrooms, where British schools did not exist, were often

better buildings than those otherwise available in the community. They became centres for educating the people as well as
places for worship, and they provided day-school facilities and
Sunday school tuition. As we shall see in Chapter 5, the Sunday
schools were family and comprehensive schools, accommodating
young people and adults of various ages, abilities and occupations. Architecturally, the chapels, unlike the Anglican churches,
were not designed specifically for devotional and liturgical
purposes. Rather, they were communal centres for educational
activities, lectures, eisteddfodau, concerts, adult classes, penny
readings, and meeting-places to discuss politics. As Professor
I.G. Jones has argued in so many of his writings, for the vast
majority of people the distinction between the religious and the
secular simply did not arise. The social aspects of religion were
inescapably present in their everyday lives. As such, the chapels
were vital ingredients in the communities, and Nonconformity
was a community-religion and community-culture.

The Established Church

The unmistakable failure of the Established Church to adapt
to the new environment actually predated the spread of
industrialization and urbanization. The emergence and growth
of Methodism is significant simply because it displayed the
weaknesses of the church in those years before the rapid
developments in industry. Traditionally and constitutionally
the Church in Wales was part of the Church of England, and the
four Welsh dioceses were part of the province of Canterbury. In
a strictly legal sense the Church of England did not exist, but
was comprised of twenty-six dioceses and thousands of parishes,
and its property was scattered over a vast number of trusts and
endowments, which were not at the disposal of a corporate, legal
body known as the Church of England. The administrative
machinery of this Church was devised for a more placid,
agricultural society. It had served the rural communities for
centuries and, if it was to adapt to industrial society, it needed
the sanction and approval of Parliament.

Towards the end of the eighteenth century the problems
confronting the Established Church were exacerbated by the
accelerating pace of industrialization and population growth.

The population of Wales increased from 587,245 in 1801 to 1,163,139 in 1851, and the greatest impact was felt in the industrial districts of Glamorgan and Monmouthshire: the population of Glamorgan expanded from 70,879 in 1801 to 231,849 in 1851, and Monmouthshire's from 45,568 to 157,418 in the same period. Not only was the population increasing, but it was also being redistributed. In 1801 not one of the old counties had more than 12 per cent of the total population and none less than 3 per cent. By 1851 there had been a dramatic redistribution: Glamorgan now had one-fifth of the total population, and the percentage of every county, with the exception of Monmouth, was less than it had been fifty years previously. By 1881, Glamorgan had one-third of the total population and, by the turn of the century, it had 42 per cent. By that time the percentage share of the counties of Anglesey, Brecon, Cardigan, Merioneth, Montgomery and Radnor had fallen to below three per cent of the total. The country was pouring its people into the industrial valleys of south Wales.

The Established Church found itself almost powerless to act in this situation. As already mentioned its administrative structure was one major difficulty. The country was divided up into parishes, and each parish was provided with a church and a priest. The diocese had no funds as such, and the parish depended on the tithe and other rent-charges for the mainten-ance of its priest and a glebe-house. Churchwardens relied on the church rate for the maintenance and repair of all the church buildings. The parishes and parish boundaries were legally constructed and there was no administrative body within the Church which was legally empowered to alter these boundaries or to restructure the parishes themselves. The Established Church in Wales was, therefore, organized on a parochial basis and, in 1831, it ministered to 1,045,958 people. There were 853 parishes in Wales, and nearly half of these were to be found in the large, rural diocese of St David's, the largest but one in the whole of England and Wales. The most urgent administrative need was to subdivide the large upland mountain parishes into smaller units, and to provide church buildings near to the centres of rising population. In the diocese of St Asaph, in north-east Wales, there were such unwieldy parishes as Henllan (14,334 acres) and Llandrillo (28,200 acres). In the diocese of

Bangor, the parish of Llangurig covered 50,000 acres; and the parish of Llanbadarn Fawr in the diocese of St David's stretched over 52,420 acres. But the worst problems of all were in the diocese of Llandaff, in south-east Wales, which had to serve the rapidly increasing population of the industrial and manu- facturing districts of Glamorgan and Monmouthshire. In parishes such as Bedwellty (16,210 acres), Mynyddislwyn (15,938 acres) and Ystradyfodwg (24,515 acres), a few scattered mountain-top churches had served a pastoral community for many centuries; but they were totally inadequate for the industrial villages in the valleys. It was here that 'religious deprivation' was most acutely felt, namely the ignorance of the truths of Christianity which could be attributed to a lack of provision of places for religious instruction and worship.

Even if the church in the diocese had the authority to subdivide the larger parishes or to amalgamate the smaller units, the financial resources were not forthcoming. It has been widely recognized that the Established Church in Wales has always been a poor church, and largely because of the geographical terrain and the nature of the land. Tithe incomes had been smaller in Wales than in the rich agricultural counties of England. Some of the large parishes such as Bedwellty and Mynyddislwyn in the Llandaff diocese, and Beddgelert, Llandygái and Penmachno in the diocese of Bangor, had no tithes annexed. In 260 parishes no tithes were payable to the parish priest, and of these nearly one-half were in the diocese of St David's. In 1831 the total rent-charges accruing to the Church in Wales amounted to £304,563 15s.0d. Of this, only £155,456 14s.4d. found its way to the parochial clergy. The remainder went to ecclesiastical appropriators and lay impropriators. This was a sad loss of income to the parochial clergy, and it was not uniform throughout Wales. In the diocese of Bangor, two-thirds of the rent-charges were kept by the clergy. It was the south Wales dioceses which suffered most of all: in St David's there were areas where less than one quarter of the income was retained by the parish priests, and this was most pronounced in the counties of Carmarthenshire and Cardiganshire. In the whole of St David's diocese, out of 115 benefices, seventy-five were in lay hands and only thirty-seven in ecclesiastical hands. The remainder of the ecclesiastical income of Wales went to four

English bishops, and some of the lay patrons who took the tithe from Welsh parishes included the following corporations: Oxford University; Eton College; Christ's College, Cambridge; St David's College, Lampeter; Abergavenny Grammar School; Trinity House; and a number of charities.

Lay influence was not confined to the drawing of tithes, for many of the lay patrons had the advowson of parishes. This was the right of presentation to a vacancy in a parish; and an example of this was the Blaenavon Iron Company, which was sold in 1833. Among its advertised assets was the advowson of the living of Blaenavon. In the diocese of Llandaff the bishop had the right of presentation to only one parish, Bassaleg. This meant that the bishops of Llandaff had little control over appointments to livings in their diocese. All they could do was to protest, as they did in the case of Llanilltud Fawr, which was controlled by the dean and chapter of Gloucester. It was usually these men, and not the bishops, who appointed monoglot Englishmen to Welsh livings.

The bishops fared no better than the parochial clergy. The north Wales dioceses were usually far better placed than their southern counterparts. The bishops of St Asaph usually drew a solid income of £6,301 per annum, and the bishops of Bangor a comfortable £4,464. But the bishops of St David's must have encountered some difficulties in running their massive diocese on an income of £1,897 per annum, and the bishops of Llandaff must have found the task well-nigh impossible on £924 per annum. The bishops of St David's were often forced to augment their incomes by accepting nominations as deans of Durham, while their colleagues at Llandaff usually became deans of St Paul's. There were a number of clergy who were quite prepared to take advantage of the weaknesses inherent in the Church. Episcopal nepotism was worse in the diocese of St Asaph than almost anywhere else, and there were six clergymen who enjoyed between them an income of £13,839.

The education of the clergy in the Welsh dioceses was an additional embarrassment. In the years 1750–1860 the bishops appointed to the diocese of Llandaff were almost all distinguished scholars. Herbert Marsh (1816–19) was regarded as one of the foremost men of letters of his day at Cambridge, and he was Lady Margaret Professor of Divinity when he was appointed to Llandaff. He had expressed some concern at the nature of theological training, but there is no evidence to suggest that he attempted to introduce reforms. The next bishop, Van Mildert (1819–26) was Regius Professor of Divinity at Oxford, but there is no reason to believe that he produced any schemes for the reform of theological training. His successor, G.H. Sumner (1826–7), stayed for only a year and had little time to attend to the problems of his diocese. Edward Copleston followed in 1828 and remained Bishop of Llandaff for twenty-one years. He was Provost of Oriel College, Oxford, and took an active role in the reform of the ancient university. In 1850 he was succeeded by Alfred Ollivant, a former vice-principal of St David's College, Lampeter, and Professor of Divinity at Cambridge.

From 1816 to 1850 the see of Llandaff had been occupied by a succession of learned men and during this period about one quarter of the ordinands had emanated from the universities. Graduates were not always, however, fitted for theological and parochial training, and it seems that university students read little theology and only infrequently attended lectures delivered by the professors of divinity.

From 1750 to 1850 by far the greatest number of ordinands were literates, that is, men who had neither attended a university nor a theological college, but who seem to have come straight from one of the ancient grammar schools in the diocese — from Abergavenny, Cowbridge, or Usk. Most of these literates would have been immersed in a curriculum of English, Latin and mathematics, but there is no evidence of a divinity school until 1821, when a letter of that year refers to the 'Usk Divinity School' attached to the grammar school. There was no attempt to train these literates in their native language, and this was a major obstacle to effective parochial work. In the adjacent diocese of St David's the Ystradmeurig Grammar School could boast of a six-to-seven-year training in classics, divinity and mathematics, provided against a Welsh background. This made Ystradmeurig unique among Welsh grammar schools. The provision of competent clergy to man new churches and parishes was of paramount importance to the Established Church in Wales. The problem of staffing parishes with Welsh-speaking clergy had not been unknown in the eighteenth century, but it arose in a far more acute form in the 1820s onwards, especially in the industrial areas of Glamorgan and Monmouthshire. When Edward Copleston became Bishop of Llandaff in 1828 he discovered that thirty-three churches in Glamorgan and nine in Monmouthshire conducted their services in Welsh; twenty-seven in the former and 104 in the latter county held English services; and forty-seven churches in Glamorgan and fourteen in Monmouthshire held bilingual services. The pressures to remedy this state of affairs grew steadily in the 1830s and 1840s, and led to the gradual reform of the Church.

It would be most unfair to create the impression that the history of the Welsh Church in the first half of the nineteenth century was one of constant failure. As we shall see in later sections on the Church and the development of education, the foundation of the National Society in 1811 and its subsequent growth made a remarkable contribution to elementary education in the decades before the 1847 Blue Books. Its mistake, however, was to train children in a language which most of them could not understand: and it perpetrated this error in spite of the outstanding achievements of that parish priest from Llanddowror, Griffith Jones, in the second half of the eighteenth century. Still there is no denying the Church's significant contribution to primary education in Wales in the first half century.

The Temperance Movement and the Churches

The working classes were attracted to Bacchus as well as to God, and the public house was the other institution which was well represented in the rural and industrial communities. The pubs, like the chapels, were usually simple buildings, organized around two sets of rooms: the bar, with its lesser rooms; and the upstairs 'long room'. Throughout the nineteenth century, Welsh religious leaders had argued that eighteenth-century Wales had been a land of excessive drinking and that the religious revival had brought the people to their senses. Drink certainly fulfilled a number of important social functions in the nineteenth century: in some areas water was unsafe to drink; beer was often cheaper than other beverages; drink was reputed to enhance the physical strength and stamina of the imbiber; at sales and auctions alcoholic drinks were abundantly supplied; in some parishes the incumbents provided drinks for those paying their tithes; drink was a useful election device, and local and parliamentary candidates often incurred enormous expenses in supplying alcoholic refreshment; the pub was an important social and communal focus — the masculine republic — and there were few other counter-attractions before the 1850s; the public house was also a meeting place for various organizations and a centre of recreation — friendly societies met there, eisteddfodau were often held there, and some denominations were forced to use the long rooms for their earliest religious services.

Drink and drunkenness soon became problems in the industrial communities, and also in the rural hinterland. In west Wales, for example, the number of persons licensed for the general sale of beer increased from 158 in 1830–1 to 1,226 in 1831–2. Opening a beer house was, in fact, one way of moving on to the electoral register. In the industrial districts the predominant cause of drunkenness was the wretchedness created by the industrial environment. Intemperance caused poverty, but poverty also caused intemperance, and throughout the nineteenth century the areas of greatest drunkenness in Britain tended to be the large coalfield areas. Industrialization and urbanization had created so many difficulties for the people who lived and laboured in the new areas: industrialization had produced regular cycles of unemployment which made sobriety less attractive; higher wages were a temptation for the labouring classes to spend excessively on drink; the nature of work in the industrial communities — heavy, monotonous, and dangerous — was a factor in the equation that linked drink to the environment; the industrial process attracted migrant labourers and thousands of young people into the social maelstrom, free from the restraints of their old rural communities; housing and settlement patterns often created unhealthy villages and communities and exacerbated existing difficulties; and there was the absence of other forms of relaxation. In Merthyr Tydfil, the industrial metropolis of the Principality, offences caused by drink increased in the period from 1842 to 1860 and ran at an annual average of 58 per cent of the Glamorgan total. The period 1868 to 1881 was the high watermark for apprehensions and convictions for drunkenness in Wales. At Swansea, drunkenness as measured by convictions for the offence almost trebled between 1869 and 1873, and the total for Glamorgan in 1881 was 7.3 per 1,000.

The temperance movement originated in America in the mid 1820s and soon spread to England. The British and Foreign Temperance Society was founded at London in 1831. The first society among Welsh people was formed at Manchester in October 1831, and a local branch of the British and Foreign Temperance Society was established at Swansea in 1833. In south Wales the temperance doctrines of moderation and teetotalism made slow progress and total abstinence probably made its first appearance in the area in October 1836, when the Cardiff Total Abstinence Society was established. Temperance and total abstinence propaganda aroused strong feelings in Wales in the 1830s and 1840s, and critics of teetotalism saw it as an intolerant and exclusive creed. The redoubtable and combative Revd David Rees, Llanelli, an early supporter of the temperance movement, soon realized the explosiveness of the issue and, in 1841, he refused to publish temperance news in his independent journal, *Y Diwygiwr*, because it was too contentious.

Prior to the temperance movement many ministers of religion and clergy were stout supporters of John Barleycorn, and public houses were often associated with the chapels. Vestry meetings often indulged in beer parties, and even as late as the 1860s the London-Welsh would proceed directly from the chapel to the public house. But the dominant themes in the temperance campaign were those of self-respect and example-setting, and clergy were urged to be total abstainers. Many were, however, suspicious and opposed to total abstinence. Eben Fardd and others believed that the temperance message conflicted with the basic tenets of their theology, for a man's health could not be controlled by earthly circumstances, but was the product of divine guidance.

The temperance campaigners realized from the outset that it would not be easy to attract support for their campaign. Temperance robbed people of their only compensation for dullness and drab surroundings, and it failed to offer some additional freedoms as did the factory and the anti-Poor Law movements. The temperance message had to be presented in a colourful and attractive way. The form was as important as the content, and temperance societies gradually resorted to calling themselves 'orders'. They developed as ceremonial and communal orders, adopting regalia and ornate ceremonies in an attempt to draw people away from the pubs. The struggle against drink soon assumed the appearance of a military campaign:

> Come and join our noble army
> Be ye soldiers brave and hardy.

Temperance societies realized that they could only succeed in spreading their social gospel if they provided alternative sources of recreation. They set up coffee taverns, literary societies, workmen's libraries, and the like, in an effort to provide counter-attractions for the multitudes. In 1854 the Gymanfa Ddirwestol Gwent a Morgannwg (Gwent and Glamorgan Abstinence Council) was established at Merthyr so as to promote congregational singing among the labouring groups. The whole idea was to make temperance a way of life, and some have gone so far as to suggest that the temperance movement transmogrified into a separate denomination.

All the denominations, however, were equally the products of an evangelical revival which had swept through Wales in the eighteenth century, and all had grasped the essential Reformation truth that faith alone can save souls. The denominations understood also that, numerically, Christians were in a minority and that they were commissioned by Christ to preach the word to the vast majority of the indifferent and the openly hostile. It is for this reason that the temperance movement assumed the characteristics of a moral and religious crusade, and from the 1840s onwards the Dissenters and the Church seemed to co-operate in organizing a temperance campaign. Relations between them had been strained in the 1830s and early 1840s, but the shock of Chartist insurrection, the impact of economic depression, and the repercussions of the 1847 Blue Books on education all coalesced to create a united religious front in the 1850s and early 1860s. Between 1850 and 1855 the Established Church in Wales and the Nonconformists built churches, and from 1855 to 1860 they concentrated on erecting reading rooms and temperance halls. In the 1860s there was a changed mood as co-operation turned to competition. The activities of the Liberation Society were revitalizing Nonconformist ranks, and the 1859 religious revival had enhanced the numbers and the confidence of the Dissenters; while the Church was showing signs of division over ritualism. After 1860 the temperance issue played less of a part in uniting the Churchmen and the Nonconformists.

Among the various denominations the Calvinistic Methodists seem to have been the staunchest supporters of temperance; and in 1835 the Annual Association of Calvinistic Methodists in south Wales expressed its approval of the principles and objects of the British and Foreign Temperance Society. Total abstinence, however, became more of an improbability as the years advanced and in the 1860s and 1870s some members of the denomination were even permitted to keep pubs. The Independents seemed to lack a positive stance towards the issue and had no central organization until 1872 when the Union of Welsh Independents was formed. The leading individual supporters of total abstinence among the Welsh Independents were the Revd David Rees, Llanelli, and Ieuan Gwynedd. But temperance could be a divisive issue and it split the ranks of more than one congregation. The Revd William Rees (1839–1919) was locked out of his chapel at Llechryd, Cardiganshire, in February 1880, by the diaconate and some members of the congregation on account of his indomitable support for the temperance movement. There were many Baptist ministers who supported temperance throughout the century, but the vast majority adopted a realistic view of the drink question, emphasizing the importance of personal decision. In general, the Baptist associations merely urged individual churches to support the campaign and did not attempt to compel them to carry the temperance banner.

Revivals and Revivalism

Most of the historiography of Welsh religious revivals was compiled towards the end of the nineteenth century and the beginning of the new century. In 1898 Edward Parry produced *Llawlyfr ar Hanes y Diwygiadau Crefyddol yng Nghymru*, a list of

Welsh religious awakenings since the Reformation. The book was written from a theological standpoint, tending to chronicle the revivals as miraculous events. Like most contemporary writers Parry viewed revivals as, 'outpourings of grace from above'. Until the 1820s religious revivals were interpreted as occasional visitations, divinely inspired to rouse congregations and to bring new converts into the religious camps. They were seen as miraculous acts of divine grace.

But there were new approaches looming from America and these were associated with revivalists such as C.G. Finney and Calvin Colton. In 1832 the latter wrote, *The History and Character of American Revivals*, a work which captured the attention of the British public. Colton argued that revivalists had purposely set out to preach their congregations into a state of hysteria. He admitted, therefore, that non-spiritual factors could be used to hasten a revival. His new emphasis was on the need to create, by human means if necessary, a certain feeling among members of the community that would prepare them for an eventual religious visitation. The revivalists could use either of two methods to create the necessary preconditions: one means was to exert intense psychological pressure on prospective converts and to hold an 'anxious meeting' either during or after a normal service; the other way was to use external social events to generate a pathological fear of impending disaster and to create a general unease among the congregation. Colton's arguments greatly influenced the Welsh preacher, Williams o'r Wern, who placed similar emphasis on revivals within his own churches. Williams was especially important in the 1839–40 revival in north Wales and he introduced the idea that revivals should be actively encouraged. He wanted to save souls, but he also realized that chapel debts needed to be cleared and, within a few months, the Independents had collected £18,000 towards a debt of £34,000. The idea of a prepared revival was fairly well established in Wales: what was new was the emphasis that revivals should be directly encouraged by specified means.

Following Colton, the most prominent pioneer of the new active and open methods of promoting revivals was C.G. Finney who published his ideas in *Lectures on Revivals of Religion* in 1831. Finney was a professional revivalist who devised a particular system whereby people were brought by public expression to testify to their true conversion. He exerted a great emotional pressure on individuals, and his personal approach seemed to suit Welsh rural communities where congregations had become well established. Wales was slow to accept the new religious concepts from America, for there were no native professional revivalists in the country. Christmas Evans and John Elias were itinerant ministers not revivalists. Finney's ideas were accepted in Wales largely because he had experienced frontier conditions in America and his *Lectures* were concerned with reviving a church that was slumbering. He provided a viable model for revival at the local level and useful guidelines for the promotion of small-scale revivals in specific localities.

Although Welsh revivals were influenced by the American experiences, they were not dependent upon the American revivalists. Wales had developed its own tradition of revivalism since the evangelical awakening of the 1730s, and much of the religious expansion which occurred in the immediate aftermath of the French wars was directly caused by a most powerful revival, the awakening that started at Beddgelert in Caernarfonshire from 1817 to 1822. Revivals were a reaction to the social pressures of the age and ministers capitalized on certain tensions within communities. In 1817 the source of the tensions was the pitiful condition of the lower classes after the post-war depression. Over-population, the effects of the enclosure movement, and bad harvests in 1817 made the conditions of the poorer classes almost intolerable.

There were a series of revivals in the years from 1820 to 1850 and perhaps a closer inspection of these will help us to understand the nature and mechanism of a revival. A revival had begun at Caeo in Carmarthenshire in 1828, and it soon spread to most parts of south Wales. In November 1828, it had reached Swansea and Neath, and in 1828–9 it was disseminated through the industrial districts. This was the first revival experience that many of these areas had witnessed. Religious revivalism was the language of the lower classes; it was an expression of the discontent and disappointment that were keenly felt in the new industrial communities. The 1828–9 revival was directly influenced by the general deterioration of social conditions in the parish: the effects of cholera; the dangerous employment; and the depression in the iron and coal industries. Trade had become so depressed that there occurred a fall of 5*s*. per ton in the price of pig-iron and 10*s*. on bar-iron. In order to offset this price reduction, many ironmasters resorted to the practice of cutting wages. A widespread protest ensued, with Llanelli colliers coming out on strike, and workers in Merthyr Tydfil and Monmouthshire finding it impossible to get paid. In July 1829 Monmouthshire colliers withdrew their labour amidst an atmosphere of violence and distrust. At the Bute Ironworks a serious riot erupted when Welsh workers sought to eject all Englishmen from the district.

Such manifestations of resentment against immigrants from England and Ireland were recurring themes in early revivalism in industrial south Wales. The revival seemed to be a particularly Welsh phenomenon, intolerant of the non-Welsh population and stoutly defensive of the indigenous Welsh immigrants. An essential feature of this xenophobia was the notion of the revival as a rural, Welsh phenomenon. In some ways the Welshness was an attempt by the first generation immigrants to recall and re-create past values. The revival had been an integral part of their rural heritage and they preserved it as a 'badge of nationality' in the face of alien immigration. It might also be argued that these first generation immigrants were endeavouring to introduce an element of order into the social chaos of their Klondike-like settlements. Whatever the rationale, the effects of the 1828–9 revival were physically and numerically significant. At least 2,000 new members were captured in Carmarthenshire, and Glamorgan could boast of twenty-seven new chapels built in the years 1828–30.

In 1831–2 there followed another revival. On 17 August 1831, the *Rothesay Castle* had gone aground off the coast of Anglesey in a ferocious storm. Only twenty-one of the 130 people on board the ship were saved, and this disaster struck a note of doom in the community at large. The Revd John Elias and his ministerial colleagues sensed the feelings of the neighbourhood and helped the revival on its way. The visitation of Asiatic cholera in 1832 merely accentuated the problems of the district and, by July 1832, there were thirty deaths in Caernarfon alone. The cholera also spread to south Wales, where the ironworks were already experiencing a lean period. In 1831 Merthyr had been the scene of a major insurrection, and nascent unions had already permeated the coalfields in the north and south. As in the northern counties, so in the south the Calvinistic Methodists had expressed total opposition to oath-taking and unionism in general at the Tredegar Association in October 1831. The Wesleyans were also clear in their condemnation of secret societies; while the Baptists and Independents were less decisive and unanimous in their opinions. The revival was Nonconformity's answer to the problems of this world and, in a sense, it merely postponed those problems to a later date.

The awakenings of the period 1837–42 injected a new element into revivalism: the theme of temperance. The first temperance revival was at Bala when an American preacher, the Revd B.W. Chidlaw, visited the area. He advocated total abstinence and he claimed that 5,000 people had signed the pledge in the Bala district in 1841. In 1839 the North Wales Temperance Association was recruiting 9,000 people into its local societies. The revival then fanned outwards towards the south, making an impression on the industrial and manufacturing districts. Its success was attributable to a variety of factors: the industrial depression which had appeared in 1838 was worsening in the years 1842–3, and there were savage cuts in wages and mass unemployment in the industrial and rural pockets; it was a period in which scores of petitions were sent to the House of Commons complaining of the Corn Laws, the Poor Law and high taxes; temperance was a viable proposition in a society in which money was scarce and food in short supply; the movement had much to offer as a social anodyne in terms of economic and social distress — its recreational activities, the colour and pomp of its ceremonies, the regalia and positions of responsibility in temperance societies, all provided lively and meaningful alternatives to the drab economic circumstances of the period.

The year 1849 witnessed another big revival across the Principality, and it appeared in response to a number of economic and social stimuli. The same year 1849 saw one of the worst outbreaks of cholera in the century, as Asiatic cholera struck rural and urban centres alike. By September 1849, it had claimed 1,500 lives in Cardiff and, in industrial villages like Aberavon and Taibach, it wiped out whole families. The poorer classes were confused, disheartened and disillusioned and many turned to Divine Providence for an explanation of the epidemic. It is claimed that people gathered in their thousands in prayer meetings, 'anxious meetings', and in temperance societies in an attempt to propitiate the Divine Spirit. Other factors which had certainly paved the way for this revival were the Chartist actions of 1848, and the long and bitter strikes among the colliers of Merthyr Tydfil, Aberdare and the Rhondda valleys.

Thus, the churches' responses to the political, economic and social grievances of the period were to concentrate on temperance and revivalism. The denominations, strongly evangelical in their theology, emphasized the centrality of individual responsibility and worth, and claimed that individual evils were responsible for the social iniquities of the period. The majority of Welsh clergy found it difficult to understand what lay behind such protest movements as Chartism or the Rebecca Riots. Certainly, the denominations seemed to condemn Chartism: the Baptists gave it lukewarm support; the Calvinistic Methodists were stubbornly resistant; and the Independents were as independent as usual — some stoutly opposed the movements, such as the Revd Richard Jones, of Sirhowy Ironworks, who excommunicated all Chartists from his congregation; while others, like the Revd Benjamin Byron of Hope Chapel, Newport, were openly sympathetic. The Revd Evan Jones (Ieuan Gwynedd) printed Chartist propaganda in his journals. The Unitarians, in their free-thinking manner, gave consistent support to Chartism and to other popular movements, but they were not in the mainstream and their influence was severely constricted. The denominations as a whole tended not to support working-class insurrection, and some would go so far as to claim that the temperance movement and the revivals of the early 1840s were diversionary tactics, encouraged by the ministers, clergy and other interested groups to turn people away from Chartism, Rebecca and other public, and often violent, expressions of discontent.

SUGGESTED READING

E.T. Davies, *Religion in the Industrial Revolution in South Wales* (Cardiff, 1965).

E.T. Davies, *Religion and Society in the Nineteenth Century* (Llandybie, 1981).

I.G. Jones, *Explorations and Explanations* (Llandysul, 1981).

I.G. Jones, *Communities* (Llandysul, 1987).

W.R. Lambert, *Drink and Sobriety in Victorian Wales, c. 1820–c.1895* (Cardiff, 1984).

Articles:

E.T. Davies, 'The Education of the Clergy in the Diocese of Llandaff 1750–1866', *J.H.S. Ch. in W.*, XXVI (1979).

W.R. Lambert, 'Drink and Work–Discipline in Industrial South Wales c.1800–1870', *W.H.R.*, 7 (1974–5).

5. Education Before the Blue Books

INDUSTRIALIZATION in Wales during the nineteenth century produced a variety of new problems, most of which were associated with the remarkable growth and concentration of population in the mining and metallurgical areas. After 1800 the growth of population in the counties of Monmouthshire and Glamorgan was phenomenal. From 1801 to 1851 the increase for Glamorgan was 223 per cent, and for Monmouthshire 244 per cent, whereas the national average for Britain was around 93 per cent. In the inter-censal period 1841–51 the population of Glamorgan had multiplied by more than 35 per cent, as immigrants from rural Wales, nearby English counties, and Ireland, swarmed in. Living conditions in the newly-industrialized communities were deplorable and, in those places where works' proprietors built houses for their work-force, they usually did so without paying much attention to the comforts, health or decency of the people.

Population growth and rapid industrialization also raised another problem, that of education. It is perhaps fair to say that the provision of elementary education for the working classes attracted more public attention in Wales during the greater part of the nineteenth century than any other issue. Basic elementary education in Wales before 1840 was provided mainly by the Sunday schools and by clusters of private adventure schools which offered some form of instruction for a 1d. a week for those who could afford it. The two voluntary societies, the National and British societies, had penetrated the Principality in the years before 1840, but their activities were circumscribed. The infamous Blue Books of 1847 show that, although there were hundreds of schools of one kind or another in Wales, most were in a languishing and totally unsatisfactory state. Countless government reports in the first half of the century drew attention to the lamentable state of education and to the 'education destitution' which existed, in particular, in the industrial areas of south Wales. We shall turn our attention now to those schools and educational societies that operated in the period before 1847.

The British Schools in Wales

The movement to establish British schools is usually associated with the activities of the British and Foreign School Society, which was founded in London in 1814 to promote the education of the labouring and manufacturing classes of every religious persuasion. It was a movement initiated at the beginning of the nineteenth century by Joseph Lancaster, the Quaker pioneer of the Lancasterian, or what he called the British, system of education at his Royal Free Schools, Borough Road, London. The system was based on the following principles: instruction should be available to the whole community; the teaching of the dogma of any religious sect should be excluded from schools; the Holy Scriptures should be the only religious textbook used; and scholars should attend places of worship chosen by their parents. In short, the system proclaimed the virtues of unsectarianism.

In the years 1806 to 1814, the period when Lancaster was personally involved with the development of the movement, he influenced the course of events by personal contact with various areas. In the year 1806–7 he made a short tour of south Wales, visiting Cardiff, Neath, Swansea, and Carmarthen. In 1806 several gentlemen of various denominations in Swansea and district had corresponded with Lancaster and discussed the outlines of his system. Soon they formed 'The Swansea Society for the Education of the Children of the Poor', to establish first a boys' and later a girls' school. At a general meeting in the Town Hall on 29 January 1806, the Society formulated rules for the conduct of the school: instruction was to be given only to the children of parents too poor to pay for their schooling; instruction would be given in reading, writing, and the first rules of arithmetic; the principles of religion and morality were certainly not to be neglected, and all pupils were expected to attend a place of worship every Sunday. The venture was supported by gentlemen from various backgrounds and the

Swansea Lancasterian school was opened on 30 June 1806. It was the first Lancasterian school established in Wales.

Lancaster visited south Wales in the autumn of 1807 and, at a later stage, he referred to the success of his movement in Carmarthen, Swansea, and all over south Wales. His system was certainly creating an interest, and especially where Quaker families had settled in connection with the copper, iron, and coal industries. Lancaster was, however, a little prone to exaggeration and the recorded number of schools at this time does not justify his optimism. The years 1808–14 were much more fruitful. In 1808 two schools were opened in Swansea and one near Cardiff. At Swansea a new Lancasterian boys' school was opened in Goat Street in 1808, with provision for 300 boys. A committee of ladies formed in 1807 established a Lancasterian girls' school early in 1808 to educate girls from poor homes to become useful domestic servants. The rules for admission were the same as those for boys, with the addition of instruction in needlework. Another Lancasterian school was opened in 1808 at Melingriffith, near Cardiff, by John and Samuel Harford, members of a wealthy Bristol Quaker family of industrialists. They were interested in the welfare of their employees at Melingriffith Tinworks, and in October 1807 they invited Lancaster to address a local meeting on his system of education. The meeting decided to establish a Lancasterian school and the Harfords headed a subscription list.

A school at Neath Abbey, Glamorgan, had been established by Peter Price, a Quaker ironmaster. He came to Neath in 1799 to manage Neath Abbey Ironworks and he erected a school for the poor children of the district. His son, J. Tregelles Price, an elder of the Society of Friends, followed him as manager and he retained close links with the school. In January 1809, the Borough Road School in London arranged for him to have a copy of Lancaster's Spelling Book, a number of slates, and other literature. J.T. Price remained a loyal supporter of the British school movement and of the Neath Abbey School.

In north Wales the movement seems to have made little impact in this initial phase, for a variety of reasons: the comparative poverty of the Nonconformists meant that they were unable to provide building sites for schools; the gentry, the landowners and the clergy supported the church schools, and the National Society made considerable strides in the area after 1811. There are, however, two examples of Lancasterian schools being established. The first was near Wrexham, where the Stanton theatrical company gave a public performance in October 1800 to raise funds to establish a Lancasterian school for poor children in the area. The second was attributable to William Alexander Madocks's efforts. A local industrialist and philanthropist of some importance, he enclosed 1,000 acres of Traeth Mawr, Caernarfonshire, and built Tremadoc, where he opened a Lancasterian school in the Town Hall in 1810.

Other schools followed in Brecon in 1811 and in Usk in July 1813. Apart from these, few others were established before 1814. The only schools mentioned in the report for 1812 were Swansea, Neath Abbey, Abergavenny, and Machen. In April 1814, Lancaster severed his connection with the Society and the so-called Lancasterian era came to an end.

In the years from 1814 to 1833 the British and Foreign School Society built on the foundations of the Lancasterian era. But the Society's impact in Wales in this period was negligible. In 1819 it admitted that its restricted funds prevented it from giving assistance. Its reports for the years 1814 to 1833 do not provide information on the movement's progress in Wales but, in June 1820, we are informed that fifteen schools had been established in Wales since 1806 and that others were being considered for the future. Over half the schools recorded in the 1820s had been established in the preceding, Lancasterian era. The period 1814–33 was, therefore, one of consolidation with some limited expansion.

Throughout this phase, the Swansea schools continued to grow and in 1815 the boys' school was advertised as a school where masters could be trained for a premium of £2.2s.0d. By 1825 the number of boys admitted since 1806 had reached 3,281. The Swansea girls' school had experienced mixed fortunes and had succeeded in alienating its founder, Richard Phillips, by introducing a particular form of prayer and taking the majority of the pupils to church. Phillips responded by building another girls' school, which was opened in 1821 and was conducted on the principles of the British and Foreign School Society.

In February 1824 the Neath Abbey School was reorganized and reopened, under the charge of a master who had been trained at the Swansea British Boys' School. Within three months of its reopening there were eighty pupils in the school, and in 1825 a new schoolroom was erected to accommodate 120 children. A girls' and an infants' school was started in the building at a later date. At nearby Carmarthen a Lancasterian school had been opened in 1814 for fifty boys. By 1822 over 1,000 pupils had been taught the rudiments of arithmetic and how to read and write. The headmaster of this school, who was appointed in 1822, had been trained at the Borough Road School in London.

In the same period, from 1814 to 1833, other schools were set up at Newport, Cardiff, Caernarfon, Crickhowell, Caerleon, and Ebbw Vale. The Newport British Boys' School was opened in March 1815, largely as a result of a subscription of £100 from Sir Charles Morgan, the MP for Monmouthshire and president of the Newport British School Society. It accommodated 133 pupils aged from six to twelve years and, by 1831, 1,136 pupils had been admitted to it. At Cardiff, the Free School was established under the patronage of the Marquis of Bute in 1815. The British and Foreign School Society provided a master, and it supplied most of the equipment and lesson materials.

In August 1833 there came the first government grant to education; the money to be divided between the two societies, the British and the National. This aid was provided for the erection of schoolhouses and carried the condition that building proposals needed the approval of either of the two societies. Because these grants were dependent upon a stipulated amount of local voluntary contributions being available, much of the Principality was too poor to satisfy the regulations and only a small portion of the money secured by the British and Foreign School Society reached Wales. It would seem that only about three or four per cent of a total of £50,000 flowed into Wales. During the initial years 1833–4 the applications for aid from Wales were quite insignificant. One such application had come from Bangor seeking £105 towards the estimated cost of £210 to erect a school for 200 children. A letter was also received from Templeton, in Pembrokeshire, noting that there was no school for the children of the poor within an area of two miles and that over 200 children were in need of instruction. Reports show that a school was established at St Dogmael's in Pembrokeshire in

1834 under the auspices of the Society. A new girls' school, with a qualified teacher from Borough Road, was opened at Newport on 1 January 1834. Overall, it is estimated that fourteen places, scattered in north and south Wales, received grants to build British schools in the years from 1835 to 1840. These grants varied from £18 for a new school at Heneglwys in Anglesey, to £125 for a school in Haverfordwest. Other places which were given financial assistance were Holyhead, Morriston, Bangor, Narberth, Port Madoc, Talybont, and Mumbles.

In April 1839 State intervention took a further step when the Government announced that the Committee of the Privy Council had been set up to superintend the application of money voted by Parliament for educational purposes. The Committee would only consider applications in relation to the schools of the British or National societies. In the succeeding years there followed a marked increase in the number of applications for aid and the British Society reported in 1841 that seventeen places in Wales had applied to the Committee for grant aid. Some of the places seeking aid to build schools were Rhosllannerchrugog, Llangollen, Penmachno, Llantrisant, Ynyscedwyn, and Neath. Places seeking assistance to pay teachers' salaries were Cefn Canol, Llanarman Dyffryn Ceiriog and Llanfachreth. Applications for a grant to meet general expenses were sent from Bedwellty, Llanfawr, Corris and Aberllefenni, and Dyffryn.

In December 1839, the Committee of Council instructed H.S. Tremenheere, HMI of grant-aided schools, to inquire into the state of elementary education in the mining districts of south Wales, and particularly Monmouthshire, the scene of the recent Chartist disturbances. Tremenheere reported in February 1840 that, in five parishes which were the focus of the disturbances, there were only two British schools, out of a total of forty-seven schools in operation. In March 1840 the Committee responded to the report by offering the twenty-nine mining proprietors in Monmouthshire the opportunity to seek assistance in establishing schools in their localities. There was no immediate widespread response from the industrialists, although a little later more industrialists did seek to develop a closer association between their works and the British and Foreign School Society.

In the years from 1841 to 1843 there were some substantial grants to schools in Wales. One of the most notable was for a school at Ynyscedwyn, at the top of the Swansea Valley, to accommodate 307 children. The Committee awarded £250, which was exactly a half of the estimated building cost. With the gradual encroachment of the state there came a limited increase in the number of British schools in Wales in the years from 1833 to 1843. It is difficult to give precise figures, but one estimate suggests that the number of schools had increased to twenty-eight in that decade.

One important change that was occurring in the years after 1815 was the gradual transition from 'free' to 'fee-paying' schools. In 1835 the British Society reported that Neath Abbey schools, with 210 boys and 50 girls enrolled, had benefited from an agreement with the nearby iron and coal works whereby each man paid 1*d*. and each employed boy ½*d*. per week. These payments, deducted at the works' office, provided about £80 a year and enabled all the employees' children to attend the school. In 1838 the Swansea Boys' School was operating a new scheme of fees introduced in 1835 whereby parents earning under 15*s*. a week paid 1*d*. for one boy, but 2*d*. for all boys of the same family; those earning in excess of 15*s*., but under 20*s*., paid 2*d*. for one boy but 4*d*. for all boys of the same family; and parents earning more than 20*s*. paid 2*d*. for each boy.

Historians have often regarded the year 1843 as a turning-point in the history of the British school movement in Wales. In that year there was a remarkable increase in the number of British schools in north Wales, though, in the south, progress was much less spectacular. One factor which stimulated the British school movement was the excitement that built up over Graham's Factory Bill in March 1843. Its educational clauses were seen as giving the Church control over the proposed new schools and, in Wales, members of the Nonconformist camp rose in stout defence of their traditions and liberties. There was an air of frenzied activity as meetings were held at Haverfordwest in April, and at Neath and Swansea in May. The Bill was eventually withdrawn, but the agitation had concentrated the minds of the Nonconformist denominations and propelled the rise of Voluntaryism, (i.e. the anti-State aid movement), especially in south Wales.

Another factor of considerable importance which accounted for the development of the British school movement after 1843 was the publication of Hugh Owen's famous *Letter to the Welsh People*, in August of that year. This was Owen's master-plan for the provision of an efficient system of British schools throughout Wales. The scheme involved placing a British school in every district and forming a British School Society in every county. Local committees were to be appointed in every district to find a site, seek support for the school, and secure the services of a teacher. Owen outlined the facilities available at the British Society's Normal School in London, and he offered to place before the Government those applications for British schools in Wales. The response to his letter was so encouraging that he urged the British Society to send agents to Wales to promote the British school system. The Society took the hint and, by November 1843, Revd John Phillips had been appointed as the Society's agent for north Wales. Soon it was realized that the one agent could not possibly cover all the work and, by July 1845, Revd H. Pugh and the Revd J. Mills had agreed to assist Phillips as part-time agents. By 1846, thirty-one schools had been established in north Wales; and Anglesey, where Phillips lived, had the highest number of ten new schools. By May 1848, another forty-eight schools had been opened, including those in south Wales. The Voluntaryists had set up their own schools in the south, and no agent was appointed for the British Society in these parts until 1853.

In 1844 the Revd Henry Richard reported to the Congregational Union on the state of education in Wales, and this spurred some London Welshmen into action. In March 1845, twelve '*émigré*' Welshmen published a letter in Welsh journals, reminding their countrymen that, unless they endeavoured to provide education, a bill similar to Graham's could be resurrected. They also arranged a conference of all denominations in south Wales, which met at Llandovery in April 1845. The conference, which was attended by 120 representatives, agreed that the leading denominations should unite to establish undenominational schools. As an initial step, they launched the South Wales Committee of Education which, in September 1845, decided to rent a building at Brecon for use as a Normal school to train young men in the British system. This was opened on 1 January

1846 and, by November 1846, fifteen students had been given various periods of training and had left to return to their previous schools or to start new schools.

Hugh Owen did not support the policies of the Llandovery conference. He feared that the South Wales Education Committee would rake up the old sectarian differences, and he preferred to see students from Wales proceeding to the Borough Road Normal School for their training. In April 1846 he became the honorary secretary of the newly-formed Cambrian Education Society, which sought to promote the establishment of British schools in Wales. The Cambrian Education Society began conducting its own survey into the provision of day schools at the same time as the Government Commissioners were beginning their inquiry into the state of education in Wales. Major strides had been made since the early Lancasterian days, and all these developments augured well for the future of the British school movement in Wales.

The Contribution of the National Schools

The 'National Society for Promoting the Education of the Poor in the Principles of the Established Church', was founded in October 1811. It was a Church association, founded as a result of the work of individual churchmen, many of whom were already active members of the SPCK. The newly-founded National Society had an ambitious aim, namely, to provide every parish in England and Wales with a school in which the poor could be educated in the principles of the Established Church. Some of the earliest National schools in Wales were established by diocesan organizations. In 1811 a committee had been formed in Bridgend with all the clergy as subscribers. In April 1812 it entered 'into union' with the National Society and set about establishing schools for boys and girls. The first diocese in Wales, in fact, with an organization of this kind was Bangor. The absence of elementary schools in the diocese had alarmed the higher clergy and, following a public meeting on 29 December 1812, a Bangor Diocesan Committee was established, which received a grant of £30 from the National Society. This was the first grant given to Wales.

By the end of 1816 there were twenty-three National schools in Wales, five in the diocese of Bangor, four in St David's, eight in Llandaff, and six in St Asaph. In 1817, ten more schools appeared and the financial drain on the National Society's funds became quite considerable. The demand for National schools in Wales far exceeded the supply, and many of the existing schools quickly became overcrowded. The Society's funds were almost exhausted by 1823 and it became necessary to appeal, through the parochial clergy, to all the congregations in the land. As a result, funds once again began to flow into the coffers. Nevertheless, the Society was continually under financial strain and thus unable to offer annual grants. Local school committees were expected to be responsible for the upkeep of the schools and the teachers' salaries. These costs were usually met by subscriptions, collections, and parental payments. The rate was around 1*d.* a week per pupil, but there were some striking variations: at Llandaff, Glamorgan, it was 6*d.* a month, while at Margam the workers of the English Copper Company paid 1½*d.* a week from their wages so that all the children could attend free of charge.

By far the greatest single item of expenditure was the teacher's salary, and at the beginning of the century this was often low. Salaries varied considerably. For example, the schoolmaster at Carmarthen Boys' National School was paid £40 per annum and as much as he could collect from 'the pennies of the pupils'. The highest remuneration was £100 per annum, which was paid to the schoolmaster at Beaumaris. Many school committees were compelled to offer payment in kind as well as in cash. The master at Margam received £52 per annum 'with house and coals'. Many of the National schoolteachers were employed as village shopkeepers, shoemakers, small farmers, and even publicans, so as to supplement their meagre incomes.

In the period from 1811 to 1833 the National Society had already achieved much in the Principality. In 1833, 146 National schools were operating and instructing approximately 13,424 pupils. The schools were open to all the children of the poor, regardless of their religious affiliations and, according to the reports of the Charity Commissioners and the Abstract of Educational Returns of 1833, not one National school in Wales excluded Dissenters' children. The National Society had made

strenuous efforts to promote elementary education on a large
scale in the years before the introduction of the first government
grant: it had provided building grants, encouraged the formation of diocesan and district societies, and tried to increase the
value of education for the poor. But there was still much to be
accomplished: the larger towns such as Cardiff and Swansea,
were still without a National school, and many of the industrial
and rural areas were still without daily schools.

In 1812, the National Society had made it clear that all the
children who attended their schools should be instructed in the
Liturgy and Catechism. Some Anglican leaders, such as Dean
Cotton of Bangor, firmly declared that the main purpose of the
schools was to ground the children in a knowledge of the Holy
Scriptures and ensure that they were well acquainted with the
teachings of the Church. In some areas the National schools
insisted that pupils should attend the Church, and this only
exacerbated relations between the Church and the Dissenters.

Reports from National school committees from all over Wales
showed that there was a clear emphasis on discipline and moral
training, and many officials commented on the improvement in
the manners and morals of the young. At Llandovery, in 1816,
the inhabitants spoke of great advances 'in decency and
conduct' among the local children. At Holyhead, in 1819, only a
few months after the National school had opened, 'the town was
perfectly quiet'. Despite this general emphasis on discipline,
only a few of the teachers in these early National schools seem to
have been cruel. At Llangefni, in north Wales, corporal
punishment was a daily occurrence, and the children lived in
fear of being put in the 'Twll Du' (black hole) for the slightest
misdemeanour.

The curriculum of the schools was of a limited nature, with
the greater emphasis on moral and religious teaching, but
with some instruction in the three Rs and domestic crafts.
The monitorial system was used to teach the work to the
large numbers of children who were assembled in the schools.
Most of the National schools found it extremely difficult
to purchase basic resources for their pupils, and some, such
as Llangefni National School, relied entirely on subscriptions.
At Rhiwabon, in 1832, the schoolmaster had to accept a
reduction in salary so that a pound could be spent to purchase

books. Few of the schools had a library, although in 1814 the General Committee recommended that the Welsh Diocesan Committees should establish a depot of books. No action was taken until 1820, when the St Asaph Committee opened a central library in the diocese.

Teaching methods were based on a system of rote-learning, and the work involved cramming the memories of the children with the necessary information. There was a graduated system of instruction with the lowest classes often learning the alphabet and the Lord's Prayer 'off by heart', while the next class wrote on slates and learnt the Catechism and its explanation. The top class would often read portions of the Bible and learn to use simple divisions. Although the work of most schools was confined to the three Rs and religious instruction, occasionally a committee or an enterprising teacher would endeavour to provide a broader and more balanced curriculum. At Machynlleth National School mensuration was included, while at Neath needlework was taught, provided that the girls paid 1*d.* a week extra. Navigation was part of the curriculum at Caernarfon, spinning at Bridgend, and straw-hat making at Blaenavon. Most of the early patrons and promoters of the schools acted as unofficial inspectors so as to ensure that the schools were attending to their duties in an efficient manner. In many areas local committees organized their own visitational schemes: in Bangor there were daily superintendents; Bridgend preferred monthly visitations; while at Llandovery the scholars were subjected to a system of weekly examinations. By 1820 the diocese of St David's had organized its own system of inspection on a diocesan basis. An important feature of the visitation scheme in Wales was the annual public examination. On 20 October 1812, the 150 children at Bridgend were marched from the Town Hall, where the school was housed, to the Parish Church for their public examination. On 5 July 1818, the Bangor Town Band led a procession from the National schools of Bangor to Llandygái where they were publicly examined. By 1828 the National Society could proudly boast that four in seven of its schools had the benefit of visitors and the general superintendent. The inspection system, though voluntary and local, did prove quite useful in ensuring that a basic standardization of learning was maintained.

There were many obstacles to the effectiveness of the schools in Wales, of which language was one. Very few of the pupils were acquainted with the language in which they were instructed, and there seemed to be no guidance from the National Society on how best to tackle this problem. There is nothing in the Annual Reports to indicate that the Society was even aware of the existence of the difficulty. Most of the leaders of the National Society movement in Wales stressed the importance of acquiring a mastery of the English language. At Ruthin National School, Canon Newcombe, Warden of Ruthin, insisted that the children learn the Catechism in Welsh as well as in English. He believed that this was the only way of ensuring that the National system functioned well in Wales. Although a number of local committees included the Welsh language in their syllabuses, the prevailing language was English, and the schools were conducted in much the same way as their counterparts in England.

Poor attendance was a perennial problem. The school minute books disclose the various reasons for this and reveal the spirited efforts made to control the problem. When the committee at Bridgend in 1817 decided to inspect all absentees at regular intervals, the attendance rate improved. At Caernarfon, in 1819, parents were required to explain their children's absence from school for two days or more and, if the explanations were unsatisfactory, expulsion could follow. The National schools at Buckley in Flintshire and at Llantwit Major in Glamorgan had an intricate system of rewards for regular attendance.

An even more intractable difficulty was the quality of the teaching staff. Most of the Welsh schools were staffed by teachers who were usually untrained and completely inefficient. It was estimated that 90 per cent of the teachers in the elementary schools of Wales in the 1830s had not been trained. The National Society had not prepared any proposals for the training of the teachers in Wales, and every local committee was free to apply its own method. Some local societies and managerial boards were quite earnest in their attempts to train teachers, and the Bridgend National School, founded in 1812, was so progressive that it soon became known as the 'Model School'. In 1815, five masters and one mistress, all in charge of schools, had been trained there. Similar roles were performed by the St Asaph National School in 1817, and later by those at Usk, Llandaff, and Caernarfon.

The advent of state grants after 1833 eased the financial situation for the National Society, and Wales received its first Treasury grant in 1834 when £80 was given to the National school at Abergwili in Carmarthenshire. In 1835 Llanbedr in Caernarfonshire received £47, Llanllwchhaearn in Cardiganshire £40, and Llansantffraid in Denbighshire and Llandysilio in Monmouthshire each received a grant of £30. The grants did enable the National Society to undertake a minor expansionary programme and so there was a gradual annual increase in the number of schools brought into union with the National Society. Table 5.1, which appeared in the Society's 1836 Annual Report, outlines the progress made in all the Welsh counties after three years of state grants.

Table 5.1

County	Schools	Attendance	Treasury Grant, 1833–5 (£)	National Society Grant, 1833–5 (£)
Anglesey	32	2,547	156	269
Brecon	13	1,837	153	249
Cardigan	16	953	93	382
Carmarthen	32	2,421	533	614
Caernarfon	41	2,738	88	627
Denbigh	45	2,984	566	942
Flint	43	4,704	524	1,195
Glamorgan	39	2,365	166	759
Merioneth	15	996	91	87
Monmouth	35	1,994	523	885
Montgomery	20	1,228	63	885
Pembroke	16	985	553	332
Radnor	7	307	50	70
TOTALS	354	26,059	£3,559	£7,296

Despite injections of money from the Government, the finances of the National schools were nearly always in a perilous state and they relied heavily on parish subscriptions. The Newport National School, for instance, cost £1,000 to build. The Treasury provided £295, the National Society £200, and the parish had to contribute the remaining £505. When the schools fell into financial troubles, the parish incumbent could often be liable for all debts; and the fact that only the schools at Edeyrn, Aberystruth, Rochfield, Minera, and Ewloe were forced to close in this period is of great credit to the parish clergy.

The early National schools contended with many obstacles to development: finances were a major problem for most schools; administering schools in a country of sparsely-populated areas was not easy; language was an insuperable barrier for some district committees; the lack of trained teachers compounded the difficulties, as did the absence of compulsory attendance, and growingly, keen competition from Nonconformists. Yet, despite this array of obstacles, the National Society made substantial contributions to Welsh education in the years from 1811 to 1846. There were 146 schools established under the aegis of the Society and many Church schools had decided to adopt the Society's teaching system without actually seeking to be united with it. The achievements were significant and the Society proceeded in the years after 1846 to expand its frontiers and to improve the government of its existing territorial gains.

The Works' Schools

The works' school would seem to have been a familiar institution in western Europe, and in Sweden, Germany, and some parts of Holland. The Swedish schools existed in the seventeenth century, and the most prominent were found in close association with the copper industry. There was a copperworks' school in Dalarna in 1642 and, in the Uppsala region, works' schools were to be found in every works. The ironworks district in the Karlstad region also had a number of works' schools. The works' schools in Wales were closely linked to the industrial development of the country and, in particular, to the immigrant foreign and English industrialists. The industrial areas of England were peppered with works' schools in the nineteenth century: in Durham there were colliery schools, the large schools of the Consett Iron and Coal

Company, and the chemical works' schools; there were also works' schools in Warwickshire, Staffordshire, and Cornwall.

The works' schools in Wales were established by all the major metallurgical and mining industries, and it would seem that the first works' charity school was set up in 1700 by Sir Humphrey Mackworth at the Esgair Hir Mines in north Cardiganshire. Mackworth built another charity works' school at Neath around 1705. But no others of this kind were established in Wales in the eighteenth century. The initial phase of industrialization in south Wales, in the period 1750–1800, produced the first ironworks' school. This was a small venture at Capel Waun y Pound, between Beaufort and Sirhowy in Monmouthshire, opened in 1784. In many ways, this was the forerunner of the nineteenth-century works' schools: not the charitable institutions of the eighteenth century, but 'pay' schools within the voluntary system. We now turn to consider the various works' schools that existed in the nineteenth century.

The Ironworks' Schools

The first ironworks' school of the new century was established in 1816 at Blaenavon in Monmouthshire. It was founded and endowed by Miss Sarah Hopkins of Staffordshire, in memory of her brother, Samuel Hopkins, who had started the Blaenavon Ironworks in 1789. Later, it was enlarged and, by 1860, three separate schools had been built. These were run by the Hill family on the National system and a nominal charge was deducted from the workmen's wages towards their upkeep. This caused some friction between the proprietors and the employees in the Blaenavon area, since most of the latter were Dissenters.

The Neath Abbey ironworks' schools were promoted by J.T. Price, a Quaker ironmaster. The first school was opened in 1816 and, in 1825, additional accommodation was provided for boys, girls, and infants in separate buildings, and surrounded by a wall. Price was one of the first ironmasters to introduce the practice of weekly stoppages from the workers' wages, and he introduced certain medical services for his work-force. The Abbey Boys' School was divided into three classes, but there seems to have been little difference in the ages of the pupils. The children were usually withdrawn from school when they were

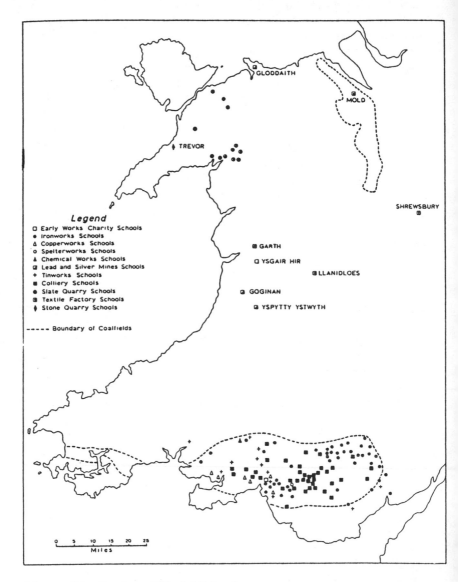

MAP 3. Distribution of Works' Schools

ten years old so that they could improve the family's wage-earning capacity.

At Hirwaun two schools existed, although only one is mentioned by name in the 1847 Education Report: the Firemen's or Furnace School established in 1820. This was owned by F. Crawshay, of Treforest, near Pontypridd, and the school was run on the basis of a stoppage of $\frac{1}{2}d$. in the pound from the workmen's wages. It seems that these schools were not well received by the parents, and the children positively hated them. One redeeming feature was the status accorded to Welsh in the schools, and another was the interest shown by the workmen in acquiring some basic knowledge. Some even recommended that winter lectures be instituted and were keen to secure a master to lead the classes.

By far the most important of all the works' schools in the nineteenth century were those established by the Guest family at Dowlais, near Merthyr Tydfil. In 1839 Dowlais alone had a population of 12,000 and, apart from Guest's original schools, which were opened in 1828 with 110 pupils, there were few others in the vicinity. These original schools had been intended for boys and girls, and some time before 1844 an infants' school had been added. In 1843 Sir John and Lady Charlotte Guest had informed the Commissioners and Inspectors that they considered the school provision in the area to be totally inadequate, and they were especially concerned about the long waiting-lists for admission. They decided, therefore, that new and larger schools should be built. Sir Charles Barry, the renowned architect, was commissioned to design the new schools which were opened in 1844, and a new Infants' School was added in 1846. With the opening of the new schools, a new staff was appointed and the headmaster, Matthew Hirst, was assisted by two trained teachers from the Battersea Training School. The Boys' School was organized on a system of graded classes separated from one another by wooden partitions and curtains. This was an innovation of considerable importance, for separate classrooms, which became known as the Prussian or German system, were not introduced into Britain until after 1870. The Boys' School was equipped with a laboratory and apparatus for chemical experiments. The First Class, which was composed mainly of the sons of mechanics, was taught a wide range of subjects, including algebra, mensuration, arithmetic, mechanics, etymology, music, reading, writing, drawing, scripture, history, and religious knowledge. In the Second Class the curriculum was a little more restricted; while the Third Class was limited to elementary instruction. It was from 1844 onwards that Sir John evolved his more ambitious educational scheme, which will be considered in Chapter 11.

Schools of the Non-Ferrous Industries

Each of the two phases in the evolution and expansion of the copper and allied industries had its own characteristic schools. The first, which was involved with the fortunes of Sir Humphrey Mackworth and his mines in north Cardiganshire, spawned the early charity works' schools. The second, which began in the early years of the nineteenth century, gave rise to the works' schools. Each of the copperworks at Swansea, Llanelli, Pembrey, Cwmavon, Neath, and Port Talbot, produced a works' school.

Two prosperous industrialists established two of the largest copper-smelting works in south Wales, the Vivians of Swansea and the Nevills of Llanelli. Their schools, the Hafod Copperworks Schools at Swansea and the Heolfawr Copperworks Schools at Llanelli, were the largest in the western part of the coalfield, catering for those workmen and their families who were engaged in the copper and allied trades. The first school in the Swansea district was associated with the White Rock, Upper and Middle Bank Copper Companies. Promoted by the two proprietors, Pascoe St Leger Grenfell and John Freeman, it started in 1806 and was maintained by stoppages of 1*d.* a week from the workmen's wages. The schools were so successful that in 1839 John Freeman gave another site which was used to build the new Kilvey Infants' School, which had over 200 in attendance in 1846.

In the Swansea area the equivalent of the Guest schools were those of the Vivian family. The Vivians had come to Swansea from Cornwall in 1800 and, by 1825, Mrs J.H. Vivian had started a small school for forty girls in the parish of St John. She had also initiated a Model Dame School in a Swiss cottage in the grounds of their residence at Singleton Park (the present site of the University campus). But these schools were quite ineffective in coping with the major problem of educational destitution in the area. By 1847, the Vivians, partly in response to Guest's ambitious scheme at Dowlais, had constructed the Hafod Copperworks Schools at Swansea. The growth of these schools and Nevill's Schools at Llanelli will be traced in Chapter 11.

Tin-plate Works' Schools

There were fewer tin-plate works' schools than ironworks' or copperworks' schools, and two factors accounted for this: first, most of the early tinworks were attached to the ironworks and were often appendages to the large ironworks; and secondly, the tin-plate industry did not expand until after 1875, and the tin-plate era coincided, therefore, with the period when the State was assuming an ever-increasing role in education and when school boards were set up to improve the school provision in many areas.

The earliest tinworks' school in south Wales was founded by the Harford family at Melingriffith, near Whitchurch, Cardiff. There was some kind of school in existence in the years 1786–7, but it was in 1807 that the Harfords invited Joseph Lancaster to address a meeting at Melingriffith. A school was opened in 1808 on the Lancasterian principles and a year later there were sixty-two children in attendance.

In west Glamorgan a tinworks' school was opened in the parish of Margam in 1829. Messrs. Roberts and Smith, who had built the tinworks in 1822, required their workmen to pay 9d. per month towards the upkeep of the school. The first school was held in a room attached to the tinworks, but in 1833 two schools were in use for boys and girls with 65 and 106 pupils respectively. There was also a tinworks' Sunday school, which was originally started for adults but later extended to children of all ages.

In 1844 a small school was started by the Carmarthen tinworks. This school was accommodated in the house of the master, who had formerly been a clerk at the tinworks. The proprietors were partly responsible for running the school, and the employees were expected to pay 1d. a week. We are also told of night schools held in conjunction with this school on five evenings a week, and free of charge for the workmen and their children.

In the Swansea Valley there were two tinworks' schools. One had been established at Pontardawe in 1846 by William

Parsons, owner of the works. The other was at Ystalyfera, a school for boys begun in 1850 on the National system. The ironmaster, J. Palmer Budd, soon ran into difficulties with his workmen, who were staunchly Nonconformist in religion. They objected to the compulsory withdrawals from their wages and went on to build their own school based on the British system and with the aid of grants from the British and Foreign School Society.

Colliery Schools

Most of the large iron or copperworks which emerged in the latter part of the eighteenth century and the early part of the nineteenth century owned their own collieries, which provided the parent works with a constant supply of cheap coal. These collieries usually had no works' schools, for the colliers' children would attend the iron or copperworks' schools. The colliery school proper was the one which was established or promoted by the owner of a colliery unattached to any other concern. Forty such schools were developed in the south Wales coalfield during the nineteenth century, whereas the north Wales coalfield had no colliery schools.

In the period before 1840 the colliery schools which appeared represented the efforts of individual proprietors and private subscribers. The first colliery school of the south Wales coalfield was set up at Hirwaun in 1820. It was situated in a room over a stable and packed with fifty boys and girls. The school was established by F. Crawshay of Treforest, near Pontypridd, and was maintained by a weekly stoppage of $\frac{1}{2}d$. in the pound from the colliers' wages. The management of the school was in the hands of the workmen and this proved to be a stumbling-block in future years. The work-force was particularly resentful of the clergy's interference in its workings, and by 1846 a schismatic group had emerged with the robust intention of building its own school on the British system.

In the parish of Llangyfelach, near Swansea, the Llewelyns of Penllergaer promoted the Llangyfelach Church School in 1822, one at Penllergaer in 1834, and a boys' and girls' school at Gorseinon in 1846. In east Glamorgan, the Marquis of Bute supported two schools at Aberdare, the 'Free' schools in 1830, and another in 1850. But the first colliery school in the Rhondda valleys was at Dinas, founded by Walter Coffin, seemingly about 1830.

There was a small colliery school at Cilybebyll, in west Glamorgan, serving the children of those miners employed in Wauncoed and Primrose collieries. The schoolroom was built by Howell Gwyn, of Duffryn, near Neath, in 1839.

The Slate-Quarrying Schools of North Wales

The provision of schools for the industrial classes of north Wales was largely met by the voluntary societies. Apart from the activities of the slate-quarry owners and some financial support from industrialists on the coalfield, the works' schools had a limited impact on the northern counties. Chirk possessed the only school established and supported by an employer of labour. Chirk Charity School was established in 1820 and the inhabitants of the parish were expected to send all their sons there. At Brymbo and the adjoining industrial townships of Broughton, Minera, Nant, and Bersham, the ironworks company had expressed its willingness to build a school. But no plans materialized.

In the slate-quarrying areas of Caernarfonshire and Merioneth, a stronghold of Nonconformity, quarry owners set up many schools based on the National system. The children attended the schools in the winter months when it was too cold for them to work in the open quarries. But the Nonconformists had often attempted to maintain their own schools in open defiance of the quarry owners' wishes and, where this was not possible, they would reluctantly send their children to the nearest proprietors' schools.

In Caernarfonshire, Lord Penrhyn, the owner of the Penrhyn quarries, was the driving-force behind the establishment of many schools for his quarrymen. The Llandygái National Schools were built for the children of the Penrhyn estate workmen by Lady Penrhyn as early as 1810. These were schools for boys and girls and the instruction was free. The school buildings included accommodation for the master and mistress and there was a generous provision of school equipment. The Ty'ntwr undenominational school was established in 1830 on a site given by Colonel Pennant. Pupils seeking admission to this school paid an entrance fee of 1*s*. and then 1*d*. per week. By 1846 there were 143 scholars in attendance.

Two other slate-mining districts in Caernarfonshire were not as well blessed with schools. It would seem that Assheton Smith of the Dinorwic quarries had made no effort to provide schools for his workmen. In the parish of Llanddwrog there was one National school: Bron y Foel School, associated with the Cilgwyn Company, and started in the 1820s. The 1847 Reports refer to it as the 'mountain school'.

In mid Wales the owners of the woollen factories made provision for education, but they did not provide schools. At Llanidloes, Messrs David Davies and Edward Hughes, owners of the flannel factories, sent about forty children to a day school in the town. At the small woollen factory at Garth, Machynlleth, the proprietors hired a woman to teach in the mill. The Independent congregation at Llanidloes set up its own Sunday school at the Glyn Factory in 1838 and instruction was given in reading, English, and scriptural geography. At least forty small children under 15 years, and forty-three over 15 attended.

The Sunday School

The Sunday school made no real impact on Wales until almost the last decade of the eighteenth century. The catechizing of scholars and teaching them to read were not new features peculiar to the Sunday school movement. They had formed the core of educational work in Wales since the time of Thomas Gouge. Indeed, there are occasional references to schools in the late seventeenth century which operated in ways quite similar to the Sunday schools. In the Independent chapel at Mynyddbach, near Swansea, pupils were catechized and taught to read soon after 1693. Had the practice spread, this small school might well have become the prototype of the modern Sunday school.

As soon as the London-based Sunday School Society was formed in 1785 there were clear signs that certain Welsh individuals were beginning to show an interest in the movement. The Bishop of Llandaff was already in communication with officers of the Society and there was a school in Cardiff by the summer of 1786. By 1789 there were Sunday schools at Holywell, Bala, Denbigh, Caernarfon, and Llanfyllin. Thomas Charles of Bala had established a few Sunday schools before 1789, but they seem to have been appendages to his circulating schools. By 1795, however, he was promoting the Sunday schools with considerable enthusiasm, soon acting as intermediary between the London-based Society and Wales. By 1812 the Society claimed to have helped 256 schools in north Wales and 186 in south Wales belonging to all denominations.

After 1800 the Sunday schools spread to all parts of Wales. In the rural areas they had already become an integral part of the life and organization of Nonconformist chapels, especially in the north where, after 1811, they were the handmaiden of the Calvinistic Methodist congregations. In the industrial south the Sunday schools were often the nucleus from which the congregations grew, and in the industrial districts of Monmouthshire and east Glamorgan the Sunday schools appeared before the places of worship. Immigrants from the rural counties of Carmarthenshire, Pembrokeshire, and Cardiganshire carried their religious affiliations with them to the new industrial zones and the Sunday schools became the focal points of these settlements. In this eastern region, which experienced the first phase of industralization, there emerged a unique kind of Sunday school, the works' Sunday school.

The proprietors of the Rhymney Ironworks provided facilities for Nonconformists of all denominations to conduct their Sunday schools: there were three Baptist, four Independent, two Wesleyan, one Calvinistic Methodist, and only the one church Sunday school in this citadel of Nonconformity. In the ironworks region thirteen ironworks had set up thirty-three Sunday schools. The Baptists had nine, the Independents seven, Wesleyans six, Calvinistic Methodists four, Established Church four (of which two were at the Guest Ironworks at Dowlais), and three were undenominational.

The Sunday schools in this eastern industrial district concentrated on providing religious instruction and on reading. Welsh was used as the medium of instruction and, for the majority of the settlers in these new industrial encampments, these schools, together with the works' schools, were the sole means of acquiring a basic level of instruction. Nearly all the dame and private adventure schools had disappeared by 1840 and the Sunday schools had fast become the principal agents of instruction. Both the perceptive HMI Bowstead and the acutely observant Horace Mann sang the praises of the Sunday schools.

The 1847 Reports provide some statistical guidelines for those seeking to compare the respective contributions of the day and the Sunday schools (Table 5.2).

Table 5.2

County	Industrial parish	Population 1841	No. attending Day schools	No. attending Sunday schools	No. of Day schools	No. of Sunday schools
Monmouth	Aberystruth	11,272	616	1,402 (2,331)	10	18
	Bedwellty	22,413	1,236	2,863 (4,842)	16	32
	Panteg	2,171	–	294 (389)	–	4
	TOTAL	35,856	1,852	4,559 (7,562)	26	54
Glamorgan	Merthyr Tydfil	34,997	2,301	4,290 (6,902)	41	36
	Michaelstone Super Avon	2,531	323	839 (1,350)	2	8
	Margam	3,526	765	597 (927)	8	9
	Glyncorrwg	634	72	45 (128)	1	2
	TOTAL	41,668	3,461	5,771 (9,307)	52	55

KEY

The attendances in these figures show the number of children under 15, and those in brackets all age groups for all denominations and the Established Church.

The figures reveal three things about the Sunday schools in the parishes: first, apart from Merthyr Tydfil, all the parishes had more Sunday schools than day schools; secondly, with the exceptions of the parishes of Margam and Glyncorrwg, more than twice the number of children went to Sunday schools in the under-15 age group; finally, if all age groups are included, over three times the number went to Sunday schools.

In the industrial areas of west Glamorgan and south-east Carmarthenshire, with their long history of industrial activity, there was a greater diversity of industry. This reduced the risks of unemployment and trade depression, and the working population in the metallurgical industry tended, on the whole, to be more permanent and less mobile than its industrial counterparts in the eastern sectors. There was a tendency, also, for the day schools to outnumber the Sunday schools in this region, as the figures in Table 5.3 will show.

Table 5.3

Area	Population in 1841	No. attending day schools Noncon.& Church	No. attending Sunday schools Noncon.& Church	No. of day schools	No. of Sunday schools
Borough of Swansea & Llangyfelach	34,697	3,423	3,320	79	55
Neath	4,970	536	757	13	8
Llanelli	11,155	976	1,918 (140 in Church S.School)	20	13
TOTAL	50,822	4,935	5,995	112	76

The statistics in Table 5.3 reveal an almost even balance between the attendances at the day and the Sunday schools in the borough of Swansea and the parish of Llangyfelach. The Assistant Commissioner in his 1846 Report on the Swansea district included details from an inquiry made in 1841 into the population of the borough of Swansea; in which he indicated that there had been an actual decrease in attendance at the Sunday schools of 11.1 per cent on the figures of 1841. One can conjecture at the reasons for this apparent lack of interest in the Sunday schools: adults were sometimes embarrassed to attend, especially when they were forced to study in the same rooms as the young people; the equipment and the teaching staff were of a poor standard; a more constant employment pattern prevented many from attending on Sundays; and the retention of children in the day schools for longer periods made the Sunday schools less effective as instructional media.

As the Sunday schools expanded, so an army of teachers was required to teach the scholars of all ages who attended. Most of the teachers were no better trained than their contemporaries in the day schools, and their limitations would often account, in part at least, for the circumscribed activities of the schools. But the denominations went to great lengths to produce publications which could be employed in the Sunday classes. A great deal of attention was paid to the learning of catechisms, and many of these were produced along denominational lines. Thomas Charles's *Hyfforddwr*, which ran into scores of editions, was the most enduring; while a catechism by Titus Lewis circulated among the Baptists, as did a similar work by Gwilym Hiraethog among the Independents. Alongside the catechism, the learning of a *pwnc* (subject) became just as popular an activity. A *pwnc* could be based on abstruse theological topics, such as the atonement, or the incarnation. Samuel Griffiths of Llandysul was a popular writer of *pynciau* among the Independents, as was J.M. Thomas of Cardigan among the Baptists. *Pynciau* and the Scriptures were learnt by rote, and schools were organized into unions of ten or twenty schools, which would meet every six weeks for interrogative and examination sessions. The examination day would be spent in catechizing, starting with the younger children and progressing along the grades. A whole day would be spent on this activity, with each school taking its turn, and the element of competition adding to the excitement of the proceedings.

After mid century more variety was added to the work of the schools and more attention was often given to singing. Sunday school hymnals were introduced and children encouraged to learn the sol-fa system of music notation. The eisteddfod also began to make an impression on the schools and this stimulated the competitive side of school life. Sunday schools became the moral conscience of the iron districts and coalfield society as they sought to inculcate the virtues of sobriety, thrift, diligence, and cleanliness upon the inhabitants of rural and industrial Wales. Bands of Hope, youth meetings, and 'Penny Readings' emerged as tentacles of the parent-body. The Sunday school became the religious, intellectual and social powerhouse of Welsh Nonconformity.

It is not easy to assess the value of the Sunday school movement in the nineteenth century, for it has suffered at the hands of those who have eulogized it too lavishly. It would probably be true to say that neither the day school nor the Sunday school showed much imagination in their approach to teaching. But HMI Bowstead does remind us of the importance of the Sunday school in his remark of 1854: 'The working classes attach the highest value to the Sunday school . . . ' What accounted for this? It would seem that there were a variety of reasons for their success: first, they were held on a Sunday when most working people could attend; secondly, the medium of instruction was Welsh, the language of heaven, and the language of the vast majority of the inhabitants of the Principality; thirdly, there were usually no admission payments and no teaching fees; fourthly, the Welsh Sunday school was an all-age, comprehensive, family school where adults worked alongside their children; finally, it has often been claimed that the Sunday school elevated the individual and gave the ordinary person a sense of importance and dignity within the community — it helped him to read, it enabled him to hold offices of various kinds, and it provided a system of values and a sense of purpose.

The Blue Books of 1847

The Blue Books of 1847 did not of themselves inaugurate a new era in Welsh education; they appeared in the middle of a decade of intense educational activity in Wales and at the end of a period of agitation and of violent protest. The Merthyr Rising of 1831 and the Chartist attack on Newport in 1839 had given the rest of Britain the distinct impression that Wales was falling under the spell of radical and violent agitators. This impression was reinforced when Rebecca and her hosts began disturbing the Welsh countryside in the years from 1838 to 1843. When the Government's Commission of Inquiry published its report on the riots in 1844, many of its comments clearly anticipated those of the Blue Books in 1847.

As already noted, the years from 1837 to 1843 were particularly significant for the British and National school movements. A wave of Anglican school-building had caused alarm among the Nonconformists and this was intensified by the prospects of Sir James Graham's Factory Bill in 1843 which, if passed, would have given control of factory schools to Anglicans. Hugh Owen's letter of 1843 urged some sections of Welsh public opinion into action, and from 1843 to 1846 British schools began to spread with alacrity through various parts of Wales.

The South Wales Education Committee and the Cambrian Education Society appeared during these years, the latter publishing an advertisement in 1845 quoting details from a government report showing that 45 per cent of the men and 70 per cent of the women married in south Wales during 1844 were unable to write their own names. During the same year 41 per cent of the men and 66 per cent of the women in north Wales were similarly illiterate. But there was hardly any need for governments to highlight this point, for Welshmen of various social groupings were only too aware of the need to provide many more schools in Wales. Welsh journals and denominational magazines like *Y Cronicl* and *Y Diwygiwr* carried articles attesting to the desire of the Radical leaders of Wales for better educational provision. The Church and the National Society were also active in focusing on the poor provision of education in Wales in the early 1840s. Even without the Blue Books of 1847, the decade would probably have been one of intense activity and discussion in the field of education.

It was the Member of Parliament for Coventry who eventually raised the matter on the floor of the House of Commons on 10 March 1846. He was a Welshman, William Williams (1788–1865), a native of Llanpumsaint in Carmarthenshire, who had made a fortune as a highly successful merchant in London and had become an acknowledged authority on financial matters in the House. His speech to the Commons fills fifteen columns of *Hansard* and displays his realistic appreciation of the material resources available in the Principality. He argued that education in Wales had been insufficiently discussed, that schools were scarce, and that governments had neglected the country. He complained that the employers cared little for the well-being of their workers and that landlords were equally negligent. He showed that south Wales had not received its fair share of government grants: since 1839, £248,000 had been voted for education in Britain, of which the five counties of south Wales, according to Williams, had received the disproportionate sum of £2,176. Sir James Graham, the Home Secretary, replied suggesting that a departmental commission of the Privy Council should be entrusted with the task of conducting the necessary inquiry. Williams accepted this motion, but it was left to the new incumbent at the Home Office, Sir George Grey, to fulfil the undertaking.

Sir James Kay-Shuttleworth (1814–77) appointed the Commissioners and prepared their instructions. R.R.W. Lingen (later Lord Lingen) was a distinguished classics scholar and lawyer, who later became Secretary to the Treasury. J.C. Symons was also a lawyer and, from 1848, one of Her Majesty's Inspectors of Schools. H.V. Johnson was called to the Bar in 1848 and was eventually appointed secretary to his father-in-law, Lord Chancellor Campbell. Not one of these Commissioners had any experience of school-teaching or of administering a system of education, and they were blissfully ignorant of the Welsh language. They were the sons of wealthy English families, and insensitive to the feelings and traditions of Dissenters. Furthermore, they chose as their assistants those who seemed least likely to endear themselves to the industrial and rural classes of Nonconformist Wales. Of the ten Assistant Commissioners, seven were Anglicans, and five of these were students of St David's College, Lampeter.

The Commissioners divided Wales into three sections: Lingen examined the counties of Carmarthen, Glamorgan, and Pembroke; Symons covered Brecknock, Cardiganshire, Radnorshire, and Monmouthshire; while Vaughan Johnson surveyed the north Wales counties. By 1 October 1846, the three were at work, conferring at Builth. They started their discussions by approaching the bishops of Hereford and St David's, and thence they went their separate ways. They had been instructed to inquire into the education of the labouring classes (including the Sunday schools) and the means by which they could learn English. They were also asked to inquire into the social and moral condition of the people.

The Commissioners applied themselves diligently to their appointed tasks and collected evidence from 334 witnesses, 80 per cent of whom were churchmen. They collected detailed figures of the scholars, the teachers, the buildings and the equipment, and they provided information on the financial arrangements of schools; they also gave verbatim accounts of their examinations of various classes. The Reports were published in three volumes, containing 1,252 pages and including statistical information on each shire, district, parish, and school. The actual accounts were detailed and rigorously compiled and they have served as a valuable source for the social historian.

The Blue Books painted a dark picture of education and school provision in Wales but, as we have already argued, Welshmen in various positions were already aware of the deficiencies and were actively trying to remedy them. Where the Reports really offended public opinion in the Principality was in their observations on the language, the religion, and the morals of the people. The Welsh were portrayed as ill-educated, poor, dirty, unchaste, and potentially rebellious. The Blue Books were critical of almost the whole population, though the Welsh language and Nonconformity were made to carry most of the blame. One particular criticism levelled at the Commissioners was that they failed abysmally in their examination techniques. Dean Cotton of Bangor accused them of asking misleading questions of the children, such as, 'Christ was crucified at Bethlehem, was he not?', and 'Peter was one of the prophets, was he not?'. Many complained of the hectoring nature of the questioning, and in a language which was almost foreign to most of the school population. Dr Lewis Edwards, the respected leader of the Methodists, claimed that the Assistant Commissioners were probably incapable of translating accurately either the questions asked in English or the answers given in Welsh.

It took some time for the literate public to comprehend the full impact of the Commissioners' work. By Christmas 1847, the storm of criticism broke, and the Revd Thomas Price (Carnhuanawc), an Anglican priest, lampooned the Commissioners as, 'libellous and mendacious foreigners' at the Merthyr eisteddfod. In 1848 Dean Cotton of Bangor published an anonymous pamphlet attacking the Commissioners for their libels on the Welsh. Evan Jones (Ieuan Gwynedd) attacked the incorrectness of the Reports in *The Cardiff and Merthyr Guardian*,

John Bull, Y Traethodydd, and in two books. The Revd David Rees of Capel Als, Llanelli, editor of the journal, *Y Diwygiwr,* attacked the Blue Books for their criticisms of Nonconformity. Most of the most telling attacks on the Reports emanated from the Welsh Anglicans, and even Sir Thomas Phillips, the famous mayor of Newport who had led the assault on the Chartists in 1839, showed in his historical survey of Wales in 1849 how exaggerated and prejudiced the Reports were.

Once the initial furore had subsided, the Reports had left a number of long-term effects on Wales. In the first place, they paved the way for Government and State intervention in education, so that by 1870 a wholly English system of instruction could be applied to Wales under Forster's Education Act of 1870. The Reports also reduced the self-confidence of Welsh people and created in many quarters a strong sense of national inferiority.

The Blue Books also succeeded in creating a united Welsh Nonconformist front. Even the Methodists were roused into action, joining the Independents and Baptists in working towards some form of political campaign. The Nonconformists began to regard the Anglicans as the outright enemies of Wales and Welshness, and the Commissioners and their Reports were seen as having betrayed the Welsh people. After 1847 Nonconformists increasingly identified themselves with Welshness and, in the 1850s and 1860s, they created the distinct impression that they alone bore the mantle of Welshness.

But, although the Nonconformists regarded the Blue Books as an act of treachery and called them by the name *Brad y Llyfrau Gleision* (Treason of the Blue Books), in memory of a Welsh legend of the Dark Ages (Treason of the Long Knives), most of the scions and intellectual leaders of the Welsh denominations quietly accepted the Reports and their long-term implications. In the 1850s and 1860s there occurred a massive cultural and political shift to a 'Nonconformist Nation', and the Welsh were encouraged to forget their past with its passion for poetry, legend and history. The new emphases were on practical knowledge, industriousness, progress, the language of success, and the Victorian ethos of self-improvement. By the 1860s the Blue Books were being forgotten. All that remained was the sense of treachery. By 1870 the Welsh had accepted the necessity of State education; the English language was the symbol of commercial and social success; the Nonconformists, so it is claimed, had welcomed the imperial culture into Wales.

SUGGESTED READING

E.T. Davies, *Monmouthshire Schools and Education to 1870* (Newport, 1957).

R.R. Davies, *et al* (eds.), *Welsh Society and Nationhood*, Historical Essays Presented to Glanmor Williams (Cardiff, 1984).

L.W. Evans, *Education in Industrial Wales, 1700–1900* (Cardiff, 1971).

R. Brinley Jones (ed.), *The Anatomy of Wales* (Glamorgan, 1972).

Articles:

L.W. Evans, 'Colliery Schools in South Wales in the Nineteenth Century', *N.L.W.J.*, X (1957–8).

L.W. Evans, 'Ironworks Schools in South Wales, 1784–1860', *Sociological Review*, XLIII (1951).

L.W. Evans, 'Copper-works Schools in South Wales during the Nineteenth Century', *N.L.W.J.*, XI (1959–60).

L.W. Evans, 'School Boards and the Works School System after the Education Act of 1870', *N.L.W.J.*, XV (1967–8).

6. Popular Protest
1815–1850

Rural Distress and Resistance c.1790–1830

THE period of the French wars had witnessed a number of protests in rural and urban Wales. In the 1790s there were outbursts against the Navy Act, enclosures, and the price of grain. In 1795 the forces of order in Denbighshire were the objects of popular hostility, and magistrates were imprisoned by the enraged crowds. Throughout the 1790s conditions were often perilous as the pressures of an increasing population, inflation, and exploitation of land, began to bite. People often fled to America in desperation, and hope of a better life. Riots became an endemic feature: between 1793 and 1795 there were riots in Swansea, Bangor, Aberystwyth, Denbigh, Bridgend, Fishguard, and Haverfordwest. There were disturbances in Barmouth and Machynlleth in 1795–6; and violent responses to grain shortages in Merthyr, Pembrokeshire, and in parts of north Wales in 1799–1800. Disorder was, in fact, widespread and troops had to be employed on several occasions to restore order.

The end of the Napoleonic wars in 1815 brought a number of crises and a general depression in Welsh farming. The drop in post-war prices for stock and dairy produce was especially serious for the poor Welsh farmer. In 1815 a marked fall in prices occurred owing to the long summer drought which forced farmers to sell their stock in large quantities. In 1816 south Wales cattle were selling at a third of their former price and sheep at a half. In 1817 and 1818 the situation worsened and farmers had to sell their animals at any price. Livestock prices continued to slump in 1821 and remained low until 1823. The fall in prices, however, was not accompanied by a corresponding reduction in rents. The fast-growing population and the lack of alternative employment led to intense competition for farm holdings. Unrealistic rent levels and sharp rises in local rates and

taxes weighed heavily on the Welsh peasant and tenant up to
the 1850s. When prices were very low, and during bank crises in
1816, 1825–6, and 1832, conditions were desperate. In 1816–17
an unprecedented number of farmers failed to pay their rents
and were forced to sell their livestock. Some tenants quit their
lands by night and took their animals with them. On the
Wynnstay estate, in north Wales, in 1823 and 1824 tenants
failed to pay rents and became day labourers, while some fell
back on the parish; others simply left for America.

This distress often reopened old wounds, especially the effects
of enclosures. In 1820 there was rioting at Maenclochog in
Pembrokeshire, where the house of a farmer, who had enclosed
much of the mountainside, was destroyed. Two years later, a
similar incident occurred on Mynydd Bach, Cardiganshire, and
another house was similarly destroyed in 1826. At Lampeter
and Aberystwyth the presence of soldiers proved only partially
effective in controlling the disorders. In one instance an
Inclosure bill was successfully opposed, and this related to land
in the parishes of Llanddwrog and Llanwnda in Caernarfonshire. There was further opposition to parliamentary enclosure
in north Wales in 1827.

The slump in industry and agriculture also produced a
banking crisis, which had the effect of further intensifying the
depression. One problem was that so many local and country
banks had sprung up at the end of the eighteenth century: one
was opened at Merthyr in 1770, with another at Brecon in 1778,
and soon they were appearing in all the larger market towns.
During the war years, these banks issued considerable quantities
of their own banknotes. However, once the war ended in 1815,
some banks, such as those at Welshpool and Denbigh crashed
immediately. In 1825 and 1826 a severe banking crisis occurred
during which more than seventy banks failed in England and
Wales. Every bank in Pembrokeshire was wiped out, and those
that survived in other countries did so by the skin of their teeth.

A factor which exacerbated the whole situation was the
reassertion of freeholders' rights by royal agents, the Church of
England, and important landowners. There were often conflicts
between landlords and squatters in the period from 1790 to
1830, and the rights of squatters were defended passionately in
many parts of Wales in the 1820s. At Fishguard a number of

people were sued for encroaching on the Crown Manor. In Denbighshire, at Llandulas, quarrymen refused to allow the Bishop of Bangor to take possession of land in the parish in 1829. The poorer people were fervent believers in certain rights and custom; and they firmly maintained that custom permitted them to use the common lands. There was frequent encroachment in the upland areas under the custom of *tŷ unnos*, whereby a man would establish freehold rights to whatever he could build and enclose in one night. The poorer sections of the community argued that this custom was sanctioned by the laws of Hywel Dda; and they often rioted in order to enforce a kind of natural justice in their localities.

The Strike of 1816

At the end of the Napoleonic wars, Wales was plunged into a general industrial depression, with low wages and unemployment. Lead-miners in Cardiganshire struck early in 1816; there were disturbances at Mold, and the cavalry was used against the Wrexham colliers. In south Wales, especially around Merthyr Tydfil, large crowds of workmen assembled in a menacing fashion. In 1809–10 the Dowlais puddlers had brought the ironworks to a standstill when they went on strike against lower wages. In 1812 Cyfarthfa puddlers had organized protest meetings and sworn the Luddite oath. It was not altogether surprising, therefore, that the great strike of 1816 was precipitated by the threat of a possible wage reduction of up to 40 per cent. Unemployment was causing considerable hardship in the autumn of 1816, and the number of persons seeking poor relief had increased rapidly. A third irritant was the system of long pay adopted by the ironmasters, namely, the giving of wages at the end of a month. Allied to this was the hated truck system. The truck shops or company shops where workers were obliged to buy their goods, were a special feature of Monmouthshire industrial society, and all the major industrial concerns owned one or more of them.

The strike of 1816 was a spontaneous outbreak by the distressed and the destitute, and a dispute about bread and wages. But the authorities in south Wales always regarded industrial workmen as possible revolutionaries. They were unable to forget that Swansea coppermen in 1793 had pointed to France as a warning; or that Monmouthshire and Merthyr ironworkers had been urged in 1801 to take up arms. Merthyr had always been associated with nascent sedition: the philosopher and Jacobin, John Thelwall, had visited the town during the rioting of September 1800; the Cyfarthfa Philosophical Society had been established as early as 1807; various radical Unitarians had begun to influence municipal affairs; and during the post-Napoleonic war years, there were supporters in the Merthyr area for such Radical campaigners as Sir Frances Burdett and Major John Cartwright.

At the beginning of 1816 the situation in the south Wales coalfield was not particularly dangerous, despite a fall in iron production and reduction in wages. But the authorities were concerned and the rector and magistrate of Abergavenny, the Revd William Powell, pressed for soldiers to be despatched from Bristol. A captain and sixty men of the 55th Regiment were stationed at Newport. Powell was still not satisfied, and, fearing a rising of the workmen in the Tredegar–Sirhowy district, he ordered a corps of the Monmouthshire yeomanry to assemble at Abergavenny for a two-day exercise. At Merthyr a reduction in pay had initially been accepted without protest; but once the links between Merthyr and Tredegar were forged, trouble was imminent. In October over 1,000 miners and colliers at Tredegar stopped work, and a half of these set off for Merthyr to persuade another group of miners to stop all ironworks in the locality. The mob visited every ironworks in the area and, although some 200 special constables had been sworn in, the constables fled in the face of the oncoming crowds. Many of the local magistrates and gentlemen were injured — William Crawshay and his brother hid in a farmhouse, while Josiah John Guest and his friends barricaded themselves in a Dowlais house and fired at the mob.

A few days later the mob returned to Merthyr again, after having visited Tredegar, Sirhowy and Nant-y-glo, and some 8–10,000 people confronted 120 men of the 55th Regiment and the Swansea Cavalry. The troops charged the mob and seized thirty of the workmen. The centre of unrest then moved from Merthyr to Newport, where colliers had gathered in their hundreds. However, the arrival of a party of infantrymen in a coal wagon from Pontypool, and some stirring speeches from the Duke of Beaufort and the sheriff soon dowsed their enthusiasm. In the winter of 1816–17 radical ideas began spreading across the coalfield: 'Orator Hunt's' speeches were translated into Welsh; William Cobbett's *Political Register* was circulated in parts of Merthyr; there were petitions for parliamentary reform; and demagogues began visiting the local public houses.

Although the reform petitions were ignored by Parliament and there was no actual rising in south Wales in these early years, it would be a mistake to ignore these demonstrations, riots and strikes, which give the impression of being spontaneous and ill-conceived outbursts. There was often a degree of organization behind the riots and many of the skilled workers, at Merthyr for instance, met in public houses and swore oaths. Emissaries and delegates were sometimes welcomed from other parts of south Wales and Britain, and this was certainly the case in 1816. The strike of 1816, therefore, should be seen as one of a number of ways of putting pressure on employers: it was a form of 'collective bargaining by riot'.

The Scotch Cattle

The Scotch Cattle (*Tarw Scotch*) was an underground movement which worked in total secrecy. From 1816 onwards the workmen of Monmouthshire and southern Breconshire developed their own particular organization in the so-called 'black domain', an area extending from Rhymney to Abergavenny, and from Llangynidr to Caerphilly. Coal and iron dominated the life of the 'black domain', which was inhabited by Welsh-speaking immigrants from the contiguous counties of Glamorgan and Brecon. The villages of the southern part of the black domain had grown up around collieries. They were smaller and different from the villages of the northern iron region, and they suffered from short-time work and recurring unemployment. Long-pay was the norm in an area where men were paid on a Friday or Saturday with the help of tickets on which were listed their weekly advances, together with charges for rent, coal, soap, equipment, the works' surgeon and the sick fund. The company shop was a central feature of the mining communities, and the payment of wages in goods had become an entrenched practice by the 1820s. In 1830 several petitions were sent to Parliament from the colliery districts complaining about the truck shops, and in 1831 the Anti-Truck Act was passed. It was, however, ineffective; no provisions were made to ensure its enforcement and employers found it easy to evade its requirements.

People in these industrial communities were controlled by their masters, and they were often distinguished from each other only by degrees of debt. The inhabitants of these districts frequently lived in a state of permanent fear: the fear of losing one's job, home, and security. The Scotch Cattle movement was largely born of these fears.

It would seem that the Scotch Cattle first appeared during the Napoleonic wars. Their leader, a man called Ned, had moved into south Wales from Staffordshire and incited the Monmouthshire ironworkers to resist the wage reductions of 1813 by adopting Luddite tactics. There were 'Cattle' in operation in the course of the strikes of 1816, 1818 and 1819, but they did not win much popular appeal until the 1820s. From 1820 to 1835, and particularly in the depressed years of 1822, 1830, 1832, and from 1833 to 1834, the 'Cattle' roamed the mining districts and terrified the 'blacklegs', the overchargers and the over-ambitious. Their secret meetings were usually held at night on the hill slopes of the Monmouthshire valleys. If peaceful methods failed to achieve the required objective, there followed another kind of meeting at which guns were fired, horns blown, and drums beaten.

The Scotch Cattle often sent warning notes and letters to their victims, and these were occasionally displayed as notices at the works themselves. A typical one ran thus:

> To all the Colliers, Traitors, Turncoats and others. We hereby warn you the second and last time. We are determined to draw the hearts out of all the men above named, and fix two of the hearts upon the horns of the Bull . . . .

The letters were intended to intimidate, as were the attacks on company property. In 1822, 1830 and 1833 wagons were set on fire and barges sunk in an attempt to prevent coal from reaching the ironworks. Those who ignored these early warnings would eventually be subjected to the midnight visit, when groups of miners, diguised in masks and cattle skins, or with faces blackened, would call at a victim's home. Their arrival was dramatic: doors were broken down, windows smashed, and furniture destroyed. Blacklegs, strike-breakers, and the dreaded contractors were usually picked out for these attacks, as were landlords and bailiffs. In May 1833 the Rhymney turnpike house was smashed, and in April 1832 almost 300 men marched down the Rhymney Valley in a raid on shopkeepers' homes.

It is very likely that the Scotch Cattle was a well-organized body, with hierarchical and regional divisions. Most of their work bore the resemblance of a co-ordinated and continuous movement. The 'Cattle' were gangs of colliers, who were often of a violent nature. They were probably Welsh-speaking Welshmen and the average age of those who appeared in courts was about 27. The purpose of most of the 'Cattle' raids was to impose collective order and action on people who lacked an industrial tradition, and it was no easy task to organize strike action across a coalfield segmented by valleys and parcelled into semi-isolated communities. But the communities had their code of conduct, and the 'Cattle' theirs. The 'Bull' could address proclamations to his '9,000 faithful children', and the communities rallied around those who were members of the herds. Colliers would refuse to work with people who had testified against their friends in court; and in court they supported each other in intransigence and secrecy. The greatest tribute to the discipline endemic in these mining communities was the immense difficulty experienced by the authorities in convicting a member of the 'Cattle'. Although the military was used on a number of occasions, it was found difficult to identify the colliers.

By the summer of 1834 the authorities were convinced that a firm line needed to be taken with the 'Cattle' and the unions in the valleys. They formed their own mountain police and required workmen to sign a declaration that they were not members of a union or a secret society. The Calvinistic Methodists and the Oddfellows Friendly Society supported this new campaign. A breakthrough came at the spring assizes of 1835 when three of the 'Cattle' were sentenced to death. Two had their sentences commuted to transportation for life, but the third, Edward Morgan, was hanged for the murder of the wife of a victim of the Scotch Cattle. Like Dic Penderyn, Morgan became one of the martyrs of the coalfield. Recent research has shown that the 'Cattle' were involved in almost every major dispute in the Monmouthshire coal and ironworks from 1822 to 1849, and it is possible that they led the Aberdare Valley strike of 1850. Frustrated, however, by their inability to make much headway on the industrial front in the late 1830s and, encouraged by the Chartist Missionaries, the colliers and ironworkers of south-east Wales turned increasingly to political activity.

The Authorities and the Forces of Order

Though the Lord Lieutenants were in charge of all county forces and acted as link-men between central and local government, the real work of maintaining the King's peace was entrusted to the Justices of the Peace. They could arrest suspects, prohibit meetings, and impose curfews. When unrest occurred they summoned the local police and specials, and they performed their duties at intercounty, county and district levels. The pan-county meetings were held in 1832 and 1834 by JPs from Glamorgan, Monmouthshire and Breconshire, to discuss the rising tide of union activity and the spread of the Scotch Cattle. At a county level, action was taken in quarter session meetings, which were held four times a year. But it was the petty sessions, which consisted of eight or more justices, which were the mainspring of government in the localities and districts. In the year of the Great Reform Act, more than one-fifth of the JPs in Wales were clergymen, and for a variety of reasons: they were usually literate; resident in their localities; they had the necessary freedom and time for such affairs; and they were often looked upon as local leaders.

Some of the magistrates were good at anticipating trouble and prepared their districts accordingly, as did the Revd William Powell of Abergavenny during the 1816 strike. But they were often criticized for their efforts by contemporaries who were ignorant of the difficulties encountered by the magistrates. The number of justices operating in a district could be painfully low: in 1827, when the population of Merthyr Tydfil was over 30,000, there were only two JPs acting for the district. Absenteeism and illness were two factors militating against magisterial efficiency, and a third was a common reluctance to incur any unnecessary expenses. A final problem was the attitude of governments and the general public. The Monmouthshire justices had little sympathy during their campaigns against the 'Cattle' or the unions, and they were regularly threatened and intimidated.

The day-to-day enforcement of the law was in the hands of the constabulary, which consisted of high, petty and special constables. The high or chief constables were chosen from among the gentlemen, the yeomen, or better class of tradesmen, and for a period of one year or longer. Service was compulsory and involved arduous administrative tasks, such as attendance at assizes. Next to them were the petty, or regular, constables, who were usually elected for considerable periods of service. They carried out a variety of duties — visiting public houses to prevent excessive drinking, seeking out troublemakers, delivering warrants — and they were poorly paid for their work. Though their job was unpopular, the constables were often an inefficient and effete group of men. At Carmarthen, during the Reform crisis, the thirteen permanent constables were unable to cope with the unrest, and help was enlisted from within and without the town. The special constables were the third group of law enforcers who could be called upon in an emergency. The magistrates could enrol any number of specials, from the ranks of the small farmers and shopkeepers, provided that five men were prepared to swear an oath that extraordinary measures were required. On occasions the specials refused to serve as in 1831, during the Carmarthen riots, when seventy-four of the 'better class of householders' repudiated the summons to attend for duty.

The special constables were called upon at certain times of the year to control the crowds: fair days and Guy Fawkes nights were usually troublesome periods for the local authorities. By the early 1830s, as panic swept through the coalfield, the specials were treated with a little more respect. In the winter of 1830-1 well over 1,000 were sworn in along the border counties, and these were often formed into semi-professional military companies. At Chepstow they were mounted and armed with sabres, while at Swansea they were promised iron pikes. The Swansea magistrates also knew that, in a crisis, they could enlist

the assistance of fifty pensioners. The outpensioners of the
Greenwich and Chelsea hospitals acted as special constables in
various parts of Wales during the early 1830s, and they assisted
as scouts and guards during the Merthyr Rising.

Local authorities were reluctant to establish a full-time,
professional police force when they could fall back on the part-
timers and specials. London policemen were rarely seen in the
Principality until the Reform crisis. Three officers had been sent
from London to Denbighshire in 1831 to investigate an attack
on coalowners. At Merthyr Tydfil three retired policemen were
appointed to organize their specials; one of these remained in
the town to become the chief police officer. The same happened
at Carmarthen when John Lazenby, one of the six metropolitan
officers sent to the town during the infamous election riots of
1831, was retained as the high constable. At Abergavenny in
May 1832 magistrates and ironmasters passed a motion to
establish a permanent police force; and, in June 1834, largely as
a result of the spread of trade unionism and outbreaks of
disturbances across the coalfield, it was decided to form a new
regular police force for Glamorgan, Monmouthshire, and
Brecknock. Several of the largest towns in south Wales had a
semi-professional police force by the beginning of 1835. The full
county police force for Glamorgan was not established until
October 1841, and the first Chief Constable was Captain
Charles Frederick Napier of the Rifle Brigade.

Also stationed in the rural and industrial districts were
various military forces. At the end of the Napoleonic War in
1815 a permanent staff of militia remained to help the civil
authorities. The Royal Glamorgan Militia, for example, had a
staff of about twenty-four men in 1816. The magistrates,
however, preferred the voluntary yeomen and infantry, who
seemed less likely to side with the demonstrators and to indulge
their political sympathies. They played an important part in
maintaining order throughout this period: they were used
during the 1816 strike; and in 1818 they quelled the cheese riots.
The yeomen were not a professional group, and were no match
for the regulars in dispersing large crowds. Only in exceptional
circumstances would the Government augment the numbers of
these forces and, during the 1831 insurrectionary atmosphere,
they were compelled to station large contingents of soldiers

in Wales. The advent of the military, however, sometimes compounded the difficulties facing the local authorities: the soldiers were a rough and ready company who upset local feelings; they were costly in the extreme, and there were frequent arguments as to who should pay for their presence; finally, there were controversies surrounding their accommodation.

The Rebecca Riots

The period from the end of the Napoleonic wars to the mid nineteenth century was one of general agricultural depression. There had been a drop in prices in the post-1815 period and corn prices fluctuated considerably in the succeeding years. Farmers throughout Wales found that they were farming at a loss, and they dismissed their workmen to reduce their bills. At the same time there occurred an overall increase in rents. During the war years rent rises had varied from estate to estate: on the Picton Castle estate in Pembrokeshire rents had risen by 77 per cent from 1790 to 1820; on the Llandeilo and Llanarthney sections of the Cawdor estate in Carmarthenshire rents had gone up by 60 per cent; and on the Nanteos estate in Cardiganshire there was a 200 per cent increase in the rents from 1790 to 1820. When war ended in 1815 and the prices of foodstuffs began to slide, there was no corresponding reduction in rents. Unrealistic rent levels and crippling local taxes weighed heavily on the desperate farming communities.

Widespread unemployment had also developed in the industrial areas and workers began flocking back to their rural home districts. This merely added to the problems already existing in the rural counties, where the population had been expanding since the eighteenth century. Between 1801 and 1841 the population of the counties of west Wales increased considerably, with that of Carmarthenshire rising from 67,317 to 106,326, Pembrokeshire from 56,280 to 88,044 and Cardiganshire from 42,956 to 68,766. Increased population, general depression on the land, widespread unemployment, and the introduction of new machinery, were sure recipes for disaster in the rural counties in the years after 1815.

There was also a cleavage between those who worked the land and those who owned it. The gentry was by now Anglicized and

Anglican, while the remainder of the population was poor, increasingly Nonconformist and Welsh-speaking. The rift between squire and peasant was based on deeply-felt differences in wealth, culture, language, religion, and politics. As the depression deepened so the clash between the two groups became inevitable, particularly as other factors worsened conditions and heightened the tension.

Tensions had existed in the country areas for a very long time, and violent protests had often erupted in such places as Carmarthen in 1801 and 1818 due to the shortage and high prices of food. There was considerable unrest throughout the Welsh countryside in the late eighteenth and early nineteenth century, and landlords' officials were frequently assaulted as they prepared to enclose lands. Threatening letters were sent to landlords, and property was often attacked in raids by day and by night. There was also the longstanding tradition of the *ceffyl pren* (the wooden horse). This involved carrying a person who was unpopular in the community on a wooden pole or ladder. An effigy was regularly used instead of the actual person, the idea being to ridicule the person concerned and to show the people's condemnation of his apparent breach of community and moral law. The *ceffyl pren* was a kind of people's justice: a form of community protest against the imposing, and often ruthless, landlords.

In the 1830s two important government decisions exacerbated the already critical economic and social situation. The first was the passing of the Poor Law Amendment Act of 1834. Poverty had been endemic in rural Wales since 1815, and various attempts had been made to assist those who were destitute and poor. The old Poor Laws had dealt harshly with so many groups in society. Since the Restoration and Settlement Act of 1662 the responsibility for the relief of the poor had fallen on the parish. The sums distributed to the poor were small, and the laws were harshly applied. Poor children were apprenticed by the parish and often brutally treated. The sick and the old were mistreated and their possessions seized if they applied for relief. The parish poor law officials were themselves a rough and incompetent band: some were quite illiterate, others were merely inefficient at their tasks. By the 1830s the problem of the able-bodied poor had reached crisis proportions, and the new Whig Government decided to pass the 1834 Act. Its provisions stipulated that outdoor relief was to cease; parishes were to be grouped into unions with boards of guardians; workhouses were to be built and those who sought indoor assistance were to be treated in such a way as to render indoor relief a less desirable proposition than outdoor assistance. The Act was savaged for its cold and cruel policies and the workhouses were dubbed the 'Bastilles' in memory of the celebrated Paris prison. Wales was outraged by the measure: the Nonconformist press was unanimous in its condemnation; petitions flowed from urban and rural centres in opposition to the Act; many magistrates and clergy declared the new law to be an unjust and cruel piece of legislation.

The second government decision which antagonized Welsh society was the compulsory commutation of tithes. At a period of depression and cash shortage, it seemed particularly insensitive to insist upon a money settlement. The Act of 1836 prescribed that tithe-owners and payers should meet to decide the value of the tithes, and that the annual payments should be calculated on the average prices of wheat, barley and oats over seven years. So, while payments to the poor were effectively reduced by about 50 per cent, the tithe charge increased by seven per cent as a result of the calculations. By the nineteenth century many landowners had purchased the right to receive tithes, and this meant that sections of the poor people were having to pay rent, local taxes, and tithes to the landowner.

Another injustice keenly felt by the small farmers and poorer inhabitants of south-west Wales in this period was that perpetrated by the nature and role of the magistracy. Local magistrates were invariably selected from the ranks of the gentry and the clergy, a factor which was bound to anger the Nonconformists. The control of local politics and justice was firmly in the hands of the gentry, who were the JPs, and they decided how local rates were to be spent. Some were indifferent to the work, and others used their power corruptly.

But the spark which ignited this smouldering pile of dis-affection and unrest was the reaction to the turnpike trusts and the toll-gates. In the early eighteenth century, Parliament had passed a law which enabled private companies, called turnpike trusts, to be set up to build and repair roads — an eighteenth-century version of privatization! By the 1770s there were trusts in the three west Wales counties. The road trusts of Wales were inefficient, largely because they were too numerous and their districts were too small. The frequency of toll-gates made the trusts oppressive and there were numerous examples of travellers having to pay twice or more within short distances. Towns like Carmarthen, a market centre, and Swansea were encircled with toll-gates; and farmers who crossed the counties in search of lime found the tolls exorbitant. The farmers of north Pembrokeshire would often travel to the lime-kilns of the south and, in order to pass through a gate in one day, and hence make a single payment, they would often queue with their carts at the first gate at midnight in the hope of completing their journey within twenty-four hours. The gates of a trust were usually auctioned and, by the 1830s, Thomas Bullin, who had exploited the farming of tolls in England, had become one of the most important farmers of tolls in south Wales. Under his regime, the whole collection process became much more rigorous.

Though the tolls in west Wales were relatively cheaper than those in other parts of the country, and the turnpike trusts only controlled about 20 per cent of the roads in the west, it was against these that the 'children of Rebecca' rode in those dark winter nights of 1839. Trouble had been brewing in the wet summer and autumn of 1838 and, in January 1839, the new workhouse at Narberth was burnt. Then, on the night of 13 May a newly erected gate at Efailwen in Carmarthenshire, not too far from the Pembrokeshire border, was destroyed. It belonged to the Whitland Trust, and the tolls were farmed by none other than Thomas Bullin. The gate was rebuilt, and demolished yet again by a crowd of around 400, many with blackened faces and dressed in women's clothes, on the night of 6 June 1839. A few nights later, another gate was destroyed a few miles away at Llanboidy. The leader of the rioters here was Thomas Rees of Carnabwth, a fist-fighter who was better known as Twm Carnabwth.

The revolts subsided for a period only to resurface in the winter of 1842. Within a few months disturbances were breaking out in Pembrokeshire, Carmarthenshire, and Cardiganshire. Bands of men dressed as women, often led by horse-riders, staged elaborate rituals before a gate and then destroyed it. Rebecca broadened her activities and attacked the workhouses.

On 19 June 1843 a crowd of about 2,000 marched into Carmarthen town and, in the company of the poorer inhabitants and the farmers, proceeded to attack the much-hated workhouse. Had it not been for the well-timed arrival of the 4th Light Dragoons, the workhouse would have been completely ransacked and almost certainly burnt to the ground. This attempt to destroy the Carmarthen 'Bastille' persuaded the authorities in London that urgent action was required to restore order to the countryside. It was at this point that Thomas Campbell Foster was sent to the area as a correspondent for *The Times*; and he soon began to despatch perceptive reports to his employers in London. He showed that the presence of the police and the military in south-west Wales merely exasperated Rebecca and her followers and made them determined to pursue their course of action.

By the late summer and autumn of 1843 the Riots had spread to the industrial areas of south-east Carmarthenshire and Glamorgan. On 2 August 1843 Rebecca attacked her first toll-gate at Llanelli, and on 6 September a crowd of over a hundred attacked the toll-gate in the village of Pontarddulais. On this occasion the authorities had been tipped off and they were lying in wait for the Rebeccaites. At least seven people were arrested and tried at the Cardiff Assizes in October 1843. These arrests did not, however, deter Rebecca from her purpose and, two days after the Pontarddulais fracas, the gate at nearby Hendy was besieged. During this incident the toll-keeper, a 75-year-old woman called Sarah Davies, was killed.

As Rebecca entered this more violent phase, the Government urged the authorities in west Wales to take more positive action against insurgents. Over 150 more Metropolitan policemen and additional marines were rushed into the area and, in the autumn of 1843, this energetic and concerted campaign by the authorities resulted in the arrest of some prominent leaders, including Shoni Sgubor Fawr (John Jones) and Dai'r Cantwr (David Davies). In December they and thirty-nine others were put on trial at Carmarthen. Both Shoni and Dai were transported to the convict colony in Australia. Although there were minor convulsions after 1844, the Rebecca Riots of 1839 and 1842–3 had, more or less, ended. The Government had set up a full Commission of Enquiry into the disturbances in

October 1843, and this published its much-awaited Report in March 1844. It made a number of recommendations for reforming the turnpike trusts: the trusts were to be consolidated, and county road boards were to be set up in Wales to take charge of them in each shire; the tolls were to be simplified and made more uniform; and the toll on lime, a particular grievance of Rebecca, was reduced by a half. Other measures also helped to relieve the distress so poignantly felt in these rural areas: a General Inclosure Act in 1845 stipulated that a local enquiry by enclosure commissioners should precede the introduction of a private enclosure bill; the repeal of the Corn Laws in 1846 had some significant repercussions, not least of which was the fillip it gave to radical, Nonconformist public opinion; and finally, a Poor Law Board was established in 1847 to render the working of the Poor Law more humane.

Chartism

One of the first Chartist groups in Wales was set up at Carmarthen in 1837 by a local solicitor, Hugh Williams. He had often visited London and met many of the leading Radicals of the day, especially Henry Hetherington. Williams campaigned vigorously for the Charter in south and west Wales and, when over 4,000 people met in Carmarthen in January 1839, they chose the reforming and zealous advocate to represent them at the National Convention of Chartists in London. Welsh Chartism has often been associated with violence, and the picture that emerges in many texts is of a short, violent and radical movement. Chartists have been condemned as criminals and atheists.

The community leaders of Chartism were a fairly well-defined group which included craftsmen, tailors, shoemakers, shopkeepers, printers, schoolmasters, innkeepers, doctors, ministers, and master colliers. The one factor in common to most of these was their religious affiliation. In areas such as Merthyr Tydfil, Blackwood and Llanidloes the Established Church was almost non-existent, and Welsh Radicals looked to the Nonconformist minister for guidance. Chartist petitions were often left in the chapels, and scores of Baptist, Independent and Unitarian ministers were enthusiastic Chartists. Chartist meetings were held in chapel buildings, and demonstrations used them as starting-points. There were several Chartist churches in Wales, and perhaps the best-known Chartist sympathizer was the Revd Thomas Davies, the minister of a Baptist chapel in Merthyr for almost twenty years. To understand Welsh Chartism one has to consider the importance of the existence of a radical tradition of a distinctly Nonconformist complexion: the heroes of Welsh Chartism were Cromwell and the American revolutionaries; the Welsh Chartist press fulminated against the Church; Chartist meetings usually commenced with a prayer, and some had a distinctly revivalist tone.

The leaders of the working-class communities adopted Chartism because it enabled them to make their mark in the world: it gave political and social expression to their feelings of being consciously respectable and intelligent. The Chartist Committee at Merthyr Tydfil penned pompous letters to *The Times*, and whole communities competed for the attention of famous Chartist speakers. John Vincent was a favourite and, whenever he appeared in the drab and craggy mining communities, gigantic tea meetings would be arranged by the ever-resilient Chartist women. These mining communities seemed to be rehearsing their self-confidence and declaring themselves the equals of the 'fools at Westminster', or 'the stupid Queen'. David Jenkin Hughes, a Llanidloes printer, considered himself something of a philosopher, as well as a Chartist leader; Morgan Williams of Merthyr embellished his 1841 election address with detailed statistical trimmings and completely confounded his opponents. Leaders like these rejected violence and endeavoured to control the outward manifestations of working-class discontent. They helped to make the movement generally peaceful and respectable, even in south-west Wales, the cradle of the Rebeccaites. Many of the Chartists rejected the attempts to unite with Rebecca, and the *Northern Star* confirmed this opposition to Rebecca:

> It would be madness, nay it would be worse, it would be traitorism to the hallowed cause of Chartism to attempt to mix it up with the present [Rebecca] movement.

Chartism in Mid Wales

Mid Wales was a centre of woollen manufacture and the textile industry had become well developed in Llanidloes and Newtown by 1838. Newtown, with a population of 4,800, in 1841, had six factories employing 192 people in 1838. Llanidloes, with a population of 2,700 in 1841, boasted of six factories employing 180 people. By the 1820s the woollen trade was susceptible to fluctuations and price movements, and crisis proportions were reached in the 1820s and 1830s. The slump of 1836–7 was probably the most severe to have affected the Severn Valley, and it followed a trade boom at the beginning of 1836. A hard winter in 1837 merely heightened the depression and exacerbated the hardship. The conditions of employment in the factories were particularly oppressive and lamentable, where a 14-hour day was common practice. In 1832 there were 270 children under sixteen years of age employed in the factories and weaving shops, and these were sometimes required to work 36 hours continuously. The wages of the handloom weavers were low: in 1838 a weaver at Llanidloes could expect to earn 7s. to 9s. a week, while those at Newtown were often paid 11s. The conditions of life were hazardous: weavers died at an early age, their homes lacked sanitation, and disease was a permanent feature of life. There were cholera visitations at Newtown in 1832, Welshpool in 1849, and a further outbreak at Newtown in 1853.

In an area where political representation was tightly controlled by the Wynn interest and the Earl of Powis, and where only 4.6 per cent of the population was allowed to vote in Newtown, 2.1 per cent in Llanidloes and 5.2 per cent in Welshpool, a tradition of industrial action had emerged among the working classes which, by 1834, had coalesced with the anti-Poor Law campaign and the agitation for parliamentary reform. From the beginning of the century the threat of wage reductions and the appalling conditions of work had produced collective action by the workers. In 1819, men had marched through Newtown and damaged property; at Llanidloes, textile workers had struck for five weeks in 1830; in 1832 there was a fresh outbreak of disturbances, and fifty special constables were enrolled to contain the troubles. In 1832, political meetings were organized in Llanidloes and Newtown and, by June of that year, almost 8,000 signatures had been submitted in support of reform. The New Poor Law also attracted some ebullient opposition and when the Poor Commissioner visited Llanidloes in the late 1830s his gig was tossed into the river.

A local branch of the Working Men's Association was active in Newtown from April 1837 and the leading-light was John Owen, a weaver at Penygloddfa. By October 1838 the branch had organized a great Chartist demonstration at Newtown, and a huge crowd of around 4,000 people attended to assent to the National Petition and to elect a representative for the proposed National Convention. The pioneers of this branch were responsible, peace-loving men like John Owen, Richard Reynolds, the saddler, Thomas Powell, ironmonger, and Jenkin Hughes, the master-printer. They were not belligerent men and they believed in conducting their cause in a peaceful manner. In the early spring of 1839 Henry Hetherington toured mid Wales and on 9 April he addressed a crowd of around 2,000 in the public rooms at Newtown. The following day, Hetherington was given a rousing reception by the Llanidloes Chartist Association. In his speeches he actively encouraged his listeners to adopt peaceful and constitutional methods to achieve their aims.

The magistrates were in a state of needless panic and appealed to the Home Office for police and soldiers to be sent to the area. T.E. Marsh, the Llanidloes magistrate, swore in 300 special constables. On the night of 29 April three London policemen had arrived in the town and taken up residence at the Trewythen Arms. Fearing that local Chartist leaders were about to be arrested, Lewis Baxter blew his horn on the streets and announced that a meeting would be held on the Long Bridge in the town on the morning of 30 April. In the midst of the meeting news was brought that three of their comrades had been arrested and were being held in the Trewythen Arms. The crowd became excited and attacked the inn. Stones were thrown, guns fired, and the doors broken down.

Although the presence of the London policemen had worsened the situation, it was really the action of T.E. Marsh which precipitated the riot. Finding himself locked outside the Trewythen, he pretended to be one of the angry crowd and smashed a pane of glass in one of the large windows of the inn. The crowd interpreted this action as a licence to riot, and Marsh slipped quietly away. It is clear that those who took part in the ensuing mêlée were not connected with the responsible leaders of the Chartist Union, but rather a crowd of teenage labourers, vociferous housewives, and several town nuisances. Lewis Baxter, the 18-year-old bugler, was one of the town's general mischief-makers, and had never taken part in Chartist meetings. Very few of the rioters were weavers, and it seems extremely unlikely that this was a Chartist insurrection. Indeed, it was the timely action of the Chartist Union in calling a counter-meeting in the town and persuading the people of their folly which prevented further rioting.

Marsh was still determined to capture the Chartists and he appealed to the Lord Lieutenant for military assistance. On Saturday, 4 May, a battalion of the 14th Light Infantry arrived from Brecon, and the commanding officer, Major Barlow, was immediately struck by the lack of rioting in the town. Nevertheless, the authorities were unfaltering in their pursuit of the Chartists and a total of thirty-two arrests was made. At the Montgomeryshire Assizes in July 1839 there were four QCs and the Attorney-General ranged against the prisoners. The Chartists were represented by Hugh Williams, the Carmarthen solicitor. Savage sentences were imposed on the thirty-two persons charged in this show-trial. But T.E. Marsh was never forgiven by the people — his haystacks were burnt and his pack of hounds poisoned. He lived in constant fear thereafter.

The Newport Insurrection of 1839

In the industrial valleys of south-east Wales, as we have seen in other chapters, communities had grown up in Klondike-fashion. The conditions of life and work were extremely precarious, and combinations amongst the working people of south Wales were quite common. After 1815 the miners and colliers were quite capable of organized and sustained action and, by the early 1830s, the workforce of the ironworks could bring out all the sale-coal colliers of the district. The strikes of 1822, 1836, and 1840 exhibited the solidarity of the workers; and on a number of occasions the whole of the Glamorgan and Monmouthshire coalfield came to a halt — in 1816, 1822, 1830, and 1832. The popularity of trade unions during and after the Reform crisis added a new dimension to the workers'

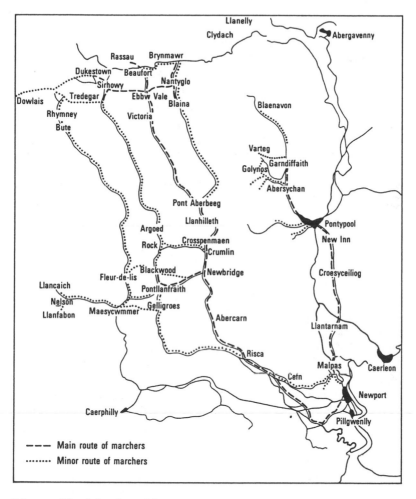

MAP 4. The March on Newport

organization. In 1831, south Wales lodges were affiliated to the Friendly Society of Coal Mining.

The Reform crisis of 1830–2 raised the political temperature throughout the land and, in November 1831, John Frost and his colleagues established a branch of the Political Union in the area. The Reform Act of 1832, however, gave Monmouthshire very little and by 1837 a Radical Association had already appeared in Pontypool. There were Radical stirrings also in Cardiff, Chepstow, and Newport. John Frost actually became a magistrate in Newport, and mayor of the borough in November 1836. In the summer of 1838 a Working Men's Association was formed at Newport, and by January 1839 there were 430 card-carrying Chartists in the borough. It was estimated also that there were 7,000 enrolled Chartists in Aberdare and Merthyr by the end of 1838. During the late 1830s support grew for the Radicals' assertions as industrial workmen flocked to join the Chartist Associations. By February 1839, Frost reported that twenty new branches had opened in Monmouthshire in the previous months. At the height of the movement's success in 1839 there were over 25,000 enrolled or committed Chartists in the district, or one-fifth of the total population. In these communities, working-class attitudes and methods of organization had imprinted themselves on the new political movement.

The authorities in Newport responded quickly to this rising tide of Radicalism: meetings were banned; special constables were appointed, and pensioners were alerted for duty; 120 soldiers of the 29th Regiment arrived in Newport on 2 May; and the Chartist leader, Henry Vincent, was arrested. In spite of these restrictions, political meetings were held across Wales and the movement grew quickly in the ensuing weeks. It was estimated that there were 4,000 Chartists at Pontypool; and by July 1839 over 1,000 had joined associations in Rhymney and Dukestown. The Working Men's Association at Merthyr was growing at the rate of 100 to 120 members a week.

It was the outright rejection of the National Petition by the House of Commons on 12 July 1839 which changed Chartist attitudes in the late summer and early autumn. As the authorities put increased pressure on the Radical movement there was a growing militancy among Chartist supporters. It was known that weapons were being made in the workshops of

Newport and in caves in the hills. By mid October a decision had been taken to prepare the valleys for a rising and, from 28 October, John Frost was the acknowledged leader of that rising. Elaborate preparations were now made throughout the district: nightly meetings, the organization of groups by districts, financial collections were hastened; soldiers were bribed to desert their platoons; and guns and pikes were being openly sold in the lodges and pubs. The leaders, including Frost, Zephaniah Williams, and William Jones, revealed none of the details and plans. Crucial decisions about the rising were eventually put to a delegate meeting held at the Coach and Horses in Blackwood on Friday, 1 November. They reckoned that they could rely on at least 5,000 armed men to march in support of the cause.

On 3 November Frost and his contingent left Blackwood at around 7.00 p.m. From Blaina, Zephaniah Williams set off at 9.00 p.m. with 4,000 men from the northern iron towns. The third contingent under the command of William Jones did not leave Pontypool until about 7.00 a.m. on 4 November. Jones had tried to muster additional forces and had delayed the start. In the meantime Frost and Williams led their exhausted and soaked contingents on the march to Newport. The authorities were prepared: Thomas Phillips, the mayor, had sworn in about 500 special constables, and thirty soldiers had been sent to the town. On the evening of 3 November they set up their headquarters at the Westgate Hotel. Frost now concentrated his attack on the Westgate. After the soldiers had opened fire on the crowd, panic followed and most of the Chartists fled. In the confusion it seems that twenty-two of the Chartists were killed and two of the soldiers. Even though most of the Chartists fled back to the valleys, the authorities did not feel secure until larger numbers of troops were moved to the coalfield and the leaders of the rising captured.

After the rising all manner of enquirers and government officials were sent to the area to investigate the causes. Subsequent historians have tended to interpret the rising in two ways: it is seen either as a peaceful demonstration that went sadly astray; or it has been construed as part of a national conspiracy to overthrow the Government. One recent historian, Dr D.J.V. Jones, has argued that the events were so extraordinary in design and execution, that the rising can be interpreted as a mass movement. The degree of planning was unique and it would seem as if Thomas Phillips, the Mayor of Newport, was correct in his assumption that the local rising was originally conceived as part of a general insurrection. John Frost, however, had probably criticized the bolder plan of attacking four or five towns simultaneously; his proposal was a modified version, which included the assault on Newport.

Whatever the intention, by the end of November most of the leaders were in prison. Sixty of the most important Chartists had been arrested and they were put on trial on 10 December 1839. The Chartists were found guilty in January 1840 and the three leaders, Frost, Williams and Jones, were sentenced to death. Chartists all over Britain campaigned against the sentences and on 31 January 1840, it was decided that they should be transported for life. Williams and Jones never returned to Britain, but Frost returned to a hero's welcome in 1856.

Chartism after the Newport Rising
The failure of the Newport Rising did not destroy the Chartist movement in Wales. By the end of 1841 there were new Radical stirrings on the fringes of the south Wales coalfield at Llantrisant, Cardiff, Caerleon, Monmouth and Abergavenny. Chartist lodges in the Aberdare and Merthyr district may even have increased in size. After 1840 these lodges became the centres of popular Radicalism in the south, and almost 14,000 signatures were collected there for the National Petition in 1842. In the early 1840s Chartists in south Wales set up their own press, dominated street politics and fought local elections. Secret meetings at the Coach and Horses in Merthyr in 1842–3 discussed some of the arguments that had been rehearsed during the 1839 rising. In the Monmouthshire valleys there were sufficient examples of workers' solidarity in the sale-coal collieries: in 1841, 1843, and from 1847 to 1853 there were workers' combinations operating against the employers.

In mid Wales, also, organized Chartism survived well into the 1850s. The Chartist movement received a new lease of life in 1842 as trade became depressed. In 1847 the Education Commissioners indicated that the local Chartist organization was sound and active. In the 1850s, the Severn Valley supported Julian Harney's papers, *The Red Republican* to 1850 and thereafter, *The Friend of the People*. In Ernest Jones's paper, *Notes to the People*, there were many references to Chartist activists in the Severn Valley. The Chartists at Llanidloes responded to Jones's call for a 'People's Paper' to be founded in January 1852. In June 1853 Ernest Jones and R.C. Gammage, the historian of the movement, undertook a six-week tour of mid Wales. But by the time that Ernest Jones called for a new conference to be held in London, Chartism in Montgomeryshire was displaying signs of decay.

In the 1850s many Chartists concentrated on social amelioration, and lectures assumed a new degree of importance as media of communication. Morgan Williams had helped found the Merthyr subscription library in 1846; Henry Vincent often toured and lectured on such themes as democracy and liberty, moral elevation, the promotion of knowledge, and temperance. At the same time, Chartists tried to penetrate local politics: many played an important role in trade unions and the co-operative movement; others pressed for political reform and slowly paved the way for the great Liberal victories from 1867 onwards. At Merthyr, for example, Chartists had worked tirelessly to ensure that the people would be represented in Parliament. Some of the old Chartists actually survived into the early part of the twentieth century. William Price, a flannel weaver of Cross Keys, and a Chartist in 1839, died in 1906 at the age of 90. David Morris, the last of the mid-Wales Chartists, died in 1901, by which time he had become an enthusiastic supporter of the ILP.

SUGGESTED READING

D.J.V. Jones, *Before Rebecca: Popular Protests in Wales, 1793–1835* (London, 1973).

D.J.V. Jones, *Chartism and Chartists* (London, 1975).

D.J.V. Jones, *The Last Rising* (Oxford, 1985).

Ivor Wilks, *South Wales and the Rising of 1839* (London, 1984).

D. Williams, *The Rebecca Riots* (Cardiff, 1986, first published 1955).

D. Williams, *A History of Modern Wales* (London, 1982).

G. Williams (ed.), *Merthyr Politics* (Cardiff, 1966).

Articles:

O.R. Ashton, 'Chartism in Mid-Wales', *Montgomeryshire Collections*, 62 (1971–2).

A.V. John, 'The Chartist Endurance: Industrial South Wales, 1840–1868', *Morgannwg*, XV (1971).

D.J.V. Jones, 'Chartism in Welsh Communities', *W.H.R.*, 6 (1972–3).

D.J.V. Jones, 'Chartism at Merthyr — A Commentary on the Meetings of 1842', *B.B.C.S.*, XXIV (1972).

7. Political Developments
1815–1850

The Background to Welsh Politics

THE constitutional structure of parliamentary representation was the ancient one surviving from the Act of Union. This sixteenth-century legislation had given Wales twenty-seven Members of Parliament. Each of the counties received two members, and this was on the English model. The county franchise was in fact an extension of the English system, with the uniform 40s. freehold qualification. In the boroughs, each shire town, except in the county of Merioneth, returned one Member of Parliament. By the terms of the Act of Union, all the ancient boroughs that contributed towards the payment of the wages of the parliamentary representative were to participate in his election. In this way there evolved the distinctly Welsh system of contributory boroughs.

All candidates for a seat in Parliament during this period were required by law to have an annual income of at least £600 from land if they sought election for a county, or £300 if they stood for a borough. In south Wales, however, these legal requirements were not the decisive attributes, for the influential families there set their own standards in lineage, estate, independence, constitutional loyalty, and attention to the welfare of the county. No candidate, even for a safe seat, wanted to be thought lacking in these essentials. The Welsh gentry regarded distinguished lineage and ownership, by inheritance, of an ancient and honourable Welsh estate as essential requirements for election purposes. Many families claimed descent from the princes, or the great chieftains, or from the noble families of Wales. All, save one or two borough candidates, paid respectful attention to the sentiments of the gentry. This sentimental appeal to lineage caused many Englishmen who married Welsh heiresses to change their names when they took possession of an estate. Pryse of Gogerddan and Morgan of Tredegar were outstanding examples of this. In Glamorgan, in 1820, the need to present candidates as Welshmen gave the contest the semblance of a charade. The Morgan estate brought Sir Christopher Cole as its candidate, and introduced him as a Cornishman, 'the Welshman's first cousin'. The Welsh language was, however, usually excluded from such appeals to Welsh sentiment, and pride in a Welsh lineage did not extend to the language. Some election addresses were printed in Welsh, but English was the language of the gentry and of political discussion.

No candidate for parliamentary election in the years from 1790 to 1832 presented himself as a Whig or Tory, but there were many who claimed to be Independent. Independence could mean a whole host of things: it could be independence of an aristocratic patron; independence of a dominant group of families; independence of the ministers; or of a parliamentary connection; or independence of the electors themselves; or, indeed, independence of fortune. Sir Christopher Cole, when challenged in 1817 that he stood as the nominee of the Morgan estate, replied that he was an independent person: 'I am not rich, but I am rich enough to be independent.' Independence served as a suitable rallying-cry for both sides in Breconshire between 1816 and 1818 in the great contest between Sir Charles Morgan and Thomas Wood. Wood was the son-in-law of a peer, the nephew of a marquis, the brother-in-law of Viscount Castlereagh; and Morgan's supporters castigated him as a dependent candidate. Wood's supporters, on the other hand, responded by declaring that Morgan was the opponent of independence: he was guilty of oppressing his tenants as his forebears had done. In their constituencies, most members were 'independent' in whatever sense such a description presented them in a good light to their constituents.

All candidates were expected to profess loyalty to the constitution, especially during the period of the French Revolutionary and Napoleonic wars. After the 1815 peace they continued to do so, for it was generally agreed that the constitution was a blessing conferred on those who were fortunate enough to live under it. Most candidates set themselves up as guardians of the constitution. They were opposed to any changes in the Catholic Laws, in the Corn Laws, or in the laws and practices governing elections. Candidates who showed any interest in Catholic emancipation or electoral reform were at an immediate disadvantage. John Moggridge, an avowed champion of electoral reform, was defeated in the Monmouth boroughs in 1820. Sir William Paxton alleged that the anti-Catholic cry was whipped up against him in Carmarthenshire in 1807. Appeals to constitutional loyalty subsided in later years, although south-west Wales remained a constitutional stronghold. In 1823 the Revd David Archard Williams took over the editorship of the *Carmarthen Journal* and made it a Church and Tory paper. He exhorted his readers to attend meetings, to sign petitions and to support the constitution. He described Sir Robert Peel's Catholic Emancipation measure of 1829 as the, 'breaking of the Constitution Bill'.

Parliamentary candidates were expected to pay special attention to the needs of their constituents, and these were widely interpreted. Support for social functions and charities was important, as were economic and professional favours, magisterial activity, and the promotion of local interests in Parliament. The county families followed a seasonal round of balls, assemblies, theatrical and musical entertainments, hunt and race meetings, fêtes and regattas. Members and their candidates were judged by their readiness to join in the social round. Benjamin Hall, whose election for Glamorgan in 1814 was first viewed with grave misgivings, quickly commended himself to the Glamorgan families. He revived the Glamorgan races, acted as steward, and gave public breakfasts and suppers.

Members of Parliament could also reward their supporters by helping them to obtain ministerial favours. The younger brother of John Hensleigh Allen of Cresselly, Member for Pembroke boroughs, became a clerk in the Petty Bag Office in 1824, and a clerk in Chancery the following year. But Roger Samuel, who left Carmarthen in 1821 with a letter of recommendation, failed to find employment in London. Members, on the whole, did their best to secure posts for their loyal supporters. All members were expected to attend Parliament as frequently as possible and, as already mentioned, to attend to the economic and social interests of their constituencies. There was a minor revolt in industrial Glamorgan in 1807 when John Llewelyn of Penllergaer canvassed constituents in protest against the Member's apparent neglect. In the industrial counties of Glamorgan and Monmouthshire the old qualifications for candidacy and membership were losing their hold on the constituents. In Glamorgan, Benjamin Hall proved the value of a man of business. Sir Charles Morgan was successful in Monmouthshire because he assumed the traditions of his mother's family and extended his interests in agriculture to embrace ironworking, land transport and shipping. New needs and old attitudes could not be indefinitely reconciled by equivocal electioneering, and an ominous sign of change was the call for reform.

Reform, Radicalism and Riot

The parliamentary reform movement dated back to the mid seventeenth century. In 1780 there had been responses from Wales to the Revd Christopher Wyvill's proposals to increase the Welsh county representation by four Members. Reform committees were established in Flintshire and Breconshire, and there were also individual members of the London Corresponding Society in Wales. In 1799 Cardiff was cited in a House of Lords Select Committee as a town in correspondence with the Society.

The years after 1815 saw the birth of a new reform movement in Wales. Inflammatory notices were posted outside ironworks at Tredegar and Merthyr in 1816–17, and copies of Henry Hunt's Spa Field speech were sent to Merthyr in December 1816 and translated into Welsh. At Neath and Merioneth, extracts of Cobbett's *Political Register* were translated into Welsh. However, of over 400 petitions sent to Parliament in 1817 calling for reform, only one emanated from Wales, and this was the result of a county meeting called at Usk, Monmouthshire, in February 1817. The petition was presented to the House of Commons on 17 February and made specific requests for the reduction of taxes and the introduction of triennial parliaments.

By the 1820s reform meetings were being held in many parts of Wales. The Breconshire meeting of 20 January 1821 was instigated by Walter Williams, the Whig member for Radnorshire, who voted for a petition to the House of Commons calling for reform. A reform petition from Monmouth Corporation was presented in Parliament on 28 March 1822 by Joseph Hume, the Radical MP for Aberdeen, who had been made an honorary freeman of Monmouth in the previous October. A further petition from Monmouthshire emanated from a county meeeting at Usk in May 1822. At a Carmarthen meeting of January 1823, convened to discuss agricultural distress, George Thomas, the leader of the local Whigs, blamed the distress on the defective state of the representation of the people. There were several demands from Wales for reform, and the call was often based on the belief that reform would ameliorate material conditions. Reform petitions frequently became the barometer of social conditions and, when agriculture improved in the mid 1820s, little was heard of reform.

The Tory administration of Lord Liverpool showed no interest in parliamentary reform, while the Whig opposition was not yet united on the subject. Lord John Russell's reform motions of 1821-3 and February 1830, were all heavily defeated. Reform was not an issue in the general election of August 1830. Soon, however, the political spectrum changed and reform became a distinct possibility. When the Duke of Wellington resigned in November 1830, after defeat on the Civil List, the Whigs, headed by Lord Grey, formed an administration and pledged to introduce a measure of parliamentary reform.

There was a renewed wave of interest in the subject. At a Newport meeting on 20 December 1830, John Frost, a local Radical, succeeded in getting a resolution passed calling for shorter parliaments and the free exercise of the franchise. At Merthyr Tydfil there was a call for annual or trienniel parliaments, vote by ballot, and the enfranchisement of all those who paid national or local taxes. At Carmarthen there was a heated clash in the borough meeting between the local Whig leader, George Thomas, who called for a second member for each Welsh county, and Hugh Williams, a Radical and future Chartist leader, who demanded the ballot. Local reformers also became active in Montgomeryshire, and there was a disturbance at Newtown in January 1831 on the part of local weavers. A reform meeting was held at Holywell, Flintshire in January 1831, against a background of colliery discontent. On the eve of reform, there was thus considerable political activity in Wales, but no coherent reform movement.

The first Reform Bill presented to Parliament gave only one additional Member to Wales, to augment the total allocation to twenty-eight. The Glamorgan boroughs were to be divided into two, while a new constituency was to be grouped around Swansea. Cardiff would return a separate Member, representing also Llantrisant and Cowbridge, and there were three newly-enfranchised boroughs at Merthyr, Aberdare and Llandaff. The unique Welsh contributory borough system made it possible for the franchise to be extended without an increase in the number of seats. In addition to Merthyr, Aberdare and Llandaff, sixteen boroughs were to be enfranchised as contributories.

The Bill met with an enthusiastic reaction and countless reform meetings were held throughout Wales. The alterations to the borough system were described as judicious, but many boroughs still had their grievances. The only disenfranchisement was that of Cricieth from the Caernarfon group, and no reason was given for it. The newly-enfranchised boroughs acknowledged the commercial importance of Wrexham and Holywell in north Wales; Newtown as the centre of the mid-Wales flannel industry; and the port of Llanelli in the coal trade of south Wales. The enfranchisement of Llanelli stunned interested parties in Carmarthen. The *Carmarthen Journal* commented that it was, 'a piece of pure political meddling for which there exists not a shade of necessity'. The newspaper spoke of the move as a political disenfranchisement contrary to Carmarthen's chartered rights. Resolutions expressing alarm at the enfranchisement of Llanelli were passed by an overwhelming majority.

The Reform Bill in its original form did not become law. The important division on the second reading took place on 22 March 1831, when the Bill was carried by 302 votes to 301. On 19 April 1831, the Government was defeated on an important amendment and resigned. A general election followed at which reform was the only issue. It was an electoral issue in at least twenty-one Welsh constituencies. Nine reformers were elected unopposed and eight anti-reformers. In two constituencies, Carmarthenshire and Monmouthshire, anti-reformers declined re-election rather than continue to oppose reform against their constituents' wishes, and they were replaced by reformers. At Carmarthen itself there was violence at the poll.

The Carmarthen Riots of 1831

The borough of Carmarthen had a long history of violence associated with parliamentary and borough elections. In the mid eighteenth century there had been serious rioting and shooting in the town, and by the end of that century two rival factions had emerged: the Red party of Dynevor, and the stronger Blues represented by the Whig houses of Golden Grove and Cwmgwili. In 1796 when the Red candidate, a London banker, was illegally elected for the borough, pistols were fired in the streets and inhabitants barricaded their homes. In 1802 rioting broke out during the expensive 'Lecsiwn Fawr' for the county constituency. Elections were also contested in 1812 and 1818; and in 1821 the Red party wrested the seat from the Blues, and the victor, John Jones of Ystrad, became a popular hero.

This long tradition of bitter conflict may partly explain the turbulent conditions during the Reform crisis. There were also economic and social forces at work. On two occasions in 1800 and 1818 the situation caused by food shortages had been dangerous enough to warrant the stationing of troops in the town. The winter of 1830–1 again brought difficulties: the poor were given assistance; the wages of sailors and labourers were low; work was difficult to find; and craftsmen and tradesmen were affected by a slump in agriculture. To make matters worse, the forces of order were not strong and showed little interest in maintaining it. Only thirteen permanent constables had been appointed, and the London police constable, who had been sent to Carmarthen on a previous occasion, had not been rendered much support and had died of drink problems. There were no soldiers within sixty miles, and the magistrates had little knowledge of legal matters.

The renewed interest in parliamentary reform gave the Blue party its chance. The resident MP, John Jones of Ystrad, had voted against the Reform Bill on its second reading on 22 March. The Blue party grasped the nettle and attacked Jones for his anti-reform stance. Captain John George Phillipps of the house of Cwmgwili was put forward as a supporter of 'Reform and Retrenchment' in opposition to Jones. The election began on Friday 29 April, at the town hall, and a mêlée broke out during which the MP struck one of the crowd. The magistrates, fearing more troubles, ordered the special constables to appoint 140 additional constables. Over a half of those approached refused, and on 2 May the magistrates decided to ask the Government for a permanent military garrison in Carmarthen. A party of around twenty men of the 93rd Regiment were sent to the town, and fifteen voters were arrested.

The House of Commons debated the new Reform Bill from June to September and the magistrates, when they realized that a new election would be held, appealed to the Home Office for help to control the town. In answer to their request, six policemen were despatched from London, fourteen dragoons were drafted in, and sixty-one special constables were sworn in. Despite these precautions, the new election was no less violent and, during the evening of 19 August, the six policemen and a number of special constables were assaulted in Spilman Street. The violence continued even into election day. John Jones was returned as Member for the borough with a majority of 71. He showed great personal bravery in agreeing to be carried shoulder-high through the streets of Carmarthen for, as soon as he was seated, he was pelted with stones. One struck him on the forehead and blood streamed down his face. John Jones left the town that evening and, after his departure, a pitched battle took place.

The Carmarthen riots had no effect on the actual election result. Yet they were significant in two ways. First, they were the outward sign of a social disorder and the violent sections of the community were the small craftsmen, the carriers, blacksmiths, shoemakers and tailors. Also, unemployment was endemic; and 'idle and disaffected' sections were prepared to commit outrageous acts of violence even after the August election. Second, the respectable people of the borough, the better class of householders and the middle-class reformers, supported the rioters and refused to serve as special constables. Since the end of the Napoleonic wars the Carmarthenshire landowners had become increasingly unpopular and, within four months of the passing of the Reform Act, reformers were demanding the ballot as a means of curtailing the worst aspects of landlordism. It is against this background of middle-class support that the Rebecca Riots can best be comprehended.

The Merthyr Riots of 1831

The riot of 3 June at Merthyr was a massacre and more died on that day than at Peterloo in 1819. Merthyr had been a cockpit of industrial unrest since the early part of the century. Bread riots in 1800 were followed by strikes of skilled workmen at Dowlais and Cyfarthfa in 1810 and 1813. This unrest reached a climax on Saturday, 19 October 1816 when a mob of 8–10,000 faced the ironmasters. But it was the tenacity of the 1831 riots that took the authorities by surprise and, despite the presence of 800 soldiers, workmen held the town from midday on Friday, 3 June, until the following Monday. The riots seem to have been an isolated event and it is difficult to pinpoint the causes: the whole of Britain in 1831 was caught in a maelstrom of unrest, and Merthyr was no exception; the Reform crisis had dominated the political scene for some time and in June 1831 the Second Reform Bill was introduced to Parliament. It was not until the Bill was rejected in the autumn that violence erupted in Bristol and other centres. Industrial unrest seems to have played a minor part in the disturbances and there had been few industrial or unionist activities in the 1820s. The Scotch Cattle, bands of colliers dressed up as cattle or women, had ransacked the homes of blacklegs and enforced solidarity in the strikes of 1822, 1823, 1827, 1829 and 1830 in Monmouthshire, but there is no evidence to suggest that they infiltrated the ranks of Merthyr's work-force. By the winter of 1830 lodges of the Friendly Associated Coal Miners' Society had been formed in Flintshire, but unionism does not seem to have engulfed Merthyr until the autumn of 1831.

The violence at Merthyr does seem to have been peculiar to that town and we must try to explain it accordingly. There was a long political tradition in Merthyr and, as early as 1800, John Thelwall, the leading philosopher of the London Corresponding Society, had attended meetings of workmen as they prepared for the bread riots of that year. There were secret political meetings on Aberdare mountain and members of the Cyfarthfa Philosophical Society (founded in 1807) read the works of Tom Paine and Voltaire. In 1815 the speeches of Henry Hunt were translated into Welsh and distributed throughout the town. By 1830 there was agitation against the truck system and the Corn Laws and, led by the ironmaster William Crawshay, the townspeople petitioned for radical parliamentary reform. At Merthyr and Aberdare 'political-union' clubs were formed which included shopkeepers, miners and professional people. In Merthyr, therefore, as in London, Manchester and the other towns, there was a popular movement for reform, and parliamentary affairs held the attention of the working classes. The inhabitants of the town agreed upon an illumination as a token of their support for reform, and people who did not light up their windows ran the risk of having them smashed. A number of reform meetings were held and workmen were encouraged to protest against Colonel Wood, the Breconshire MP. On 9 and 10 May 1831, the workmen of William Crawshay, led by the ironmaster, roamed the streets of Merthyr burning effigies and expressing disapproval of those known to support Wood. Shopkeepers' homes were attacked and the local squire was the victim of an assault.

Financial and economic factors played an important part in the riots: one source of discontent was the reduction in wages which was precipitated by a period of over-production resulting in a sudden slump. Crawshay had been forced to inform his ironstone miners on 28 March 1831, at Cyfarthfa and Hirwaun, of an imminent reduction in wages. His father, William Crawshay Snr., had advised him to deal strongly with any trouble-makers, and on 24 May he discharged eighty-four puddlers. The Court of Requests was a contributory factor in the troubles. This had been established in 1809 for the recovery of small debts, usually by taking and selling debtors' furniture. As the violence spread at the end of May it was the local shopkeepers and the officers of the Court of Requests who became the principal targets of the rioters.

As violence erupted a mob virtually took control of the town, and the forces of law and order were forced to beat a retreat to the Castle Inn. The mob waved the red flag as they roamed the district and urged workmen to desert their posts. Once they pressed against the soldiers, who had taken guard outside the Castle Inn, the temperature mounted. The soldiers fired and the

High Street became a scene of desolation. As the mob withdrew, the bodies of six men, one woman, and a boy of twelve years were taken into the coach house of the inn. It is estimated that sixteen were fatally wounded and many seriously injured during the riot. By July, twenty-six of the Merthyr rioters were in Cardiff jail, and Richard Lewis (Dic Penderyn) was eventually hanged. He died protesting his innocence.

Interpretations of the riots have differed over the years, but it is now accepted that they were a unique popular disturbance. They were not so much the result of a conflict between employer and employee: in a sense the roots of Chartism can be seen in this reform demonstration in 1831, when some of the working classes became disillusioned with constitutional means of pleading reform.

The Events leading to the 1832 Reform Act

The Whigs returned to power and introduced a Second Reform Bill which contained certain modifications: Amlwch and Llangefni were to join Holyhead as contributories to Beaumaris; St Asaph was to be granted the status of a parliamentary borough contributory to Flint; Cricieth was to keep its status as a contributory borough to Caernarfon; in Pembrokeshire, Milford Haven, originally intended as a contributory to Haverfordwest, was to be transferred to the Pembroke boroughs constituency; and Glamorgan was to be awarded a second county member. The committee stage of the Second Reform Bill lasted from July to August 1831, and on 14 September 1831, it was announced that Carmarthenshire and Denbighshire were to receive an extra county member each. The Second Reform Bill was passed by the House of Commons on 21 September 1831 by a majority of 109, but on 8 October 1831 the Lords rejected it by 199 votes to 158. The news was greeted with shock and dismay in Wales. Lord Hereford, returning to his residence in Abergavenny, was pelted with mud for having voted against the Bill. There was a disturbance at Brecon in November, and at Carmarthen farmers were urged to refuse payment of tolls.

The Whigs eventually remained in power and introduced their Third Reform Bill on 12 December 1831. There were changes in points of detail affecting Wales: Llandaff and St David's, originally intended as contributories to Cardiff and Haverfordwest, were withdrawn; Monmouthshire was allocated a third county member, possibly as a concession to the Welsh mining industry; Merthyr Tydfil was still not allocated a member and was once more attached to the Cardiff group. Eventually, however, the Government conceded and Merthyr was given its own member. Monmouthshire, in return, had to forfeit its proposed third county member. The Bill was carried on the third reading through the House of Commons by a majority of 116. The Lords passed it on 13 April 1832, by a majority of nine.

The 1832 Reform Act did have some important consequences for Wales: it increased the number of Welsh seats from twenty-seven to thirty-two; the three counties of Glamorgan, Carmarthenshire and Denbigh were awarded second members; new borough constituencies were centred at Swansea and Merthyr; and eighteen new boroughs were enfranchised as contributories.

Political Dissenting Societies and the Origins of the Disestablishment Campaign

The Toleration Act had not always spared Dissenters from the spiteful activities of the squire, parson and the mob. In November 1732 a group of leading London Dissenters, among whom Welshmen were prominent, assembled to consider the best ways of repealing the Test and Corporation Acts. An organization was created consisting of a committee annually elected from the general body of delegates, and this grouping became known as the Protestant Dissenting Deputies. Its task was to protect the civil rights of Dissenters and it involved them in two different but related kinds of activity: first, it involved them in political action, since their basic concern was the repeal of all penal legislation affecting Dissenters; its second function was the defence of the existing rights of Dissenters as defined in the statutes. They prosecuted the brutal persecutors, appealed to higher courts against magistrates' decisions and often took action against clergy. In these ways, the Dissenting Deputies became the main instrument in the creation of a cohesive body of Dissenting opinion in the country. In the years up to 1810 more than thirty cases out of a total of about 250 which were dealt with by the Deputies concerned Welsh congregations.

The other Dissenting Society was the Protestant Society for the Protection of Religious Liberty. It was founded in 1811 and existed until 1857, though its effective life lasted until 1839. Its aims resembled those of the Dissenting Deputies, for it aspired to repeal those laws which prevented the enjoyment of religious liberty and it involved itself with the defence of particular congregations. The Protestant Society looked for support to every congregation in England and Wales, though Welsh subscriptions were never considerable, totalling only about £55 up to 1834. It was, however, the first of the great Dissenting societies to make a sustained attempt to organize Dissenting opinion along political lines in the provinces. The Revd Thomas Charles of Bala was among the early members of the committee and he was one of the deputation called to protest against Lord Sidmouth's Bill of 1811 which intended to place severe restrictions on the licensing of Dissenting ministers. This attempt to meddle with the Toleration Act had provided Nonconformists with an excellent lesson in how to organize public opinion and frame petitions. Similarly, the campaign to repeal the Test and Corporation Acts indicated the growth of a liberal and effective Nonconformist opinion. Of the Welsh churches, 185 sent petitions to the House of Commons and 126 to the House of Lords. Apart from a few Unitarian churches, these were all Independent and Baptist congregations.

During the 1830s and 1840s there slowly emerged a united Nonconformist front. In 1830, the Baptist journal, *Seren Gomer*, commenced a long argument about the nature of the Church and the validity of its connection with the State. The Independent journal, *Y Dysgedydd*, carried a similar discussion in its pages, and both journals attacked the tithes as unfair. By 1833 disestablishment, and the whole question of the separation of Church and State, were beginning to enter the discussion. In that year, Hugh Pugh, the Independent minister of Llandrillo, Merioneth, founded a society called, 'The Young Men of Penllyn and Edeyrnion', which was concerned with the principles of voluntary support for religion.

However authoritative the Independent radicals might be, they could hardly have launched an effective campaign for disestablishment if the Methodists had continued to side with the Church and from 1830 to 1852 the support of the Methodists became crucial to their success. Various events introduced the Methodists to active politics in the period: the struggle for the abolition of slavery provided one such experience, and meetings were held in May 1828 at the Town Hall, Swansea, and in August 1828, at Cardiff to send a petition to Parliament in favour of abolition. The campaign for parliamentary reform attracted large numbers of Dissenters and, at Carmarthen, in October 1832 there was a huge meeting attended by over 100 Dissenting ministers and thousands of their members in support of parliamentary reform. Sabbatarian legislation pushed the Methodists ever closer to active participation in politics and the formidable John Elias was himself involved in this cause. The Nonconformists gradually adopted a more humanitarian attitude and accepted the Methodist logic of a compulsory observance of the Sabbath. When Elias died in June 1841 it was obvious that a new generation of more liberal leaders was moving to the forefront of Methodism, and it seemed as if a last stand to preserve the link between the Methodists in Wales and the Church had been broken.

The issue that possibly did most to convince the Nonconformists that piecemeal redress of grievances should give way to the more radical demand for disestablishment was the Church rate. Welshmen noted with approval the formation of the Church Rate Abolition Society in October 1836, and they began adopting tactics that could frustrate the church vestry in its attempts to collect the rates. Packing the vestry with a sufficient number of Nonconformist parishioners was one such stratagem, which was used at Swansea, Newport (Mon.), Fishguard, Merthyr, Llanelli and Llanrhidian in 1836. In the three succeeding years, this tactic was again employed to good effect. Soon there were meetings to form branches of the Abolition Society in Wales; in November 1836 a branch was established at Abergavenny; and another in December at Haverfordwest. In the early months of 1837 some 2,328 petitions were sent from all parts of the country to London protesting against the Church rates.

By the beginning of the 1840s Welsh Nonconformity was poised for a concerted campaign in support of disestablishment. On 12 June 1843, a meeting was held at Pendref Chapel, Caernarfon, to plead the case for disestablishment. Other meetings were to follow at Llanrwst and Llangefni in north Wales. Throughout the 1840s the Nonconformists began to present a united front in their attack on the Church and two developments, in particular, strengthened their cause: one factor which brought Methodists and Dissenters closer was the campaign to repeal the Corn Laws; the other catalyst was the 1847 Education Report, which raised the question of the relationship between the demand for disestablishment and Welsh nationality.

Political Reform Societies

Political dissent, parliamentary reform, and free trade: these were the issues which formed the core of much of Victorian pressure group activity. We have already considered the genesis of the political Dissenting movement, and the evolution of Dissenting opinion away from concern with single grievances towards an attack upon the Church establishment. This theme will be developed in later sections on the work of the Liberation Society and on the disestablishment campaign. This section will concern itself with the other two issues, namely free trade and parliamentary reform.

Free Trade and the Anti-Corn Law League

The early operations of the League were greeted in Wales with apparent indifference. Public attention was focused on the Chartist movement and there were few signs of support for the League in Wales before 1840. The Anti-Corn Law movement in Wales dates from the employment of Walter Griffith as agent, and his experiences epitomize the reception of the League in Wales: there was considerable public ignorance on the matter; the Established Church was hostile; local landowners were opposed; local corporations, under the control of the land-owners, frequently refused the use of town halls, as at Bangor and Carmarthen; and many Chartists attacked the League as a rival organization. Its supporters were few: there were those

Dissenting ministers who were attracted by the moral and religious arguments, and the Corn Laws were seen as an aspect of a whole system of monopoly and privilege under which the Dissenters suffered. Many Nonconformist ministers participated in the free trade movement, for example Revd William Williams (Caledfryn), the Independent minister at Caernarfon from 1832 to 1848. In August 1841 it seems that some twenty-five Welsh Nonconformist ministers attended a conference in Manchester to discuss the Corn Laws. A ministerial conference was convened on 30 November 1841 at Caernarfon, which stretched over three days. It attracted large numbers of Independent and Baptist ministers, but not the Methodists, who were still reluctant to participate in political activity. The first Anti-Corn Law Society in Wales was established at Llangollen in May 1840.

Several free trade associations were formed in Wales, and in 1840 they were most conspicuous in the north-east. Later, important branches were established at Caernarfon, Carmarthen and Swansea. The most active local branch in the early years was that at Caernarfon, formed in February 1841. From 1842 onwards the centre of League activity moved from Caernarfon to Holywell in the north, and to Swansea in the south. Wales was eventually divided into districts, and north Wales was run by Walter Griffith, and the south by John Jenkins. Once organized, the League concentrated on manipulating the electorate. It sought a thorough knowledge of electorates, and endeavoured to influence the voting registers by legal wranglings in the courts and by assisting people to purchase the 40s. freehold in order to acquire the vote. The League also scrutinized the electoral registers, and in the Carmarthen boroughs the free trade party gained a total of forty-four votes over the opposition in the 1844 registration. At Swansea, sixty or seventy sympathizers were said to have been recovered to the registers.

After 1842 the League's major provincial activity centred on fund-raising, and in this it was supported by the Nonconformists, and the denominational press. *Y Diwygiwr*, the Llanelli-published Independent journal, agitated for, 'Crefydd rydd a bara rhad' (free religion and cheap bread). On payment of a minimum of a 1d. and 1s. maximum, individuals could be issued with official membership cards. Despite constant appeals for financial help, contributions from Wales fell steadily in the years 1842–6, and the League never attained a position of strength in the industrial regions. The most important source of support for the League in Wales came from the Independent and Baptist ministers and it might even be possible to portray the conflict between the Leaguers and opponents as 'chapel v public house'. Leaguers rarely spoke at public houses for they were usually the regular rallying-points for protectionists and Chartists. The League attracted its support from the 'respectable classes', and so the labouring and working classes were not prominent supporters.

Parliamentary Reform and Radical Politics

The number of Chartist societies in Wales reached a peak in 1839. There had been a marked decline in organized Welsh Chartism, and in west Wales it was almost a spent force. Yet there were still Chartist groups in action, and it would be imprudent to overestimate the decline of Chartism as a political force in the early 1840s. Welsh Chartism persisted for some considerable time, and the survival was, in part, attributable to the formation of the National Charter Association (NCA). It was formed in Manchester in July 1840.

At this conference Merthyr Chartists were still prominent, and David John committed the south Wales localities to support the newly-formed NCA. Morgan Williams, another loyal south Wales Chartist, was elected to the executive of the NCA in June 1841. Local Working Men's Associations soon began to transform themselves into branches of the NCA, and there were nine in Wales by the end of 1841. In June 1842, a Mr Simeon of Bristol lectured in south Wales and inspired the formation of a Chartist Association at Morriston and several other places near Swansea. Others were set up at Mold, Pontypridd and Newbridge. Many of these Welsh branches enjoyed no more than a transient existence in the 1840s and soon faded into oblivion. In the old strongholds, at Merthyr and Newport, the branches were more resilient and Chartism was still active in 1847. The *Northern Star*, the Chartists' own newspaper, circulated widely in south Wales at the end of the 1840s.

The Chartist press, the NCA branches, lectures and lecture tours, and public meetings were still used to great effect as methods of pressuring the Government and those in positions of power. Petitioning was also maintained and in 1842 the NCA embarked on a second national petitioning campaign. Wales is reported to have contributed nearly 50,000 signatures, mainly from the Merthyr area. Elections were also fought on a national and local level: in the 1841 general election two Chartist candidates offered themselves for election in Wales; while in the localities Chartists still campaigned at Merthyr, Swansea, and Newport. Membership of the NCA branches in the 1840s was buoyant and the *Northern Star* gives us some numerical indications for 1842: there were 300 members at Merthyr; 120 in Aberdare; 90 each in Swansea and Newtown; 60 at both Newport and Abergavenny; 30 at Pontypool, Monmouth, Llanidloes and Cardiff. Chartist sympathizers always outnumbered the actual members and at public meetings in 1843 the Merthyr NCA could still attract audiences of 1,000 people.

The membership of these branches suggests a non-violent, Chartist approach in Wales at this period. The NCA branches were dominated by shopkeepers and tradesmen, and some professional people. The participation of Dissenting ministers gave the NCA a respectable and middle-class colouring. Men like the Revd Thomas Davies, Merthyr Baptist; John Davies, Aberdare; Benjamin Byron, Newport; William Williams, Aberdare; David John, Merthyr; and John Jones, Aberdare, all supported Chartism and opposed physical force. Indeed, it could be argued that Welsh Chartism had a distinctly Nonconformist complexion at this point; and that it used every constitutional weapon at its disposal to agitate for the reform of Parliament.

Another body which pressed for parliamentary reform in the 1840s was the National Complete Suffrage Union (CSU). It was formed in November 1841 largely as a result of dissatisfaction with the Anti-Corn Law League's progress. The earliest branch in Wales was formed at a meeting near Tredegar in April 1842. Most Welsh involvement in the movement occurred in the second half of 1843 when the CSU was on the wane. In many places, several prominent Chartists were enthusiastic towards the new movement and Merthyr Chartists, in particular, were among the foremost supporters of complete suffrage.

One final association, which was of great importance in Wales, was the Religious Freedom Society formed in 1839. Branches were soon established at Swansea, Bala, Tywyn, Machynlleth, Dolgellau, and many other centres. This was yet another society devoted to the principle of religious freedom and the security of the Nonconformists. It was one more stepping-stone in the growth of Radicalism. By the 1840s there existed in Wales a favourable climate and also a foundation upon which a movement for radical Dissent could build. The foundation of the *Nonconformist* in April 1841 represented a significant watershed in the growth of political, radical Dissent. The 1840s were significant for the Nonconformists in many ways, and they launched themselves into a number of causes and controversies. In 1843 Sir James Graham introduced his Factory Bill which, in part, provided that each child should be placed under Anglican control. There were Nonconformist protests throughout Wales, and the ministers led the way. In Merthyr alone, 20,000 people signed petitions objecting to the education clauses. The Government announcement of an increased grant to Maynooth College, a Catholic Institution in Ireland, evoked some sharp responses from the Nonconformists and public meetings were held all over Wales. Even the normally conservative Calvinistic Methodists threw themselves into this debate. In Cardiganshire alone, about seventy petitions, comprising over 21,000 signatures, were organized. The other event which focused Nonconformist thought was the 1847 Education Report, which has been discussed in considerable detail in Chapter 5.

SUGGESTED READING

G.E. Jones, *Modern Wales* (Cambridge, 1984).
I.G. Jones, *Explorations and Explanations* (Llandysul, 1981).
I.G. Jones, *Communities* (Llandysul, 1987).
P. Morgan and D. Thomas, *Wales: The Shaping of a Nation* (London, 1984).
G. Williams (ed.), *Merthyr Politics* (Cardiff, 1966).

Political Developments

Articles:

D.J.V. Jones, 'The Carmarthen Riots of 1831', *W.H.R.*, 4 (1968–9).

D.J.V. Jones, 'The Merthyr Riots of 1831', *W.H.R.*, 3 (1966–7).

R.T. Jones, 'The Origins of the Nonconformist Disestablishment Campaign', *J.H.S. Ch. in W.*, XX (1970).

D.A. Wager, 'Welsh Politics and Parliamentary Reform, 1780–1832', *W.H.R.*, 7 (1974–5).

D.A. Wager, 'Carmarthenshire Politics and the Reform Act of 1832', *Carmarthenshire Antiquary*, 10 (1974).

8. Industry and Communications 1850–1906

The Woollen Industry

IN the second half of the nineteenth century the small villages of the middle Teifi Valley — Llandysul, Drefach, Felindre, and others — became the main centres of woollen manufacturing in Wales. There was a long and respectable tradition of textile production in the area and, at the turn of the nineteenth century, the woollen trade in Carmarthenshire was supported by the County Agricultural Society. The parishes of Llangeler and Penboyr had become important centres of a thriving domestic industry and, by the early 1800s, a rudimentary factory system had evolved in the middle of the Teifi Valley. The area entered a period of unprecedented expansion around 1850 as power looms were introduced in west Carmarthenshire and south-east Cardiganshire, and the parishes of Llangeler and Penboyr again figured as the centres of expansion. A large portion of the demand emanated from the mining and metallurgical districts of south Wales, and much of the production was concerned with supplying flannel for shirts and underwear for the industrial workforce. Such was the pace of development that, from 1850 onwards, workers from other areas were gradually attracted into the Teifi Valley. The census returns for the parishes of Llangeler and Penboyr illustrate this growth:

	Llangeler	Penboyr
1851	1,681	1,271
1861	1,573	1,146
1871	1,611	1,154
1881	1,640	1,284
1891	1,880	1,428
1901	1,930	1,381

The larger woollen factories were built near the railway, which transported coal for driving the mills. The Carmarthen to Lampeter line opened in 1864 and, in the next thirty years, woollen mills were opened in the villages along this line, like Pencader, Bronwydd Arms, and Llanpumpsaint. As the figures show, after 1870 the growth was largely uninterrupted and the mill owners took full advantage of the expansion of industrial south Wales. They, or their agents, would often visit the coal and tin-plate districts to attract orders for the industry. They would also attend the seasonal fairs to canvass support and to ensure a stable demand for their products.

The conditions of work in the industry were often quite wretched; particularly for the children and young people who started work at ten years of age and laboured from 5.00 p.m. to 8.00 p.m. in the evenings, and on Saturday mornings. Their parents usually toiled from 7.00 a.m. to 7.00 p.m. and the wages they received were not high: spinners were paid at the rate of 18*s.* per week, rising to a maximum of 25*s.* after five years' service; while the weavers were paid a piece-rate, from 1*d.* to 18*d.* per yard.

In north Wales, and especially in Caernarfonshire, the woollen industry assumed a prominent role in the years after 1850. A large number of mills operated in the county and they were concerned mostly with supplying a local market. The number of people employed in the woollen industry in Caernarfonshire increased from 100 in 1831 to 145 in 1897. It was not until the First World War that a number of Caernarfonshire mills closed; and a surprising number actually overcame the difficulties of the 1920s and kept open to 1938.

The woollen industry flourished until the end of the First World War, and in the period from 1914 to 1918 the price of wool actually reached a record level. With the end of the war, and gradual decline of the industrial districts of south Wales, the woollen industry entered a period of unending depression, and the price of wool collapsed from 4*s.*6*d.* a pound to 9*d.* pound within a matter of a few months.

The Iron Industry

In the anthracite districts of the western part of the south Wales coalfield the ironworks had increasingly produced bars for tin-plate manufacture. After the 1860s, however, decline set in and only the Ystalyfera and Amman Works produced any noteworthy output of pig-iron after 1870. As pig-iron production gradually ceased, so many of the works in this district concentrated on tin-plate manufacture. In north Wales also the output of iron ore fell rapidly after 1865 and employment in the industry slowly sank.

Major difficulties had surfaced in Merthyr Tydfil, the cradle of the Welsh industry, in the 1870s. The basic problem was that local ironstone was losing quality and becoming more expensive to mine. Since the 1830s new areas of iron production had arisen in Scotland and in the north of England, and these gradually challenged the south Wales industrial giants. Both Dowlais and Cyfarthfa had been importing ores from Whitehaven as early as the 1850s. A decade later, Dowlais had experimented with ore from Spain and Cuba, and in 1873 Dowlais, together with other iron companies, had formed the Orconera Iron Ore Company of Bilbao, Spain. This ore was first used in August 1876.

The declining quality and increasing costs of local ore resources were only one problem confronting the industry. The renegotiation of land leases was another stumbling-block, and especially for Cyfarthfa and Dowlais in the mid nineteenth century. The original Cyfarthfa lease had been obtained in 1765 for a 99-year period, at an annual rent of £100; while the Dowlais lease, which was due to expire in 1847, had been granted at a yearly rent of £26. During the process of renegotiation the landowner, the Marquis of Bute, and his agents could not help noticing that Dowlais alone had amassed an annual profit of £172,746 in 1847. There was considerable pressure, therefore, on the Cyfarthfa and Dowlais Iron Companies to pay much more substantial annual rentals, and, during the negotiations, it appears that the ironmasters, Crawshay and Guest, were tempted to sell up and leave the iron trade altogether. At Cyfarthfa, William Crawshay II was prepared to sell the works for £400,000 in 1865, but he was dissuaded from doing so by his son, Robert, who actually managed the works. Eventually, after prolonged discussions with the landowner and his representatives, Guest settled for a yearly rental and total royalty payment of £30,000 to £33,000 per annum. Crawshay offered £5,000 a year rent for the minerals and £2,000 for the land, the works, and the houses. This latter offer was eventually accepted by the landlord.

During the period from the 1830s to the 1860s there were many other problems facing the iron industry, not least of which was the introduction of new techniques, such as the hot blast, and Hall's so-called 'wet puddling' process. Eventually, the strains became unbearable and one of the big four, Penydarren Works, was forced to close in 1858. The Hirwaun Works followed in 1859, and Treforest in 1867. The expansionary period of the early nineteenth century had gradually given way to more difficult days, and technical changes were occurring so quickly that many firms just could not reserve the necessary funds.

The Slate Industry

In the period after 1830 the slate industry continued to expand and registered some impressive successes. The Dorothea Quarry in the Nantlle area increased its production from 3,497 tons in 1860 to 10,501 tons in 1867; the peak year being 1873, with an output of 17,422 tons. The total value of the slates sold had increased from £4,234 in 1865 to £14,738 in 1875, and profits reached their peak in that year. The famous Dorothea, the largest and most profitable concern in Nantlle, had benefited from the improved transport facilities provided by the Nantlle Railway. In 1873 it employed almost 500 men. Slate quarrying had also established itself in the Llanberis district, and the Dinorwic Quarry had enhanced its work-force from 1,900 in 1863 to 2,850 in 1873. The Penrhyn Quarry, in the same district, had 1,608 employees in 1835 and 3,000 in 1863.

Most of these quarries, situated in mountainous terrain and at some distance from the sea, benefited greatly from the opening of the Chester to Holyhead Railway in 1849 and from the extension of the railway system in the 1850s and 1860s. The expansion of the slate mines near the village of Ffestiniog was hindered by the lack of rail transport until 1868. In that year, the line from Blaenau Ffestiniog to Ffestiniog was opened, largely as a result of the promotional activities of Samuel Holland and family. This was fortunate timing and coincided with the boom years from 1868 to 1873, when prices rose considerably. The industry became a major employer in this period, and the census returns show that the number of slate workers increased from 7,946 in 1861 to 13,576 in 1881.

The boom period was, however, short-lived. From 1876 to 1880 the value of slates exported fell by more than a third — largely because of the fall in commodity prices in the western hemisphere. This fall ushered in a period of general stagnation, often referred to as the period of the Great Depression, which continued, with some productive interruptions, to the end of the nineteenth century. There were three major waves of recession in 1879, 1886, and 1894, which were separated by the two boom years of 1883 and 1890. In fact, the peak year for the export of slates was 1889, when exports reached 79,912 tons, valued at £278,840. The trend was, however, one of depression and steady decline after 1880, and there were a number of reasons for this. In the first place, there was a depression in the building trade and this reduced the demand for slates in the 1880s. Output at the Penrhyn Quarry fell from 130,000 tons in 1862 to 111,000 tons in 1882, and at the Dinorwic Quarry from 98,000 tons in 1862 to 87,000 tons in 1882. Secondly, industrial disputes in the building and slate industries exacerbated the situation and contributed towards the reduction in output. A third factor of considerable importance was the reduction in the quantity of slates exported — from 79,912 tons in the peak year of 1889 to 1,592 tons in 1918. The decline in the German demand for Welsh slate was the main reason for this. In 1876 exports to Germany had accounted for 72 per cent of the total exports, and the drop in sales affected some areas more than others. The Ffestiniog district was one of those worst hit by the fall in demand — before 1913 Germany had taken between 35 per cent and 45 per cent of the slate shipped from Porthmadoc, and this had amounted to 39,000 tons in 1894, 21,000 tons in 1900, and about 11,000 tons in 1910. This decline in the export trade to Germany had been brought about largely as a result of the imposition of duties and tariffs on imported slates in the 1890s.

From 1891 to 1898 there was an increase in the home demand for slates, as a result of the sudden expansion in the building trades. The building industry was intimately linked to the sphere of home investment and, when British investment abroad diminished in the 1890s, funds were released for investment in the domestic markets. A programme of slum clearance was carried out in the large conurbations, in Birmingham, London, Liverpool, and Glasgow, and municipal buildings were erected in the large urban centres. All this stimulated the slate industry and many of the old ghost-quarries were reopened.

Towards the end of the 1890s depression clouded the industry yet again, as foreign competition became much keener. After 1898 the American industry affected the home market, as did the importation of slates from France which, in 1899, amounted to 46,000 tons. By 1901 depression tightened its grip partly as a result of the Boer War, which was followed by a high bank rate and a scarcity of money in the markets. Unemployment in the building industry, which had averaged $6\frac{1}{2}$ per cent in the years 1901–5, often topped the 10 per cent mark from 1906–10. This had deleterious effects upon the slate industry, and unemployment became a permanent threat in the period from 1906 onwards, so that the number of persons actually employed fell from 13,000 in 1909 to just over 8,000 in 1918. In the same period, output tumbled from 402,184 tons in 1909 to 101,315 tons in 1918.

Tin-plate Manufacture

The British tin-plate industry expanded at the cost of other European countries and, in the period from 1800 to 1891, its output increased by nearly 1,500 per cent. This expansion was caused by the increase in home demand, as the following figures indicate:

Year	Home consumption in tons
1805	1,500
1837	9,000
1850	12,000
1890	130,000

In the first half of the century the markets for tin plate grew consistently and production expanded, as follows:

Year	Tonnage
1805	4,000
1837	18,000
1850	37,000
1860	77,000
1870	150,000
1881	302,000
1891	586,000

Between 1800 and 1850 nineteen new works were built in south Wales, and the eastern half of the coalfield tended to predominate. W.E. Minchinton has shown that, by 1850, 25 out of a total of 35 British tin-plate works were situated in south Wales. By 1880, the area contained 64 of a total of 78 such works, 41 of which were located in the western half of south Wales.

There were a number of reasons why the industry should have settled in the western segment of south Wales: there were accessible supplies of coal and limestone; sufficient water from the Afan, Neath, Tawe, and Amman rivers; the coastline had good harbour facilities and, in particular, the port of Swansea, which were well placed for the import of iron ore and tin; in south-west Wales there were four competing outlets for the kind of labour required, and tin-plate workers could be recruited from the copper and old charcoal industries. Some owners actually brought their traditional skilled work-force with them when they purchased tin-plate works. In 1822 when the Margam Works were set up by Messrs Roberts and Smith, they brought most of their old employees with them from the Carmarthen Tinworks. As tin-plate manufacture developed in the Swansea area, so a tradition emerged for sons to follow their fathers into the industry. One other important factor was the development of the Siemens open-hearth process in the 1870s. Dr C.W. Siemens had perfected a technique for producing a soft steel which could be used in tin-plate production. The steel was first used in 1875 at the Landore Siemens Steel Company, near Swansea, where Siemens conducted most of his experiments.

The production of open-hearth steel was to ensure the dominance of the Swansea area in the industry, and tin-plate manufacture became a west Wales concern.

Tin-plate manufacture of a kind had been practised in western south Wales at a very early date and, in the Swansea Valley, the process started when Thomas Lewis leased the old Ynyspenllwch grist mill, near Clydach, and converted it into a rolling mill. In 1746 he leased the adjoining forge and ironworks and in 1748 formed a partnership with Rowland Pytt of Gloucester. Pytt and Lewis joined John Miers in 1754. The year 1835 was of particular importance, for both the Pheasant Bush Works, Trebanos, and the Pontardawe Works were established. In 1848 the Ystalyfera Iron Company expanded rapidly and added a tin-plate section to its ironworks. The period from 1836 to 1848 had been a difficult one for the industry; but conditions improved in the 1850s with the arrival of the Crimean War.

The character of the tin-plate industry was small scale; the works being usually small concerns and the investments not extravagant. In 1848 the Ystalyfera Works was considered to be one of the largest units of production, with twelve mills. This small-scale production largely persisted and, by 1890, only one works had erected more than twelve mills, namely, the Llanelli Works of E. Morewood and Company. The presence of small-scale units attracted a large number of producers, and the industry certainly did not resemble the copper industry of Swansea, which was controlled by an oligopoly of wealthy families. The Welsh tin-plate maker has been accused of being largely unadventurous, too individualistic, and possibly not adaptable enough as an entrepreneur.

Whatever the faults of the entrepreneurs, the south-west Wales industry thrived in the second half of the century, and largely as a result of the rapid growth of the international market. There were two expansionary periods between the mid 1870s and the imposition of the infamous McKinley tariff of 1891. The first was from 1876 to 1882, when eighteen new works were established, thirteen in Glamorgan and five in Carmarthenshire; and the second lasted from 1886 to 1891, when ten works were built, seven in Glamorgan and three in Carmarthen. The last few years of the 1880s are regarded as one of the most prosperous periods in the history of the trade. Table

8.1 provides some indication of the growth, and the industry's distribution in the period 1870–1905:

Table 8.1 Number of Tin-plate Works, 1875–1905

| | *Works* | | | | *Mills* | |
	1875	*1885*	*1891*	*1905*	*1891*	*1905*
Glamorgan	27	44	51	46	277	266
Monmouth	16	20	15	11	86	50
Carmarthen	14	17	20	18	119	105
Rest of Britain	20	17	12	8	43	32
TOTALS:	77	98	98	83	525	453

The numbers of workers employed in tin-plate manufacture were never as large as those in the coal industry, but there was considerable expansion as Table 8.2 shows.

Table 8.2 Numbers employed in tin-plate industry

Year	*Numbers employed in the industry*
1800	1,000
1834	4,000
1851	5,200
1871	9,200
1880	15,500
1891	25,000

The most serious challenge to Welsh tin plate came from America. Attempts had been made to establish a tin-plate industry in the USA in the early part of the century, but the real threat emerged with the introduction in 1891 of the McKinley tariff on tin plate imported into the USA. The immediate effect upon American production was minimal, but the British industry suffered a severe setback, and British exports to the USA plunged from 325,100 tons in 1891 to 63,500 tons in 1899. Many works in south Wales were forced to close, while others like the Panteg, Gilbertsons (Pontardawe), Bryn (Pontardawe), and the Raven (Glanamman) were converted to the production of black plate or galvanized sheet. Almost alone among firms in the tin-plate depression, Richard Thomas and Company took advantage of the closures to increase their ownership of tin-plate works. In the meantime, Welsh exports plummeted from 421,797 tons in 1890, valued at £6.4 million, to 266,693 tons in 1896, at a value of £3.0 million.

At the end of the 1890s trade did improve and by 1913 exports were ten per cent higher than they had been in 1891. Rising home consumption was the major influence on the industry up to 1914. Output, which had been twelve million boxes in 1891, fell to a nadir of nine million boxes in 1896, and then revived to almost seventeen million boxes in 1912. In a similar vein, the labour force, which had peaked at 25,000 in 1891, fell to 16,000 in 1898, and then attained new heights at almost 29,000 in 1913.

The Steel Industry

The transition to steel production required considerable capital and most of the ironworks could not meet the challenge. Many were forced out of business as a result of two revolutionary inventions which transformed the industry. The first came in 1856, when Henry Bessemer produced steel in his 'converter' by blowing hot air through liquid pig-iron. A decade later, C.W. Siemens used the open-hearth system to produce steel by burning coal gas. This effectively raised the temperature of the air blown into the furnace. The temperature of the molten iron was thereby raised to 1,750 C, and this led to the production of steel.

Many ironworks were reluctant to adopt the new processes but, in 1856, the Dowlais Company was one of the first to take out a licence from Henry Bessemer to use his method for steel production. In that year, Dowlais had undergone a complete reshuffle of its managerial team and the trustees appointed William Menelaus as general manager. He and his energetic new breed of managers were eager to try the converters and, from the early 1860s, Bessemer converters were installed in the works. The first ingot of Bessemer steel was rolled into rails in June 1865. In 1866 it produced 2,257 ingot tons of Bessemer steel, but only rolled 762 tons of finished steel, and there was still no steelworks at Dowlais. In the late 1870s, however, the attractions of higher profits, increasing orders and sales, eventually persuaded the Dowlais managerial team that the time was propitious to venture into steel production. The new general manager, E.P. Martin, who had considerable experience of steel-making in America, decided that steel mills should be built and, by 1882, Dowlais had three mills. By 1897 the steel-making capacity of Dowlais included the original Bessemer plant, consisting of four converters of 15 tons capacity, and two new 20-ton converters. There were also two recently-built 25-ton open-hearth furnaces.

By the mid 1880s all the other ironworks on the northern outcrop of the south Wales coalfield had closed and four companies joined Dowlais and Ebbw Vale in installing Bessemer converters. The works were Rhymney in 1877, Blaenavon in 1878, Tredegar in 1882, and Cyfarthfa in 1884. Cyfarthfa had experienced stormy times in the early 1870s and, by the end of the decade, the conversion to a steelworks was imperative. The works was built in 1884 but, by March 1902, Cyfarthfa had effectively merged with Dowlais. Cyfarthfa soon foundered on the rocks of international competition and closed in 1910. Dowlais responded to the challenges and prospered at least until the outbreak of the First World War.

A major problem confronting the south Wales ironworks in the second half of the nineteenth century had been the need to import foreign ores and, by 1900, they were almost entirely dependent upon them. At the turn of the century some 800,000 tons of ore were being imported annually through Cardiff, 340,000 tons through Newport, and 170,000 tons through Swansea. The costs of transporting the heavy ore imports from the coastal ports to the inland works became prohibitive, and this was one nail in the ironworks' coffin. An additional factor was the urgent need for the Welsh iron plants to reorganize to meet the challenge of steel production. Many found the competition of the 1870s unbearable and simply could not overcome the apparently insuperable obstacles to change. In the county of Glamorgan, only Dowlais and Cyfarthfa remained as Bessemer steel-making plants, and Cyfarthfa's days were soon numbered. The management at Dowlais proved more far-sighted and recognized the advantages of a coastal location. In 1888 Dowlais started to build its new plant at the East Moors site, in the Cardiff dockland. The first iron was produced there in 1891, and the steelworks and plate mill operated from 1895. This first breakaway from an inland location was also the only one of its kind in the period before 1914.

In the western end of the coalfield, the Landore Siemens Steel Company had been set up in 1868 with C.W. Siemens as a major investor and L.L. Dillwyn as chairman. In 1873 Landore was producing 1,000 tons of steel a week. The significant expansion occurred after 1875 with the transition from iron to steel in shipbuilding. By 1879 almost a half of Britain's open-hearth steel came from south Wales, but there were still only three plants in the Swansea district capable of producing steel: Landore with twenty-four furnaces, and Elba (Gowerton) and Morewood's (Llanelli) with two furnaces apiece. The 1880s proved to be the turning-point in the transformation from iron to open-hearth steel when the tin-plate manufacturers turned to steel. Many new steelworks soon emerged along the coast of south-west Wales: the Upper Forest and Worcester in Morriston (1886), Gilbertsons of Pontardawe (1890); and the Briton Ferry Works (1890). The tale was not one of uninterrupted success, as the closures of works at Birchgrove in 1895 and those at the Cwmbwrla in 1898 were to show. Many of the Siemens steelworks were short-lived and most were abandoned at least once. The major development in the western region, as far as the future prospects of the industry were concerned, was the decision of the Gilbertsons of Pontardawe to build a steelworks on a twelve-acre site at Port Talbot in 1901. The industry was well and truly launched in south Wales.

The Coal Industry

Expansion was the keynote of the industry after 1850 in Britain and, in particular, in the south Wales valleys. British production increased from 57 million tons in 1851 to 287 million tons in 1913. South Wales's contribution rose from around $4\frac{1}{2}$ million tons in 1840 to $8\frac{1}{2}$ million tons in 1854, to 50 million tons in 1912, and to 56.8 million tons in 1913. This general expansion tended to camouflage pockets and periods of decline. One of the marked trends in the Welsh coal trade after 1840 was the decline in the relative importance of house coal and anthracite.

The export of steam coal was the most dynamic section of the industry up to 1900, and it reflected the great expansion of steam power in world shipping. This extraordinary demand for steam coal led to the rapid industrialization of the Rhondda valleys. In 1850 the area around Pontypridd was largely rural, whereas by 1900 it was a heavily industrialized and densely populated area. By 1913 the export of steam coal amounted to 50 per cent of south Wales production. Anthracite coal production, confined largely to the western rim of the coalfield in west Glamorgan and Carmarthenshire, had also risen from 1.8 million tons in 1897 to 4.8 million tons in 1913, in response to the rapidly rising demand in the 1890s from western and southern Europe. By 1900 south Wales was the most important coal-exporting area in Britain and by 1880 the Bristol Channel ports (Bristol, Cardiff, Newport, Swansea) could compete on equal footing with the ports of north-east England for coal shipments. In fact, historians have often noted that, in the period from 1890 to 1910, the export of coal from south Wales constituted nearly a third of the total world exports.

The industrial expansion of the south Wales valleys occurred in those decades when the industrial sector of England expanded least and a marked inverse relationship may be detected between the rate of growth of the English and Welsh colliery districts. Welsh coal was largely for export and the Welsh mining districts therefore tended to fluctuate in response to the wider export markets. English coals, on the other hand, which were consumed in the home market, were sensitive to changes in domestic investment and home capital construction. The population graphs of the colliery districts of England and south Wales are a mirror image of each other, that is, they move in opposite directions. In the 1880s the distinctiveness of Wales becomes even clearer for, as the rural crisis began to bite, so the absorptive capacity of the south Wales coalfield increased abruptly. At this point, when British emigration tended towards a peak, Welsh emigration dropped to a negligible level. In the 1900s nearly 130,000 people moved into south Wales, and there was an overall net gain of 100,000 people. The demographic changes and their impact on labour and language will be explored in more detail in Chapter 13.

Productivity in the coal industry advanced smoothly until, in 1883, output per man reached the all-time peak of 333 tons per annum. In south Wales the trend was similar with the output per man year at 309 tons in 1883, but declining thereafter to 212 tons in 1912. One reason for this was the sheer abundance of labour in the area. An additional problem was the existence of a large number of small firms, especially in the 1850s and 1860s. This tended to hinder the innovative capacity of the industry, and it certainly had an effect upon industrial relations in the region. The figures for 1913 show us that there were 49 firms in Monmouthshire, 162 in Glamorgan and 49 in Carmarthenshire, making a total of 260. If we compare these with the figures for 1862, the corresponding totals are 62, 138, and 66, making a grand total of 266 firms. A large number of firms had existed, therefore, since the 1860s and differences in size and efficiency among the firms were often quite considerable. This made for an uneven performance throughout the coalfield, and many firms opted for the possibility of becoming limited liability companies, so as to spread the risk. J.H. Morris and L.J. Williams have shown that this device was often no insurance against disaster. They traced the fate of fifty-three out of sixty-four companies formed in the period 1856–67 and the results were extremely revealing: three were abortive; ten had failed by 1864; a further thirty-one had failed by the end of 1870; and two more had failed by 1874. Only seven were still in existence in 1875.

From the mid 1880s companies were more carefully floated and the larger steam-coal companies had considerable success in the field. Some have argued that the Rhondda pioneers were nearly all of native stock and, as late as 1906, a number of steam-coal companies were largely supported by local shareholders. Many Welshmen did fail in their coal ventures and there was increasing immigrant influence in areas other than the Rhondda. In Ebbw Vale and Tredegar two large companies pursued a policy of appointing Englishmen to their boards; and, eventually, immigrant influence became of widespread importance. Even in the Rhondda there was increasing evidence of immigrant penetration. The Maerdy collieries, which had been started by Mordecai Jones of Brecon, one of the more famous Rhondda pioneers, passed into the hands of Locket's Merthyr Collieries (1894) Ltd. in which only one director was a Welshman.

As the south Wales coalfield became more export-oriented, so there was a tendency to produce men who were well versed in financial and commercial activities and less well acquainted with the actual mining process. These commercial entrepreneurs were often remote from the daily life of the mine and detached from the cyclical problems of the industry. The cyclical nature of the industry was of immense importance, for it produced sharp variations in prices, and hence in wages, during the period 1870–1903. The average price per ton per annum of coal at the pit head in south Wales indicates the cyclical fluctuations:

Year	Price
1882	5s. 9.96d.
1886	5s. 1.44d.
1890	10s. 3.48d.
1896	6s. 0.48d.
1900	12s. 0.95d.
1905	8s. 9.15d.

These cyclical fluctuations arising from the increasing dependence on export markets, together with the existence of a large number of small mines, and the persistent structural and geological difficulties, all posed serious problems for the coalowners in the culminating decades of the century. Perhaps a further difficulty was that expansion had attracted waves of immigrants into the coalfield, with expectations of mass employment and of continuously rising living standards. Part of the problem of industrial relations in the closing decades was that volatile economic and social circumstances created feelings of uneasiness and uncertainty throughout the coalfield.

Were the 1890s a Turning-Point in the Economic Life of South Wales?

One influential school of economic historians has argued forcefully that the 1890s witnessed a turning-point in economic growth and that from then on through to the outbreak of the

First World War, there was a fall in the rate of growth. To support this argument they have pointed to such indicators as the gross domestic product for the British economy, which, in the period from 1856 to 1899, had averaged 2 per cent, before falling to 1.1 per cent for the years 1899–1913. It would seem, according to their arguments, that a declining rate of growth had set in during the 1890s.

If we turn to the major Welsh industries there is a broadly consistent and similar picture. The rate of growth of coal output fell quite sharply in the 1890s, as did the output of the tin-plate industry. From 1874 to 1914 the rate of growth in the coal industry was 4.21 per cent per annum, that is, until 1890; thereafter it was 2.88 per cent. Output per man per year also diminished from around 300 tons in 1888 to less than 250 tons in the years preceding the First World War. Recent research would tend to suggest, therefore, that Wales also experienced a break in its economic growth around 1890.

A powerful counter-argument has emerged to show that there was, in fact, no discernible downward trend in productivity. The two sudden reductions in productivity would rather suggest that *ad hoc* factors were of importance in the overall equation. At the end of the period the Eight Hours Act, coupled with the Cambrian strike of 1910–11 and the national strike of 1912, had effectively reduced the productive capacity of the coalfield. The Coal Mines Regulation Act of 1887 had reduced the number of hours that boys could work, and this was followed by Mabon's Day, introduced in 1888, which reduced the number of days worked by declaring the first Monday of each month a miner's holiday. The overall effect would have been punitive on productivity. It has also been argued that the 1880s were, in a sense, responsible for the apparent decline of the 1890s. From 1880 to 1888 there had occurred a particularly high level of labour productivity and, after an unusually high proportion of capital investment, there was a reversion to a more normal level of productivity in the 1890s.

Another indicator of growth in the Welsh context was the absolute level of output, manpower and exports in the decade before 1913. The annual output of the coalfield grew by over 20 million tons and an additional 13 million tons were exported from south Wales ports. In the same period some 100,000 more men were employed. Later we shall see how this fits in with Professor Brinley Thomas's thesis on population change in the region. The south Wales coalfield, for example, absorbed 70,000 additional miners in the decade before 1913. As a result of this, the population of Glamorgan increased by 30 per cent, and that of Monmouthshire by 33 per cent, and even that of Carmarthenshire by 18 per cent. There was an overall net gain by migration in the period, and the Glamorgan and Monmouth coal area gained 130,000 persons in the decade 1901–11. This was quite unique in the British economy.

The coal industry dominated Welsh economic life at the turn of the century, even in Flintshire and Denbighshire where an additional 2,000 miners were employed in the decade after 1901. It is significant that these two counties were the only ones in the north to record a population increase of over 10 per cent for the decennial period.

In other ways, too, coal had a kind of multiplier effect on the economy. The growth of the housebuilding industry in south Wales up to 1910 was quite exceptional; and the railway building and docks construction programmes were further proof of the expansionary tone. In the decade after 1890 the Barry Railway opened an additional 32 miles, the Cardiff Railway 23 miles, the Rhondda and Swansea Bay 17 miles, and the Port Talbot Railway 21 miles. The expenditure on docks in Wales in the years from 1890 to 1910 was actually higher than it had ever been. The Barry No 2 Dock was opened in 1898. At Cardiff, the Queen Alexandra Dock was opened in 1907, and the Bute Docks extended in area by almost one-third. At Newport a dock extension of twenty acres was opened in 1898, and Swansea saw the completion of the extension to its Prince of Wales Dock. By 1909 the King's Dock was also opened at Swansea. All this would seem to suggest that the Welsh economy in the decades from 1890–1913 was buoyant and pulsating with energy.

The Railway System after 1850

As we observed in the last section on the growth of the railways in Wales, a large part of the system was opened between 1858 and 1868. By 1854 Wales was effectively framed on three sides by railways and these included the Chester to

Holyhead, as well as the South Wales Railway, which was opened in sections from 1850. The real problem in the 1850s was to penetrate the hinterland; and in 1853 authorization was given for the construction of a line to Montgomeryshire, to run from Llanidloes to Newtown. David Davies, Llandinam, or 'Davies the Ocean', that energetic and versatile Victorian entrepreneur, had tendered to build the first portion of this railway. He made such a profound impression on the directors that he was awarded the contract for the second section of line. The line reached Llandinam in August 1856, and the actual railroad was completed in 1859. Aberystwyth was eventually linked with Oswestry and Shrewsbury in 1864. In that year the separate companies responsible for the route from Oswestry to Machynlleth amalgamated to form the Cambrian Railways, and this combine engulfed the coastal lines.

Three long lines of railway communication were completed in the period 1862–7. The first ran westward from Rhiwabon, on the GWR from Birmingham to Chester, to Dolgellau, where it joined the Cambrian. It was 45-miles long and was the work of four separate companies. The Mid Wales line which opened in 1864 ran from Llanidloes to Tal-y-llyn, and connected with the Brecon and Merthyr. The third route was the Central Wales which ran from the Craven Arms, on the Shrewsbury and Hereford Railway, to Llandovery, whence it linked to Carmarthen, Llanelli, and Swansea. This was 120-miles long and opened, in sections, from 1858–67. It facilitated a route from the Midlands and north of England to south-west Wales.

In south Wales, with the expansion of the coal trade after 1850, two main lines were serving the district, and both were incorporated into the Great Western after 1863: the South Wales Railway ran parallel to the coastline to Gloucester, and thence to London; the Newport, Abergavenny and Hereford line ran from north to south along the eastern edge of the coalfield. Yet by far the larger part of the coal was transported by sea, through Cardiff and other ports, and possibly for the simple reason that the South Wales Railway was broad-gauge, while all the local lines, and the Newport, Abergavenny, and Hereford line, were narrow. The coal interests eventually succeeded in pressurizing the Great Western to abandon the broad gauge in south Wales in 1872 .

In eastern Glamorgan, the Taff Vale Company enjoyed a monopoly in the Rhondda valleys and had the support of the Marquis of Bute. In 1859 when the East Dock was completed, the Marquis decided to ally himself with the Rhymney Railway, and the Taff Vale was forbidden access to the Dock until 1866. In 1871 the Rhymney Company opened its separate lines to Cardiff and it extended northwards into the Aberdare Valley and, in 1886, to Dowlais and Merthyr.

By the 1870s there was growing congestion at the docks in Cardiff and on the railways leading to them. The Bute trustees and the Taff Vale Railway Company were largely to blame for this; for neither had made any real efforts to extend their facilities so as to keep pace with the expansion in the coal industry. Coal was often delayed at the docks; the siding accommodation was inadequate, as was the provision for unloading. Trains were often at a standstill for seven or eight hours, and the coalmasters became increasingly impatient with the situation. By 1883 they could wait no longer for the railway company or the landowners to act and, on their own initiative, they promoted a new railway line down the valley to a new port at Barry. In 1888–9 the railway and docks were opened at Barry and siphoned a large portion of the profits of trade out of the Taff Vale coffers. Worse was to come as another new railway was built to Newport in 1886, followed by the Rhondda and Swansea Bay line carrying trade to Briton Ferry, Port Talbot and Swansea in 1890. The cumulative effects on the Taff Vale Company were quite enormous as revenue fell by a third in the three-year period, 1888–91. In the long run, however, and in the early years of the twentieth century, all these railway companies could live comfortably off the revived coal trade. The Taff Vale Company eventually regained its prosperity and the success story of Barry was almost unbelievable. Its shares reached dazzling heights and, in the period 1898–1914, they paid larger than average dividends.

We should remember, in conclusion, that the railways not only had beneficial effects in promoting the economic life of the community, but that they often produced sad and costly social results. Train disasters, for example, could have haunting effects on communities. The Abergele rail disaster of 1868 killed thirty-three people when the Holyhead mail collided with some runaway trains filled with casks of paraffin. Among those who perished in the flames were Lord and Lady Farnham, who were identified by their watches. Ten years later twelve people were killed and over thirty injured in a collision on the Rhondda branch of the Taff Vale, just half a mile above Pontypridd. At the inquest, signalman William Roberts, who had served the Taff Vale for over 30 years, was found guilty of gross neglect by the presiding coroner. Companies such as the Taff Vale did make strenuous efforts to ensure that their railways were well maintained and that the staff were clean, courteous and efficient, as rule 40 of the Taff Vale Railway rule book reminds us:

> Every person is to come on duty daily, clean in his person and his clothes, shaved, and his shoes blacked.

SUGGESTED READING

C. Baber and L.J. Williams (eds.), *Modern South Wales, Essays in Economic History* (Cardiff, 1986).

A.H. Dodd, *The Industrial Revolution in North Wales* (Cardiff, 1951).

J.G. Jenkins, *Life and Tradition in Rural Wales* (London, 1976).

J. Lindsay, *A History of the North Wales Slate Industry* (Newton Abbot, 1974).

W.E. Minchinton, *The British Tinplate Industry* (Oxford, 1957).

W.E. Minchinton, (ed.), *Industrial South Wales, 1750–1914* (London, 1969).

J.H. Morris and L.J. Williams, (eds.), *The South Wales Coal Industry, 1841–75* (Cardiff, 1958).

J. Simmons, *The Railway in England and Wales, 1830–1914*, I (Leicester, 1978).

A.H. John and G. Williams (eds.), *Glamorgan County History*, 5 (Cardiff, 1980).

H. Williams, *Railways in Wales* (Swansea, 1981).

Articles:

G.M. Holmes, 'The South Wales Coal Industry, 1850–1914', *T.H.S.C.*, (1976).

F.Ll. Jones, 'Wales and the Origins of the Railway Revolution', *T.H.S.C.*, (1983).

H. Thomas, 'The Industrialization of a Glamorgan Parish', *N.L.W.J.*, XIX (1975–6).

W.G. Thomas, 'The Coal Mining Industry in West Glamorgan', *Glamorgan Historian*, VI, (1969).

9. Agriculture and People 1850–1906

General Features and Trends

THE years following the repeal of the Corn Laws in 1846 were generally prosperous for the Welsh farmer. With the exception of wheat, the Welsh rural economy was largely protected from heavy foreign imports, and its livestock farmers shared in the growing prosperity of British meat and dairy producers. Pastoral prices were particularly buoyant in response to the growth in home demand and Welsh store-cattle prices rose by 56 per cent between 1856 and 1878. In general, agricultural prices peaked in the early 1870s; though there were exceptions, as the downward trend in wool prices demonstrated.

The prosperity of the years from 1846 to 1875 was built on rather unstable foundations and, by the early 1870s, foreign imports were flooding the home market at comparatively low costs. The advent of the railways and steamships, together with the introduction of the elevator system, made it much easier for foreign goods to penetrate the home markets. The large inflow of corn depressed prices from the mid 1870s, and a series of bad harvests from the mid 1870s, in 1878–9, and again in 1893–4, compounded the problems facing farmers. These low and poor yields were no longer offset by higher prices, once imported grain could effectively flood the markets.

The so-called 'great depression' of 1873–96 did not affect Wales as badly as the corn-growing areas of England, where the price of grain fell sharply. Wales had a proportionately low acreage under corn and so the depression did not bite so deeply. Important corn-growing areas in Flintshire, Denbighshire, the Vale of Glamorgan, and in south Pembrokeshire did suffer from the fall in corn prices in the period from 1873 to 1896. The actual price-slide in Wales started in 1874–5, when wheat and barley prices tumbled. From 1867–71 and 1894–8 wheat prices actually fell by 51 per cent, barley by 42 per cent and oats by 37 per cent. From the 1870s dairy farmers also suffered the effects of foreign competition as improved refrigeration techniques permitted the importation of frozen and chilled dairy products. Consignments of butter, cheese, bacon, and eggs from Europe, and cheese from America began to infiltrate the home markets. But as imports increased, so did home demand, stimulated by a rising population, and this led, in turn, to an expansion in domestic production.

The depression in livestock and dairy farming started in the mid 1880s and lasted until 1896. The overall falls in Welsh markets are illustrated in the following data: from 1877 to 1880 and from 1894 to 1897 store cattle fell by 20 per cent, fat cattle by 19 per cent, fat sheep 18 per cent, and fat pigs 18 per cent. Growing imports of wool and periods of bad weather resulted in a drop of 45 per cent in wool prices from 1872–4 and 1891–2. After 1897 prices did recover steadily, though the exceptionally high prices of the 1870s would not be seen again in the period before 1914.

There is little doubt that agricultural conditions in Wales had improved markedly from the mid 1850s, for a variety of reasons: landowners were tending to invest more money in improving their properties; farmers were taking advantage of the better markets for their products; the railway network opened up the rural areas to the growing urban and industrial centres; the rise in livestock prices from mid-century tended to favour the Welsh farmer; and the south Wales farmers had an expanding and readily accessible market for their products in the mining valleys of Glamorgan and Monmouthshire. Improved economic conditions led to a fairly widespread revaluation of rents on Welsh estates in the period from 1850 to 1880. Rent increases ranged from 5 to 30 per cent, and the actual valuation depended on such factors as land elevation, fertility, the availability of railways and good markets, the previous level of rents, and the all-important question of the demand for land.

In the years from 1867 to 1914 there was a rise of 10 per cent in the cultivated land area in Wales. The higher level of industrial demand, the enclosure of the commons, and the coming of the railways all contributed to increased cultivation. In south Wales the growing population of the industrial areas significantly increased the demand for corn, and this produced a growth in corn acreage between 1816 and 1849. From the mid 1850s the relatively higher prices in the livestock sector attracted British farmers towards grass, and the area under permanent grass increased between 1870 and 1914. In the same period, arable cultivation decreased from 42.7 per cent to 24.8 per cent of the total cultivated area. This extension of grassland was the basic feature of Welsh farming in the late nineteenth century and was reflected in the increased numbers of livestock. From 1870 to 1914 the number of cattle rose by 24.1 per cent, sheep by 26.7 per cent and horses by 37.7 per cent.

Throughout most of the century the basic characteristic of Welsh farming was its small margin of profitability. After the 1870s an improvement in Welsh farming practices did produce an increase in output, and crop yields on Welsh holdings augmented in the years from 1886 to 1914. Welsh agriculture now became far more capital-intensive, with a greater use of machinery and artificial manures, and the important question is how could this capital growth have occurred at a time of falling prices? There are a number of possible answers to this: first, the railways and improved communications gradually ended the traditionalism of Welsh farmers and made them more receptive to new ideas; there was a greater emphasis on lambs and younger store cattle, and this produced a quicker turnover of capital and a fall in labour costs; thirdly, increased efficiency on the land protected farmers' incomes and produced higher real income, out of which savings could be made; finally, increased savings and borrowings from banks enabled farmers to multiply their investments.

Agricultural Societies Post 1850

As we observed in our last chapter on agriculture, the old county agricultural societies were gradually giving way to local farming clubs and debating groups by the middle of the nineteenth century. In Pembrokeshire a farmer-dominated Agricultural Society had been established in 1844, but had attracted little support largely because the farmers found the membership fee too excessive. The North Cardiganshire Society collapsed in 1885 through lack of support, and yet the Montgomeryshire Society, founded in 1870, went from strength to strength. Local societies fluctuated considerably as membership responded sensitively to short-term exigencies.

The cultural isolation and poor communications of Wales had always impeded significant progress in agricultural practices. But there were some hopeful signs towards the end of the century. The agricultural departments of the university colleges of Aberystwyth and Bangor, founded respectively in 1891 and 1888, both strove to extend the scientific approaches to agricultural practices from the 1890s onwards. Rural schools also tried their hand at extra-mural work and organized classes in their localities. Thomas Jones, the headmaster of Penmorfa Board School, Penbryn, Cardiganshire, and his pupil, Tom Elias, formed an agricultural class for farmers of all ages in the Rhydlewis area of Cardiganshire in 1893. From the 1880s the Board of Agriculture subsidized the establishment of travelling dairy schools and agricultural classes. Yet little seems to have been achieved by the time of the Land Commission in 1896.

The relative smallness of most Welsh farms and their modest financial reserves reduced the opportunities for economies of scale, and even some of the earliest co-operatives foundered as a result of these problems. The St Clear's Farmers' Butter Company, founded in 1890, and the Lampeter Co-operative Agricultural and Dairy Society, established in 1899, both died early deaths. But there were still some visionaries who were prepared to invest their time and energies in developing the co-operative societies. One such was Augustus Brigstocke of Blaenpant, near Newcastle Emlyn, who saw co-operation as a means of improving the buying power, the marketing facilities, and the agricultural education of the members of the co-operative. A substantial landlord and a Liberal, he founded the Teifi Valley Agricultural Society Ltd., in 1902 as a bulk-buying organization in which members invested small sums of money. The Society spawned similar groupings such as the Emlyn, Llanarth, New Quay, Llandysul Agricultural Society, and the Cradoc Co-operative Society in west Brecknockshire, all of which were established in 1902. Largely as a result of Brigstocke's enthusiasm, thirteen co-operative societies were operating in Cardiganshire in 1904 and, in Carmarthenshire, the Carmarthenshire Farmers were soon to become one of the most effective co-operatives in Britain. Brigstocke eventually endowed a university scholarship in agricultural co-operation tenable at Aberystwyth.

The language barrier was, however, still a major stumbling-block to the development of Welsh agriculture, and there was little material on Welsh agriculture in Welsh. By the 1930s there were probably only four Welsh-language volumes on the subject. Towards the end of the nineteenth century the Board of Agriculture had displayed some concern and in 1893 had begun to publish Welsh versions of its advisory pamphlets. Bilingual forms for official June Agricultural Returns did not become available until 1907.

Landownership after 1850

The best source for an analysis of the structure and distribution of landownership in the second half of the nineteenth century is the Returns of the Owners of Land in 1873, usually referred to as the New Domesday Survey. This reveals that Wales was a land of large estates owned by a small number of landowners. Estates over 1,000 acres occupied 60 per cent of the total area of Wales, and this was much higher than the figure for England. These estates of 1,000 acres were safely in the hands of 571 owners, who were a mere 1 per cent of the total number of landowners. The small proprietors and cottagers, although comprising over 75 per cent of the landowners, held only 5 per cent of the land. J. Bateman's, *The Great Landowners of Great Britain and Ireland*, published in 1883, shows us just how many estates of over 3,000 acres were distributed throughout the various counties. The percentages of the total area were, as follows:

Anglesey	61	Denbigh	43	Montgomery	40
Brecknock	42	Flint	45	Pembroke	38
Caernarfon	67	Glamorgan	55	Radnor	37
Cardigan	36	Merioneth	48		
Carmarthen	34	Monmouth	43		

The overall average for Wales was 44 per cent.

Caernarfon and Merioneth were counties of very large properties, and six landlords, whose estates averaged over 25,000 acres, owned half of the land in Caernarfonshire. In

Merioneth, 40 per cent of the land was in the hands of five owners, whose estates averaged 24,000 acres. There was not a single estate of over 10,000 acres in Flintshire, and Carmarthenshire also had a paucity of large estates. The large estates had usually been in the hands of the same families for many generations, and only a few of them were sold in our period. In Caernarfonshire, for example, of the twelve important estates in the county in 1815, only two had been broken up by the 1890s; and the predominance of the large estates was as marked a feature of the 1870s as it had been in 1846. As we shall see, the fragmentation of the great Welsh estates was to occur after 1910.

After 1870 there was an increasing tendency for tenant farmers to purchase their own farms and, in the late nineteenth century, there emerged a new group of freeholders who had recently purchased their properties. As the landowners sold the outlying parts of their estates, the tenants borrowed from one quarter to one-third of the purchase money, at a rate of about 4 per cent interest, in order to snap up the land.

Land Tenure and Land Hunger

By the second half of the nineteenth century the agricultural land of Wales was occupied by tenant farmers and, in 1887, 88.9 per cent of the cultivated land was occupied by such farmers. Most tenant farmers in England and Wales held their land by leases or by yearly agreements and, by the late 1850s, yearly tenancies were the most common throughout Wales. Tenants preferred these for a variety of reasons: they were reluctant, in times of economic uncertainty and price oscillation, to commit themselves to the payment of a fixed long-term rent; they disliked the tendency for landlords not to grant rent reductions and abatements in times of crisis under lease agreements; another unattractive feature of leases was their covenanting the lessee to carry out necessary repairs. But the landlords also favoured the annual tenancies: they were reluctant to adhere to the long-lease system of fixed rents during periods of fast-rising prices; secondly, they felt that leases were conducive to careless and wasteful land holding and that tenants, secure in their farms, were neglecting their lands; one final factor was that, after the 1832 Reform Act, landlords found that yearly agreements facilitated a greater degree of political control over their tenants at election times.

The absence of leases was noted in the Welsh-language newspaper *Y Faner* in October 1857. Leases for one or two lives, or for seven, fourteen or 21-year periods were not uncommon in parts of Cardiganshire and Pembrokeshire, and in south and east Glamorgan leases for seven or fourteen years were still common. By the late nineteenth century leases were rare, and yet the annual tenancy system did not promote a continuous and frequent change in tenancy holdings. In fact, historians have observed that one of the more remarkable features of Welsh land tenure throughout the century was that families remained as tenants on the same farms from one generation to another.

Changes of tenancy became more frequent after 1870, especially on the smaller estates and more scattered properties, and for several reasons: one was that the owners of properties under 1,000 acres failed for various reasons to grant appropriate rent abatements in the years after 1878, and so, many tenants were forced to quit their homes; another factor of importance was the growing number of sales of outlying parts of large estates and of small properties. Freeholds of 1,000 acres or less often attracted high prices in the 1890s. One of the essential characteristics of the period after 1870 was land hunger. The Welshman's emotional attachment to the family farm and the local community was one reason for this, but there were also a number of other factors: few holdings became available on the market because there was such an entrenched tradition of hereditary familial succession; farmers clung to their properties for they conferred status and position in the community, and this encouraged local farmers to think of themselves as local aristocrats; the size of Welsh farms was another factor — Welsh farms were small enough to encourage even the farm labourers to seek their own holdings, and this put additional pressure on the land market; the rise in population squeezed the market even further; and the simple fact that only one member of a family could hope to succeed to a farm meant that its other members were forced to search for farms of their own.

This feverish land hunger explains why so few holdings remained unoccupied, even during the worst years of depression.

It also explains why farms were grabbed by tenants who lacked the necessary capital resources. This lack of capital was often regarded as a major cause of the poor state of farming in Wales; and landowners such as C.R.M. Talbot, of Glamorgan, and his experienced land agent, John Harvey, noted scarcity of capital as one of the real problems of the Welsh. Wherever tenants competed for holdings, landowners were usually cautious enough to choose those applicants with sufficient capital. This factor was probably more important in the choice of tenants than their political or religious affiliations. Indeed it has been shown that the vast majority of landowners would accept Nonconformists as tenants, and even allowed them to build their chapels on the estates.

From the late 1850s, with the emergence of Nonconformity and Liberalism, the incidence of political evictions in Wales increased as tenants began to display a remarkable degree of independence. This was true of the 1859 election and again in various Welsh counties in 1868. Notwithstanding some harsh examples of political landlordism, the actual number of evictions has been exaggerated and many notices to quit were subsequently withdrawn. Once the Secret Ballot Act was introduced in 1872 landlords were reluctant to interfere in the elections. Some, however, still flexed their political muscles and coercion was practised on the Picton Castle estate during the unsuccessful election contests of its owner, C.E.G. Phillips, in the 1880s. There were a few evictions in the 1870s and 1880s on the smaller estates. One notable example was on the Alltyrodyn estate, Llandysul, Cardiganshire, where the landlord evicted the tenants, the preacher and his chapel congregation. Evictions became rarer after 1868 and tenants felt more secure in their holdings. Many of the Radical allegations that landowners and clergy joined forces to persecute Nonconformists were largely ill-founded and, even during the anti-tithe war of the 1880s, there were probably only four examples of leading farmers actually losing their holdings as a result of their support for the campaign.

Size of Farms

Though the 1851 census contains statistics on farm size, it is the 1875 returns which are regarded as the more reliable and which reveal that the mean size of holdings was forty-seven acres. The smallness of Welsh farms remained remarkably unchanged over the next thirty years. It was estimated, in fact, that a farmer needed at least forty acres in Wales to make a living, and those with less than this usually turned to alternative outlets in order to supplement their incomes. In Caernarfonshire and Merioneth, where there were a large number of small farms of between three and twenty acres, farmers depended on work in the slate quarries. In Montgomeryshire and south Cardiganshire farmers often made their livelihood as weavers, blacksmiths, wheelwrights, masons and carpenters; and many of the occupants of these small holdings in south-west Wales migrated in the winter months to Merthyr Tydfil for jobs in the ironworks.

Farm holdings in Wales had been small-sized for many generations, and partly because of the old system of gavelkind which had divided the farm equally among the sons at the father's death. Physical conditions, with infertile terrain and the remoteness of so many farms from markets tended to produce a semi-subsistent pattern of farming. The craving for land in Wales had created among the farming community an opinion which was hostile to multiple holdings and the consolidation of farms. Also Welsh farmers tended to feel that they held an almost divine right of succession on the land, so that one member of a family ought to be succeeded by another. This time-honoured system created many difficulties and forced many farmers off the land and into the industrial districts of south-east Wales. Others succumbed to parish relief or sold up and emigrated. After the 1860s, however, a number of changes made it difficult for the farming community to exist on small holdings: mechanization gradually changed the process of harvesting; the weaving industry declined in mid Wales, and thereby deprived farmers of a supplementary source of income; and threshing machines replaced the old flail. Many landowners found themselves with no alternative but to amalgamate the farms on their estates in the closing decades of the century.

The Agricultural Labourer

From the available evidence we know that the agricultural labour force grew rapidly between 1801 and 1851, for the population of rural Wales grew by a natural increase of 64 per cent. However, the census data from 1851 to 1911 indicate an overall decrease in male agricultural wage-earners in Wales of 45.7 per cent, with the female labour force declining by an astronomic 94.9 per cent in the same period. This decline in the number of agricultural wage-earners was itself part of the overall fall in the number of persons employed in Welsh agriculture from 1851 onwards. In the period from 1851 to 1911 there was an overall drop of 28.4 per cent, and a particularly sharp fall in the two decades immediately after 1851. The decline in the hired labour force was, however, easily the most significant figure at 45.7 per cent, and it was the disappearance of a large segment of this group which accounts for the decline in the numbers of total agriculturalists in the late nineteenth century.

Most of those who left the land migrated to the new industrial areas of south-east Wales in search of employment. The growth of the iron industry and the independent development of the steam-coal mines acted as magnets to the rural labour force. Higher wages, shorter hours and the novel attractions of town life pulled people away from the rural areas from the 1820s onwards. Some of the migration was seasonal, especially during winter stock farming. But there was also permanent migration to the new industrial centres. The long-distance nature of much of this migration was in stark contrast to the English 'drift' migratory patterns.

There was a mass exodus of rural labourers to south-east Wales not only in response to the economic and social attractions of the new settlements, but also as a result of the harsh and brutal conditions endemic in the Welsh countryside. Population had grown alacriously in south-west Wales, and in a society in which there were few opportunities of alternative employment to the land. In response to depression and falling prices, farmers had been compelled to contract the labour force at the very time when the supply of farm wage-earners far exceeded the demand. A number of other factors combined to depress even further the state of the labour market: the 1870 Education Act had restricted the employment of young people, and this reduced the potential earnings of families; from the 1890s, boys from reformatory and industrial schools in England were used on Welsh farms as cheap labour and as a means of combating the depression; the fall in grain prices from the mid 1870s accelerated the switch to grass, and this further reduced the demand for labour; and, finally, the gradual mechanization of the industry further affected the labour market.

The working and living conditions of the agricultural wage-earners in employment improved steadily from mid-century, and it would seem that the coming of the railways was the significant factor. In 1869 William Phillips, Rating Officer of the Narberth Union in Pembrokeshire, commented on the improved wages of the farm labourers of south-west Wales over twenty-five years: 'I believe the turning-point in the labourers' advanced condition was about the making of the south Wales railway.' Wages improved down to the 1870s, when depression gradually set in. But there were signs of improvement in other areas of life as well. Before mid-century a labourer had existed on a diet of oaten or barley bread, potatoes and milk, whereas by 1870 the agricultural wage-earners of south-west Wales were consuming wheaten bread, and those in north Wales had occasional supplies of fresh green vegetables. By the 1890s meat was no longer beyond the labourer's means and those in north Wales consumed, on average, about one ounce a day. Fresh meat was still a luxury and reserved for Sunday lunch and for harvest meals. There continued to be some deficiencies in the diet, even at the end of the century; green vegetables were rarely eaten and fruit was hardly ever given to labourers.

Despite the steady improvement in the labourer's lot after 1850, there was still a singular absence of strong labour unions to fight for the wage-earners. The Lleufer Thomas Report on Welsh agriculture in 1894 spoke of a 'total absence' of farm labourers' unions in Wales. The strongest combinations emerged in Anglesey and Caernarfonshire in 1889–91 and secured a small reduction in working hours. Soon afterwards the movement crumbled. At Michaelmas 1891, the labourers of south Pembrokeshire battled for a wage rise of 2s. a week and, in most areas, the farmers compromised and the proposed union withered away.

In the years before the outbreak of the First World War there were few signs of open conflict between farmers and their workers, and labour unions were slow to develop. One reason for this was the scattered nature of the labour force, even in the 1860s and 1870s, and this restricted the influence of the press, which was such a potent factor in the farming districts of south-east England. The small-sized Welsh farms usually employed family labour and relatives, and this was conducive to a situation in which the interests of employers and workers were not in conflict. Thirdly, the ties between employer and worker were usually quite strong where there were indoor servants. Some historians have shown a close correlation between the emergence of trade unionism and the absence of the indoor servants. Relations between farmers and labourers worsened in the years 1914–18 when the increase in labourers' wages failed to keep pace with the rising costs of living.

The Land Question

Throughout the second part of the nineteenth century both Radicals and Nonconformists joined forces in attacking the owners of land in the Principality. They accused landowners of raising rents excessively as a result of improvements on tenants' property, and of pushing up rental values in response to land hunger. Samuel Roberts, Llanbryn-mair, and T.E. Ellis, the ascending young Liberal politician, were especially vociferous in their assaults on the landlords. But recent research has shown that the Radical-Nonconformist camp was often unfair and misguided in its criticisms. On the large estates, for example, it was customary for landlords to help provide the bulk of the material for the permanent improvements on their tenants' property. Scholars have shown that it was only a small number of landlords who tried to recoup their money by increasing rents annually. A further point of some importance is that the critics rarely took into account the effect of the advent of the railways and the growth of new markets in pushing up rental values after the 1840s.

Historians have also argued that landlords did not raise their rents in response to the feverish land hunger of the century. On the large estates there were changes of tenancies only when there were no relatives of the previous tenant available to apply for the tenancy. The increasing demand for farms did push up the rents on some estates but, as David Howell has lucidly shown, although such rents had increased in response to competition, the landlords had rarely exploited the situation by playing off one applicant against another. On the smaller estates of 1,000 acres or less, the position was far more precarious and the harassed and often impecunious owners were only too ready to force up the rents.

Land tenancy carried other payments as well as cash rentals, and foremost among these were tithes. Paid in kind in the early nineteenth century, they were commuted into cash payments following the passing of the Tithe Commutation Act of 1836. But even this change failed to reduce the pressure on poor farmers, especially during periods of agricultural depression and when there was a scarcity of cash and coinage. There were also religious objections among the Nonconformists, now the majority of the farming population, who resented having to pay to buttress the Anglican Church. Tithe payments had been a major grievance of the Rebecca Rioters, and, in the last quarter of the century, they again became the focus of militant attention as the prices of stock collapsed in the years 1885–6. Farmers felt aggrieved that the tithe rent charges were still too high and, in January 1886, they started protesting in Denbighshire. By early September, the Anti-Tithe League had appeared with the initial and apparent aim of supporting the farmers in their attempts to secure tithe rebates. The League was soon pushed into the more extreme position of opposing tithes in principle. The Nonconformist ministers, and notably the Revd Thomas Gee, claimed that tithe was a payment to an alien Church, and most of the officers of the League probably saw this agitation as an opportunity to argue the case for the disestablishment and disendowment of the Church.

Religious objections to tithes were clearly felt in Wales and the role of Nonconformity was crucial in the Welsh Tithe War. The south-east of England had been more heavily tithed than Wales and agricultural depression had been more heavily felt there, yet the opposition to tithes was far less forceful and vociferous than in Wales. In the Welsh rural counties the Nonconformists inspired the farmers into action and there were disturbances in Flintshire, Anglesey, Caernarfonshire, Merioneth, Cardiganshire, Carmarthenshire, and Pembroke-shire. Anti-tithe agitation soon evaporated after the passing of

the Tithe Rent Charge of 1891 which stipulated that landlords
were responsible for the tithes. This piece of legislation effectively
ensured that the landlords would now include the tithes in the
rentals, and so the situation remained almost unchanged.

In Wales the agitation was largely the result of sectarian and
political grievances, and the landlords were seen as the political
arm of the Church in the mid 1880s. There was a sharp
deterioration in the relations between landlord and tenant as
the pulpit and the press mounted a sustained attack on the
Church and the landlords. In north Wales *Y Faner*, *Y Genedl* and
the *Celt* newspapers carried influential articles on the land
question and, in the Welsh-speaking areas of south Wales, the
press was equally important in moulding opinion against the
owners of land.

By 1892 the reformers had attracted the support of no less a
political personage than W.E. Gladstone who, in a celebrated
speech near Beddgelert, pinpointed the landlords for their
unfair behaviour towards their tenants in the depression years
after the 1870s. Gladstone based his remarks on the speeches
and views of T.E. Ellis, MP for Merioneth, and soon the Liberal
Party began to focus attention on the land question. Many felt
that this could only be solved by similar legislation to that
enacted for Ireland, with a land court to provide 'fair rents,
fixity of tenure and free sale'. The Welsh situation was, however,
completely different from that of Ireland: agricultural improvements in Wales were not usually the result of tenants' work; the
evil of complete absenteeism, which was so endemic a feature in
Ireland, did not apply to the Welsh scene; Welsh tenants did not
suffer the kind of insecurity which was so prevalent on Irish
estates, and political evictions were equally rare in Wales; the
landlords' control in Wales prevented the subdivision of
holdings; landlords rarely took the religious affiliations of
tenants into account when considering applications for farms.

On the large estates the land question was, to a large extent, a
figment of the political imagination, and the land reformers had
overestimated the degree to which the traditional bonds
between landlord and tenant had slackened. There was far less
support for the land reform programme among the farmers than
the Nonconformist preachers had anticipated. During the
agricultural difficulties of the 1880s and the early 1890s the

landowner was often made the scapegoat for all the tenants' problems. There is, however, sufficient evidence to show that the large owners suffered along with their tenants. The real grievances occurred when the outlying parts of the large estates were sold, and on the estates of the smaller, hereditary owners. Recent research in this field has tended to conclude that the so-called Welsh land question was really designed as a way of promoting the Liberal cause and of liberating the rural Welshman from the traditional and tripartite grasp of Church, squire and privilege.

The End of the Great Estates

Landowners possessed 89.8 per cent of the total cultivated surface of Wales in 1887 and the concentration of land in the hands of a few landowning families was a more marked feature of Welsh society than of contemporary English society. Although land was bought and sold in the century, it was usually acquired by neighbouring landowners rather than by the tenants.

Although there was a slight movement towards owner farming in the years after 1870, there were no substantial sales in the last thirty years of the century. By 1900 only one of the great estates had been significantly affected by sales, and that was the Gwydir estate in Caernarfonshire. Of the thirty-five farms sold in that year, twenty-two were bought by speculators, seven by the neighbouring landowner, Lord Penrhyn, and only five by tenants. In some counties, such as Cardiganshire and Denbighshire, there was an absolute fall in the proportion of freeholders from 1887 to 1909.

As the rate of sales increased at the turn of the century, it was among those landowners whose major interests lay in England, and who were concentrating their resources there that the large-scale selling began in Wales. Of the 165 families who held estates of 3,000 acres or over in Wales in 1883, 65 per cent had no land outside Wales and only 7 per cent regarded their Welsh estates as mere appendages to their outside lands. It was among this 7 per cent that the big sales commenced and, at the turn of the century, one of the greatest transfers of land began with the fragmentation of the Beaufort estate in Monmouthshire.

It was in the period from 1910 to 1914 that every principal landowner in Wales, with the exception of those in the south Wales coalfield, began to sell some land and, significantly, it was the tenants who bought most of it. There were a number of reasons why the landowners should decide to part with large portions of their lands in this period: one factor was the emergence of a more democratic society, and a more democratic industrial society. Throughout the nineteenth century the ownership of land had bestowed political and social prestige on its holders, and this had far outweighed the apparent economic returns. As greater numbers of people were enfranchised, and especially in the rural areas after 1884–5, and as more democratic institutions emerged, so the political and social prestige dwindled and the ownership of land no longer seemed such an attractive proposition. A second factor of some importance was that landowners were increasingly reluctant to risk the hostility that would follow any exorbitant rent charges, and this factor was particularly important in the years immediately preceding and during the First World War.

Research has shown that death duties had little impact in the period before the First World War, for the death duty demanded by the Act of 1894 was only 8 per cent on an estate valued at £1 million. After the war the situation changed drastically for the landowners had lost large numbers of their class in active military service, and death duties had soared to 40 per cent by 1919 on a £2 million estate. The net result of these factors was a serious drain on the resources of the landowning class. Historians seem agreed, however, that the legislation of the Liberal governments in the pre-1914 era did not itself force the landowners to sell.

In rural Wales, after 1868, landowners who held English and Welsh estates, found it more rewarding to concentrate on their English lands. There is considerable evidence to show that the replacement of the landowners began much earlier in Wales and that a new freeholding class emerged much earlier in the Principality. Welsh tenants seemed to have stronger reasons for buying land and a Land Enquiry Committee survey of 1913 revealed that 66 per cent of a sample of Welsh tenants wanted to be owner-occupiers compared with only 33 per cent of a sample of English tenants.

There were a number of reasons why Welsh tenants appeared in the market at least a decade before their English counterparts: one significant factor was the often harsh and bitter memory of 1868 and the evictions that ensued; in those areas where landlords had not undertaken repairs, the loss of the landowners was not traumatic; there was the perennial reluctance of Welsh farmers to move away from their homes and backgrounds; and the diminutive size of many Welsh farms made them much cheaper than their English counterparts. But there was another reason, totally unrelated to agrarian or economic considerations, and that concerned the cultural heritage of Welsh rural society. The tenants of Wales, especially the Welsh-speaking cohort, rejected their landlords and shared no community of interests with them. They felt that the landed classes had, over many generations, alienated themselves from the Welsh society in which they lived. In Wales, land tenancy embraced a whole community spirit and a sense of history and nationality, from which the landlords had separated themselves. The landowners, sensing this alienation and rejection, finally decided to depart and sold out on an unprecedented scale.

Agricultural Development in the Nineteenth Century

Some scholars who have studied agricultural development in Wales in the last century have argued that previous discussions on the topic have tended to polarize into pro- and anti-landlord tirades, depending on the emotional reaction and content of the participants. A whole generation of writers fell under the spell of the Radical and Nonconformist populists who, like the Liberal politician T.E. Ellis, claimed that it was a harsh landlordism which explained the backwardness of agriculture in Wales. As our knowledge of the period expands, it would seem that this picture needs to be refined. The failure of the farming interest to exploit the benefits of the new technology can be attributed to a whole cluster of factors, of which the divisive aspects of religion, culture and language were by no means the least important.

There was certainly a grain of truth to the charge of 'absentee' when applied to the landlords. But the charge must not be overemphasized for, as we have already seen, most of the larger landowners actively encouraged the development of their estates, and the extraordinary success of agriculture after the Napoleonic wars, and through to the last quarter of the nineteenth century, was attributable largely to the willingness of landlords to invest capital in estate development and to exploit the new scientific and technological developments of the era. Estate papers and diaries of south Wales landed gentry reveal considerable expenditure on agricultural improvements. In Cardiganshire, the great houses of Nanteos and Gogerddan maintained profitable model demesne farms, and, in Carmarthenshire, the Edwinsford estate spent large sums on improvements. On the smaller estates, however, the squires living on 2,000 to 3,000 acres, with an income of £1,000 to £2,000 per annum, could scarcely afford social ambitions or pretensions if they were to maintain their farms. It was here that feelings of insecurity were strong, and this militated against agricultural development. The decline of the smaller estates in the nineteenth century was a factor of some importance in limiting agricultural development.

Geography was another factor. Apart from the river valleys, the plains and the lowlands, the topography of Wales lent itself to a predominantly pastoral economy. Even allowing for the almost insurmountable geographical and topographical obstacles, it has to be admitted that the tenant farmer had an almost ineluctable conservative quality which shunned innovation or technological change. Contemporary observers were practically unanimous in their condemnation of the 'hereditary prejudices', and Welsh farming in the period up to mid-century existed in a primitive, parlous and almost ghostly state. Thomas Herbert Cooke, who was the agent on the Middleton Hall estate in Carmarthenshire during the Rebecca Riots, wrote to his mother in 1842 in these revealing terms:

> My English ways do not suit Welsh farmers and my opinion of the Welsh farmers is that they know less than their horses. They are too ignorant to be taught. They are 100 years behind the worst managed English districts.

Why should the Welsh tenant farmer have been so conservative? Perhaps the small-scale nature of farming was an inhibitive factor. The fact that the Welsh farmer had never enjoyed the same standard of living as his English counterparts was certainly influential, and it effectively depressed the aspirations and the incomes of the farmers. Others have argued that the landlords, by demanding higher rents and squeezing the land market, had increased the competition for land and thereby forced Welsh farmers to maintain their insubstantial incomes by practising low-cost farming on marginal acreage. The twin pressures of landlordism and Anglicization also probably unwittingly created a conservative cultural environment which made the farmers more protective of their language, religion and of their traditional practices.

Imperfect tenurial relations could easily be considered as a stumbling-block to the development of agriculture. The lack of security implicit in the annual tenancies and the absence of compulsory tenant-right (at least before 1883) acted as a disincentive to investment. The 'service rents' featured in countless tenancy agreements, and these further exacerbated the tensions between owner and tenants. Occupants of E.P. Lloyd's Glansevin estate were under obligation to provide poultry and eggs as part of their rents, even as late as the 1840s. At Edwinsford, Carmarthenshire, service rents persisted in the early 1860s. Enclosures and the game laws compounded the ill-feeling on estates. In Wales, the inequitable distribution of the newly-enclosed land by the Enclosure Commissioners acted as an additional source of resentment and a further obstacle to agricultural development. Similarly, after the Ground Game Act of 1831 country people forfeited their right to kill the rabbits and hares feeding on their crops. Tenant farmers were angered by the sacrifice of their crops on the newly-created game preservations.

Fear of rent increases was, according to some historians, the crucial obstacle to agricultural improvement. The Welsh tenant farmers, with their indelible peasant mentalities, regarded any rent increases arising from improvements as calamitous. The possibility of rent increases, therefore, inhibited the Welsh farmers from experimenting with new techniques. It was their uneconomic attitude to farming, their preferences for hoarding money and for low rents, that probably impeded the development of agriculture and explained much of the underdeveloped nature of farming in the nineteenth century.

SUGGESTED READING

D.W. Howell, *Land and People in Nineteenth-Century Wales* (London, 1978).

A.H. John and G. Williams (eds.), *Glamorgan County History*, 5 (Cardiff, 1980).

Articles:

R.J. Colyer, 'Limitations to Agrarian Development in Nineteenth-Century Wales', *B.B.C.S.*, XXVII (1978).

R.J. Colyer, 'Early Agricultural Societies in South Wales', *W.H.R.*, 12 (1984–5).

John Davies, 'The End of Great Estates and the Rise of Freehold Farming in Wales', *W.H.R.*, 7 (1974–5).

D.W. Howell, 'The Agricultural Labourer in Nineteenth-Century Wales', *W.H.R.*, 6 (1972–3).

D.W. Howell, 'The Impact of Railways on Agricultural Development in Nineteenth-Century Wales', *W.H.R.*, 7 (1974–5).

10. Religion and Society
1851–1906

The 1851 'Religious Census' and the Strength of Nonconformity

ON the last Sunday in March 1851, the first census of religion in modern times was conducted in Great Britain. It was the first official and comprehensive count of the accommodation available for, and the actual attendance at, religious worship. It was initiated by the Government of the day, though its precise origins remain unclear, and it was planned and supervised by the office of the Registrar-General. Though it is a unique report, containing a mass of detailed and valuable statistical information, it fell far short of the objective analysis for which Horace Mann, one of the two senior officials at the Census Office entrusted with the task of supervising the census, had hoped. This was because the census was itself the product of the continuing debate between the Church of England and the Nonconformists concerning the role of the Church in society, and the widely held belief that the Established Church had no moral right to the wealth and privileges it possessed. This belief was buttressed by the general observation that a substantial part of the population had no formal connection with any organized religion. The aim of the census was, therefore, to discover the size of the worshipping population by establishing precisely how many places of worship existed and how many people had attended them on that last Sunday in March 1851.

The census depended upon the goodwill of those individuals discharged with the duty of collecting the information, and the clerks and officials delegated with the responsibility of amassing the details were forced to rely on the effectiveness of the machinery devised for this specific purpose. The religious census was taken as part of the decennial census of population. The local machinery was the responsibility of the superintendent registrars of the registration districts, and in Wales there were forty-eight of these registrars, their districts being almost coterminous with the Poor Law Unions. The districts were further divided into 181 subdistricts, each having a local registrar of births and deaths. The subdistricts were aggregations of parishes, townships, hamlets, and other divisions, of which there were 1,261 in Wales. For the purposes of the census, these subdistricts were divided into enumeration districts, usually based on existing parishes or other divisions which could be enumerated by one person in a day. Where the parishes were too large to be covered in a single day, a unit of a hundred households was aimed at.

During the week ending 29 March the enumerator was required to leave the Religious Worship forms either at the residence of the officiating minister or at that of the church warden or other official. There were two forms — Form A was for Anglican places of worship, and Form B, printed in red ink, was for Nonconformist churches. The schedules were to be collected on the following Monday (31 March), and the enumerator was to ensure that the forms had been properly completed. One further supervisory check was conducted by the registrar before he sent the forms to Horace Mann at the Census Office in London by 22 April. The final check took place at the London Census Office where twenty or thirty clerks were employed on the task (only two of whom, according to Mann, were Dissenters).

Modern-day researchers have realized that the system had deficiencies, and one weak link was the preliminary listing of places of worship. It is a serious criticism of the census that so many places of worship were not listed in the first place and Mann's officials in London did not efficiently check the lists of the Church of England against the Clergy Lists. In the western part of the Vale of Glamorgan a number of adjacent parish churches are missing, and places of worship in workhouses and gaols were not required to be returned. Another criticism often levelled at the report is that it did not define the 'place of worship' with sufficient clarity. There is no way of knowing, for example, whether the chapel officials clearly understood the meaning of 'separate' building when listing their church building. More problematical still was the recording of exact information regarding the provision made by the places of worship, that is, their seating capacity. After collecting the forms, the enumerators, together with the local registrars were expected to check the forms and correct any errors before despatching them to London; and there is evidence to suggest that this procedure was undertaken. As a rule, however, the enumerators and registrars confined their attention to information which was wrongly or insufficiently presented. But a large number of forms were defective because of the failure of the officials making the returns to understand exactly what was required. It is not clear whether the query concerning 'free' and 'other' sittings was understood. The object was to discover what proportion of the provision of seats was at the service of the poorer classes. The figures published in the report, however, do provide some useful clues as to the extent to which the provision of church sittings was freely available. The statistics show that about 45 per cent of the provision in south Wales was free, compared with an estimated 37 per cent of England and Wales.

Allowing for these errors and inconsistencies, it is probably fair to claim that the system devised by Mann did achieve a fair degree of accuracy so far as the actual counting and recording of places of worship were concerned, their denominational allegiances, and the sitting accommodation they provided. Missing places of worship, for example, can be traced in some topographical dictionaries. The accuracy of the attendance figures is probably more open to doubt than that of the accommodation figures, and it was these which prompted serious and heated debate when they were published. There were criticisms that there was a conspiracy by the Dissenters to inflate the numbers of attendants, by exaggerating their numbers or by encouraging individuals to attend additional services in chapels other than their own. It would probably be fair to say that not all ministers, churchwardens and deacons actually counted the heads of their congregations, and some were estimates. In many areas variables such as the weather, shift work, and seasonal factors affected the normal attendance rates. But the most serious weakness of the census was its eventual failure to distinguish individual attendances. Figures are given for all separate services, but there is no way of knowing how many individuals attended particular services. A large proportion of worshippers may have attended all the services, but what proportion did so, it is not possible to tell. What most historians have done, including the most recent distinguished Welsh scholar, Professor I.G. Jones, is to adopt the method of expressing the total of all attendances in each place of worship in each parish as a proportion of the total population of each parish. This device enables scholars to compare the strength or weakness of particular religious bodies in particular places.

What did the census reveal about the nature of religious conditions in Wales? It confirmed what many people had suspected for some time, namely, that Wales was very much more religious than England. According to the report, England and Wales together had a total of 34,467 places of all kinds, providing an aggregate of about 9.5 million sittings. The population of the two countries was about 18 million. Since not every individual could be expected to attend a religious service on any particular Sunday — the very young, the old, the sick, the maimed, and those who were compelled to work on the Sabbath — Horace Mann estimated that about 7.5 million came into this category, leaving 10.5 million, or 58 per cent of the population who were able to attend divine worship. If Mann's calculations were correct, then there was an overall shortage of over a million sittings, and he estimated that about 2,000 additional places of worship were required, especially in the large towns. In England the religious bodies between them provided seating for just over half the total population, or 51.4 per cent. In Wales just over 75 per cent of the total population could be seated in places of worship: 898,442 out of a population of 1,188,914. This was an exceptionally high proportion: the highest of any single region in England and Wales.

Examination of the statistics for England and Wales as a whole brings out one inescapable conclusion: those parts of the country with the densest population had the least provision, and vice versa. London, for example, could provide for only a little over 29 per cent, and Manchester for only 31.6 per cent, of their inhabitants. Mann noted that there was some kind of relationship between the relative levels of provision and the economic and social characteristics of the regions. The deficient districts were all in industrial areas, in large towns and cities. Wales was certainly no exception to this rule, for differences in the provision of facilities for religious worship corresponded to differences in local economies and societies. In the areas where industry had developed most extensively and rapidly, provision was relatively least favourable. Provision was greatest in the rural districts: Machynlleth (124 per cent), Dolgellau (116 per cent): and it was lowest in the industrial districts, or heavily urbanized districts, such as Newport (68 per cent) and Merthyr Tydfil (58 per cent).

Wales was sufficiently provided with accommodation for public worship. Merioneth and Breconshire had more seats available than they had population. At the other end of the scale, however, Glamorgan and Monmouthshire were both about 30 per cent short of seating. The regions with a high accommodation rate were invariably rural areas, and those with low accommodation rates were all industrialized regions; usually centred in relatively large towns. Wales was not only better provided for than England, but it also made more use of its accommodation. Taking the two countries together the proportion which attended was 24 per cent: but for Wales alone the figure was 34 per cent. About one-third of the total population attended a religious service on Census Sunday. The proportion was actually higher in the north Wales counties (38 per cent) than in the south (35 per cent), and higher in the rural than in the industrial districts. In Aberystwyth, Machynlleth, Cardigan and Bangor more than a half of the population attended, but in Newport, Swansea and Neath less than one-third were present.

The patterns of denominational allegiance were also revealing. In England and Wales together almost as many worshippers attended the services of the Church as attended those of the Nonconformists — 47 per cent and 49 per cent of the total respectively. In Wales only 9 per cent had attended the Anglican churches and 87 per cent the Nonconformist chapels. The proportions varied considerably from place to place, and the Anglican Church was strongest in the rural, Anglicized districts, and weakest in the industrial, Welsh-language speaking districts. For example, 70 per cent of the attendants in Monmouth district went to church, 43 per cent in Knighton, 10 per cent in Abergavenny, 9 per cent in Neath and in Swansea, 7 per cent in Bridgend, 6 per cent in Merthyr Tydfil, and only 1 per cent in Bala district. Wales was clearly a Nonconformist country and the masses had rejected the Established Church.

Not only had they rejected the Anglican Church, but they had provided themselves with alternative places of worship. Of the total places of worship in Wales 29 per cent belonged to the Church and 71 per cent to the other denominations. Of the total of 983,653 sittings, 30.5 per cent belonged to the Church and 69.5 per cent to the Nonconformists.

The Churches and Cultural Activities

The chapels and churches of the last century were supported because they were not wholly religious institutions. The chapels, in particular, had many functions to perform apart from the purely liturgical and devotional; and they became the cultural centres of their rural and industrial communities. Religion was organically a part of society and it became the means of preserving old traditions and of creating new ones. Within this chapel-centred society there emerged a folk culture, a culture of the ordinary folk — 'diwylliant y werin' —, the essence of which was the urge on the part of the industrial work-force to acquire in a small, and often humble enough way, the intellectual accomplishments and enjoyment, prestige and status of a more cultured society. This happened in a largely Nonconformist context and it displayed certain essential characteristics. In the first place, it represented the striving and efforts of a distinct group of ordinary, working people; secondly, they all seemed to share a basic desire for liberation from the traditional bonds of obscurity; an implicit aspect of this cultural endeavour was its self-help philosophy — it was local, unaided and a do-it-yourself movement; finally, it was a culture deeply embedded in the very soil of organized religion.

Why was there such an expansion and outburst of creative energy in the industrial communities, and especially among the ranks of Nonconformity, after 1850? Many factors combined to produce the conditions that were conducive to this cultural and literary awakening. The effect of the temperance crusade was one such factor. The temperance platform rallied the denominations to a single social point-of-view and it employed all kinds of devices and attractions to appeal to the ordinary classes of people. Industrialists were also eager promoters of local cultural events, for most employers of labour preferred a steady, sober and temperate squad of workmen. Most entrepreneurs hoped that reading, musical activities, eisteddfodau, literary pursuits and schooling would prevent their workmen from supporting extreme and violent causes. The energy engendered by the religious revivals of the century was responsible in part for the cultural explosion that took place in the mid-Victorian period. Again, the improvement in the economy and the changes in the transport system from the 1850s onwards stimulated the cultural life of the rural and industrial communities. Other factors promoting the spread of these cultural activities were the growth of the press, and fortuitous developments in the world of music and on the eisteddfod field; and each of these will be examined in turn.

The denominations placed great importance on the power of the printed word and they dominated the vernacular press throughout the century, at a time when the London daily newspapers had a very limited circulation in Wales. There were weekly, monthly and quarterly periodicals, most of which were denominational. After the Napoleonic wars, Nonconformist periodicals surfaced; notable among them were *Seren Gomer*, started by the Baptists in 1814, and from 1835 onwards, *Y Diwygiwr*, a periodical published by the Independents under the editorship of the dynamic Revd David Rees, Llanelli. During the 1840s and 1850s there appeared three notable periodicals. The first was *Yr Amserau*, (The Times), (1843) published in Liverpool and edited by the well-known Independent minister, William Rees (Hiraethog). Also in 1845 there began the publication of *Y Traethodydd*, (The Essayist), associated with Dr Lewis Edwards, the intellectual leader of the Calvinistic Methodists. In 1851 there followed *Y Faner*, (The Banner) launched by Thomas Gee of Denbigh, a Calvinistic Methodist preacher of note. Although it was intended as an inter-denominational journal, it was most definitely Nonconformist in tone and sympathies.

Before 1855 the national press was the preserve of the traditional holders of power who dominated Parliament. After 1861, it had become a chiefly popular institution, representative of classes with little weight in Parliament. The first cause of this change was the jolt given to the newspaper world by the Crimean War, but the real cause of the change was the repeal of the stamp duties in 1855. After that year the national and provincial newspapers were enabled to expand their circulation much more easily, and this further stimulated the nascent cultural exertions of the ordinary people. The appearance of national newspapers such as *The Times* and the *Daily Mail*, as well as the local provincials, the *Swansea and Glamorgan Herald*, *The Cambrian* and the *Merthyr Guardian*, stretched the mental capacities and broadened the experiences of the working communities. By the beginning of the twentieth century, for example, it was estimated that Welsh periodicals had a circulation of 50,000 a week, and the estimated expenditure on these was assessed at £200,000 per annum.

The social appeal of religion was further extended in mid-century, and the ties between religion and the folk-culture were strengthened even more firmly by means of the developments that took place in music circles in the late 1850s. Among a small pioneering group responsible for these significant developments, the most notable were the Revd John Roberts (Ieuan Gwyllt), a Calvinistic Methodist minister, and the Revd Edward Stephens (Tanymarian), a Congregationalist. They travelled extensively, lecturing to diverse groups on congregational music, and they published congregational hymn-books which provided a uniformity of standard in the hymn-singing competitions in the Welsh valleys. The revival of 1859 must have had a pronounced effect on musical development, for it was in that year that Ieuan Gwyllt published his congregational hymn-book, *Llyfr Tonau Cynulleidfaol* (Book of Congregational Hymn Tunes) and, in the same year, he had started what is generally regarded as the first modern *Cymanfa Ganu* (singing festival) at Aberdare. Also in 1859 the Revd E. Stephens had published his collection of congregational tunes, *Cerddor y Cysegr*, (The Musician of the Sanctuary). Tanymarian was also notable for his oratorio, *The Storm of Tiberias*, which was probably the first oratorio to have been written by a Welshman.

A key factor in the development of congregational singing and choral music was the emergence of various systems of musical sight-reading. John Hullah's system had been brought to the Swansea area some years before 1850 by its founder. He was persuaded to come to Swansea by John Henry Vivian to spend a few months giving lessons to the inhabitants, and there is evidence that large numbers from the town and the surrounding district attended. There were four from the nearby parish of Llansamlet who used to walk three nights a week to receive their lessons from eight to ten, paying a shilling an hour, and six shillings a week. These were the hymn-singing leaders in their individual churches and they, in turn, taught the Hullah sight-reading system to others. Very little is known about the Hullah system since the whole country was eventually swamped by Curwen's tonic sol-fa method of sight-reading. Wales actually became one of the strongholds of the system. Curwen's system was quickly learned by the hymn-singing leaders in all churches, and the majority of the candidates in the examinations of the Tonic Sol-fa College, when it was established, were from Wales. The spread of the tonic sol-fa system to the industrial communities of south Wales made the learning of music very much easier, and enhanced its popular appeal. The uniformity of the tonic sol-fa system also provided a basic standard in musical reading, and it was this which enabled geographically separate communities to join forces in their appreciation and performance of classical works. Henry Jones, later Sir Henry Jones and Professor of Moral Philosophy at Glasgow, spent a period of time as a village schoolmaster in the village of Brynamman, in the Swansea Valley. As an energetic, young teacher, in his second year of teaching, he was able to teach children Handel's 'Hallelujah Chorus'. One suspects that their knowledge of the tonic sol-fa system made his work that much easier.

John Curwen's sol-fa system made such an impression on individuals like Eleazer Roberts and John Edwards that his tonic sol-fa handbook and his hymn-book were published in Welsh in 1861, and sol-fa classes were soon established at Sunday schools throughout the country. The Nonconformists were led by Revd John Roberts (Ieuan Gwyllt) who published his sol-fa notation in 1863. From 1869 to 1873 he was editor of the journal, *Cerddor y Tonic Solffa* (The Tonic Sol-fa Musician). This published new music, carried information about the latest singing festivals and news from sol-fa classes, and included the names of successful candidates for the examinations of the Tonic Sol-fa College in London. Its system of training led to the awards of licentiate and fellowship diplomas. The sol-fa system had many advantages: it was a cheap form of music notation; it was effective and easily learned; and it instilled a sense of accurate time and relative pitch.

The sol-fa system had many longstanding results in the Principality: it led to the rise of good four-part congregational singing; it produced the annual singing festivals — 'y Cymanfaoedd Canu'; and it paved the way for the rise of the choirs. The mid-century onwards was the period of the great choirs in Wales, and choral societies were established throughout the country. Most of these were chapel-based from the outset, and one of the most celebrated was the South Wales Choral Union, or, Y Côr Mawr (The Great Choir). Aberdare was the centre of the choral union and the decision to form the choir was taken there on 12 February 1872. Aberdare was the centre of the steam-coal industry and the cynosure of a lively cultural tradition. Local brass bands had gathered in inns such as The Stag since the early years of the century, and a choral competition attracted seven small choirs. In 1861 a three-day National Eisteddfod in the township was visited by almost 7,000 people. In the 1860s eisteddfodau had proliferated as a result of the interest shown by local churches, Sunday schools, temperance, and friendly societies. Choirs began to combine and by 1863 the Aberdare United Choir, conducted by Silas Evans, won the first prize of £10 at the Swansea National Eisteddfod. The growth of choral combinations was aided by the formation of the Glamorgan and Monmouthshire Temperance Music Union. This particular union produced *Messiah* at Dowlais in 1861, *The Creation* at Pontypridd in 1863, and *Twelfth Mass* at Tredegar in 1864. The first Cymanfa Ganu was an offshoot of the Temperance Music Union.

The successes of the Côr Mawr, the South Wales Choral Union, at the Crystal Palace in 1872–3 were hailed by the Welsh press as a national victory. In less than three months of preparation, the choir had added eight technically difficult choruses, including a sixteenth-century madrigal, and works by Bach and Handel to its repertoire. All the works were unfamiliar, and two were to be sung in Latin. The organization required in a choral union of this kind was quite enormous: there was the selection of choristers and district conductors, planning of rehearsals, the transportation of choristers, collection of funds, and the arrangement of actual performances. Some 400 choristers were actively involved, drawn from twelve districts extending from Llanelli in the west to Blaenavon in the east.

The Established Church was certainly not to be over-shadowed by these developments, and the Revd Evan Lewis, Vicar of Aberdare from 1859 to 1866, soon established annual choral festivals for the Aberdare Valley. In 1871 the combined choirs had 204 choristers. Lewis had also been a prime mover in the establishment of the annual Llandaff Diocesan Festivals from 1861. With the opening of a Catholic church in 1868 a new event appeared, the performance of the choral mass in its proper liturgical setting. At its first anniversary in 1869, high mass was celebrated with Mozart's *Twelfth Mass*, and by members of the Aberdare United Choir, which would have included a consider-able number of Nonconformists.

In the Swansea Valley, January 1850 was a significant date in the musical calendar, for a young man of nineteen, William Ivander Griffiths, came from Aberafan to work as a clerk at the iron and tin-plate works of Pontardawe. In the small Methodist chapel in Trebanos, of which he became a member, he became secretary of the Sunday school. He also took charge of the 'singing school' and formed a free elementary music class. By 1855 a temperance choir had been formed at the new reading room and, on Sunday evenings after divine service, the choir sang oratorio choruses and other sacred music. In an eisteddfod in Alltwen Chapel at Christmas 1861, Ivander Griffiths con-ducted two different choirs in the same competition, the Pontardawe and Cwmgiedd choirs. On Easter Monday 1862 he conducted another choir from the Onllwyn area and this led to the formation of the Swansea Valley Choir. A meeting was held in Jerusalem Chapel, Ystalyfera, to make arrangements for the formation of a united choir and, in the first week, 150 members were enrolled from all denominations. The newly-formed choir prepared for the Carmarthen eisteddfod in the summer of 1862, and it would compete against other first-class choirs of the calibre of Aberdare, Merthyr and Dowlais. There were thirteen choirs of this quality in the Carmarthen eisteddfod, and the various prizes were shared by Aberdare and Swansea valleys. A sequel to this was the expansion of the Swansea Valley Choir, when singers from the lower end of the valley joined to swell the choir's numbers to between 300 and 400 members. By 10 January 1863, the choir was ready to perform *Messiah* at Ystalyfera, with soloists from London, and an orchestra from Bristol. The second performance was given in Hebron Chapel, Clydach, on 17 January, and the third on 16 February at Bethesda Chapel, Swansea.

There was one other outlet for the aspiring individual of talent, and one other indication of the socio-cultural concerns of the churches in our period: the eisteddfod. Unlike so many other aspects of nineteenth-century Welsh culture, the eisteddfod was not invented *de novo*. There were earlier precedents — but they were very different from the nineteenth-century eisteddfod. The first recorded meeting of the eisteddfod was at Cardigan by the Lord Rhys in 1176. It was a session, and it described a set of musical and poetic competitions. In the Middle Ages it was also the occasion for the bards to put their house in order. There was a Carmarthen eisteddfod of 1450 and two important eisteddfodau at Caerwys in Flintshire in 1523 and 1567. The first signs of revival came around 1700, and in the 1780s a great change took place in the nature of the revived eisteddfodau whereby they became linked with the 'Welsh Society'. The earliest of the revived institutions was the Society of Ancient Britons set up in 1715, and it spawned the Honourable Society of Cymmrodorion in 1751. They attracted so many members that they formed the Gwyneddigion in 1770. After 1815 the new eisteddfodau were held under the auspices of Cambrian societies in Wales — the initiative had, therefore, passed from the London clubs to the groups of patriots at home. The real turning-point in the nineteenth century came at the Carmarthen eisteddfod of 1819 when the Gorsedd of Bards of the Isle of Britain was introduced. It was in this period from 1819 to 1821 that four provincial societies were founded in Wales to publicize Welsh culture and to hold eisteddfodau. The provincial eisteddfodau were held from 1819 to 1858 and they introduced a number of features which still characterize the modern eisteddfod: the long prize essay, evening concerts by professional artistes, long patriotic or presidential speeches, and competitions for crafts and trades. These eisteddfodau also developed a symbolic language of decoration for public occasions, some of which is still used today.

By the late 1840s the chapels and churches gradually embraced the eisteddfod as a worthwhile institution and this paved the way for its development as a national institution. Other factors which promoted the growth and diffusion of the eisteddfod were: the furore emerging from the publication of the infamous 1847 Education Report and the desire to elevate the masses; the widespread support of the temperance campaigners and the teetotal zealots; the growth of the press and the dissemination of denominational journals; the inclusion of musical competitions transformed the eisteddfod into a competitive concert; and other important factors were the spread of the railway system and improved transport generally. The cumulative effect was to produce the first modern annual national eisteddfod at Llangollen in 1858, and there followed a remarkable series of national eisteddfodau in the next ten years; including 'nationals' at Aberdare in 1861, Caernarfon in 1862, Swansea 1863, Llandudno 1864, Aberystwyth 1865, Chester 1866, Carmarthen 1867, and Rhuthun 1868.

The eisteddfod was the forum of intense public debate on a number of issues. Some of the bards wanted to preserve it for the poets, while others promoted the utilitarian case and argued for social science sections. Perhaps the most sensitive of all the debates, and a harbinger of modern arguments, centred around the language of the National Eisteddfod. Lady Llanover had supported the Welsh language in the early eisteddfodau from 1819 to 1834. By the 1860s there was less inclination to press the Celtic connection, and a greater emphasis on the connection with England and on the moral force of Welsh language and religion. Attempts in the 1860s to create a Pan-Celtic League were discreetly concealed. People became tired of the Celtic theme, and one glance at Ireland seemed to reinforce that feeling. The eisteddfod was caught in the high-point of Victorianism and Bishop Connop Thirlwall's speech at the Swansea National Eisteddfod in 1863 epitomized the mood. In a splendid piece of oratory he urged the Welsh people to learn English and to use Welsh for tourist purposes. Much of the English press ridiculed the Welsh, and in 1867 the shock-troops of criticisms included the *London Review*, the *Pall Mall Gazette* and the *Saturday Review*. Even in the Welsh periodicals there was an anticipation of gloom and decline. Thomas Gee in *Y Faner* saw that Welsh would have to share with English and, by February 1866, he argued that it was not the eisteddfod's main function to ensure the continuation of the language. By August 1866 Gee was arguing that Welsh was safe as the language of heaven.

From eisteddfod to eisteddfod after 1858 the messages to the Welsh people were clear: the desire to celebrate the English connection; the welcoming of the 'Progress of Britain' as an economic, industrial and imperial nation; and the feeling that Welsh was safe in the hands of the preachers, while English was the language of commerce and business. There were few who challenged these commercial, utilitarian and deferential attitudes to English. In September 1866, however, a group of Welshmen from Pontypridd, Maesteg and Aberdare organized an eisteddfod at Neath — Eisteddfod y Cymry (The Eisteddfod of the Welsh). A special tent was hired from Messrs W. Eassie of Gloucester to accommodate around 8,000 people, and many notable eisteddfodwyr attended. But the event was a dismal failure and the church journal, *Yr Haul*, and various sections of the Welsh press derided the organizers. The National Eisteddfod organizers and the anglophiles, like Hugh Owen, were convinced that the failure at Neath proved that their own eisteddfod was the genuine article. A number of funereal pieces followed in the Welsh press suggesting how the Welsh should dispose of the institution: the Dean of Bangor and the Revd Latimer Jones advocated a policy of 'killing with kindness'. The tendency, then, was for the National Eisteddfod to slide gradually into English monolingualism. A resistance to this occurred in the 1890s, and it became much more active in the 1920s and 1930s. It was not until the 1950s that the 'all Welsh rule' was finally imposed in the National Eisteddfod.

Scholars have shown that Welshmen were so shocked by the 1847 Blue Books and the ferocious condemnation of things Welsh, the religion, culture, language and morality of the people, that they turned to the Nonconformists and the chapels for leadership. The new heroes were Nonconformist journalists, preachers and Radical politicians and, in their hands, the history of Wales was transformed into Nonconformist and Radical propaganda. The new Welsh self-consciousness was expressed in the life of the chapels, as the Welsh saw themselves as the most virtuous people in Europe, the most hard-working, the most God-fearing, the best at observing the Sabbath, the most temperant, and the most deeply devoted to educational improvement. At their most Anglicized the Welsh ordinary people (*y werin*), the chapel-goers, were merely aping the Victorian middle classes. The 1840s and 1850s can be seen as a kind of rupture, a turning-away from the past and its mythology, and a massive lurch towards a new, Nonconformist nation, with its spiritual heroes and recent history. The Welsh were encouraged in their eisteddfodau to work hard, to elevate themselves, to liberate themselves from obscurity, and to wear the badges of progress, industriousness and self-improvement: the symbols of imperial Britain.

The Revival of the Established Church

The parliamentary reforms of the 1830s, the successful passage through Parliament of the Established Church Bill (1836), the Pluralities and Non-residence Bill (1836), and the Dean and Chapter Bill (1840), and the establishment of the Ecclesiastical Commissioners began to make the task of re-organizing the Church much easier. The Commissioners were empowered to finance the subdivision of large parishes and provide stipends for the new incumbents, together with a grant towards the building of a parsonage house. The legislation made possible a gradual reform of the Church by attacking the root causes of its failure in the previous centuries: pluralism and non-residence were suppressed at all levels and church resources were released for augmenting and supplementing the livings of the poor clergy, and for endowing new parishes and providing additional clergy in the expanding industrial areas. The Royal Commission on the Church of England and other religious bodies which reported in 1910 estimated that at least £3,332,385 had been expended in the four Welsh dioceses on the restoration and extension of ancient churches and the building of new churches between 1840 and 1906. This worked out at an annual rate of £35,335 from 1840 to 1874, £58,590 from 1874 to 1890, and £79,407 from 1892 to 1906.

Reform took time before it embraced the Principality and the Ecclesiastical Commissioners did little for Wales in the first ten years of their existence (1836 to 1846). The absentee Rector of

Merthyr Tydfil, for example, retained his living until his death in 1844. The large industrial parishes of Llanguick, Aberdare, Merthyr Tydfil and Bedwellty, which contained over half a million inhabitants, were served by a skeletal force of little more than fifty clergy. The Established Church, for reasons which were outlined in Chapter 4, accepted its responsibilities in these industrial communities somewhat belatedly. Only eleven new churches were built in the diocese of Llandaff before 1840, and mainly in industrial Monmouthshire. By the late 1840s, however, there were signs of activity in the dioceses. A variety of reasons account for this: the 1847 Education Report had noted that there was a complete absence of any kind of responsibility among the governing classes in Wales for the poorer classes; the Chartist crisis and the Newport insurrection had alarmed the governing élite; the European revolutions of 1848 sent shock waves across the Principality; as did the outbreaks of cholera in the period 1849–50; strikes and unrest in the industrial districts exacerbated an already tense situation in the coalfield of south Wales; and finally, the appointment of Alfred Ollivant as Bishop of Llandaff in 1849 witnessed the dawn of a new era in the Established Church in south Wales.

Within a few months of becoming Bishop of Llandaff, Alfred Ollivant made an appeal to the diocese as a whole, and he based this on a letter which had been sent to him by Thomas Williams, Archdeacon (and later Dean) of Llandaff. The Archdeacon mapped out the rugged terrain for the new bishop: the unprecedented increase in the population of the diocese and an exceptionally high rate of immigration; the loss to the clergy of nearly half of the tithe rent-charge; the inadequate provision of church accommodation, worsened by the language problem which often called for two churches in parishes rather than for bilingual services; and the necessity of creating new parishes from the old, upland, medieval parishes. Williams's pamphlet formed the basis of discussions which then took place at two public meetings held in Bridgend and Newport on 29 and 31 October 1850. The purpose of these meetings was to launch a society to further church work in the diocese, and the result was the setting up of the Llandaff Diocesan Church Extension Society with the following objectives: to maintain curates in populous districts; to erect churches and licensed places of worship; and to stimulate the supply of educated Welsh clergymen. This Society provided the leaders of the established social order with an outlet for their social concerns and a new sense of social duty. Aristocrats such as the Marquis of Bute, Lord Tredegar, Lord Windsor and Lord Dynevor, supported the Society; and the lay magistrates were represented as well by H.A. Bruce, Howel Gwyn (Neath), H.H. Vivian (Swansea), and Sir Thomas Phillips (Newport). The memories of the 1839 Chartist insurrection remained vivid in his mind when Sir Thomas wrote his book, *Wales* (1849). The same feelings about social order had been prevalent in the thoughts of the young Bishop Sumner of Llandaff in 1827 when he bade farewell to Evan Jenkins, whose new church at Dowlais he had just consecrated: 'I leave you as a missionary in the heart of Africa.'

The process of church reconstruction, which attempted to tackle the major difficulty of the size of the parishes and the often great distances between the churches and the new centres of industrial populations, involved a number of distinct, though related, areas of activity. The first was the building of new churches and this proved to be the most spectacular aspect of reconstruction. In England and Wales as a whole no fewer than 2,381 additional churches and chapels were erected with the aid of the Church Building Society. In Wales an additional 827 churches and chapels were built from 1831 to 1906. The second aspect of reconstruction was the building and provision of parsonages. Many were old thatched cottages or small farmhouses, and by the 1870s many of these were being replaced by new and often quite splendid buildings. The third aspect was the building of schools. Although the National Society existed independently of the Incorporated Building Society, both societies were closely associated. They developed a pattern of growth opposite to that of the Nonconformists, namely, the church was built first, and then the school. The Anglicans built a church and hoped to fill it, whereas the Nonconformists gathered the congregation first.

The 1851 census of religious worship gives us a fairly accurate picture of the chronology of church building for the whole of England and Wales. It would seem that some 500 new churches were built in the decades from 1800 to 1830, and 2,000 from 1830 to 1850. This was an enormous increase, but it conceals intriguing and varying rates of growth, for there was an impressive acceleration in the growth-rate: from 1801 to 1811 some five or six churches per annum were built; nearly ten per annum in the years 1811–21; and nearly twenty-eight per annum in the decade 1821–31. In the fourth decade of the century came the giant step forward with an average of sixty-seven churches per annum being built; and in the fifth decade 120 per annum. The peaks of church building came in the central decades of the century. From 1840 to 1876 in England and Wales, the Anglicans built 1,727 new churches and rebuilt or restored some 7,144 old churches. The chronology of church building reflected the social and economic oscillations at a national level in these central decades from 1830 to 1870. Of the social forces, the most relentless was population change. There were three aspects of this which were important. First, there was the increase in population. It more than doubled in England and Wales between the censuses from 1811 to the 1870s; it grew from 10 million in 1811 to 22.7 million in 1871. By 1881 it was almost 26 million. In Wales the increase was from 587,000 in 1811 to 1,572,000 in 1881. The increased population required increased provision. Secondly, the increase occurred at varying speeds and at different times. In Wales there were important differences and variations in the rate of increase in each decade: the rate was high up to 1841, then fell suddenly to only a half of what it had been in the early decades, and rose sharply in 1871–81. Thirdly, we should remember that there were rapid changes in population in the rural counties as well as in the mining and manufacturing regions. The population in the rural and urban areas was mobile, and there were rapid and often unpredictable fluctuations.

A parliamentary return for 1876 records the total number of churches built and restored in Wales since 1840 as 637, at a cost of £318,362. The money was levied from two main sources, from central funds and the localities themselves. The central sources of possible assistance consisted of the Church Building Commissioners (who were taken over, after 1866–7, by the Ecclesiastical Commission), and the Incorporated Church Building Society. The pattern of financing and the relative share that came from the Commissioners and the Society changed from 1830 onwards. From 1800 to 1830 the proportion of monies coming from the public sources was around 40 per cent. Between 1830 and 1851 public grants rarely exceeded 8 per cent. During the period from 1840 to 1852, fourteen churches were built in Wales at a total cost of £38,655, of which £31,064, or 80 per cent was raised in Wales itself. Six of the twelve churches were in the diocese of St Asaph, costing a total of £15,092, of which £12,372, or 82 per cent, was collected from the parishes themselves.

The Incorporated Church Building Society was the contemporary of the Church Building Commissioners, but its brief was to assist in the provision of church-rooms in places which fell outside the scope of the first of the Church Building Acts, in parishes with a population of less than 4,000. The Society was also concerned with restoration, repairing, and the enlargement of existing churches. The dioceses of St Asaph and Llandaff received on average higher grants because they embraced the heavily industrialized parts of Wales. The Society also took seriously its obligations to assist in implementing, 'the Act for making better provision for the Spiritual Care of Populous Parishes' (1843). By this Act the Ecclesiastical Commissioners were given powers similar to those of the Church Building Commissioners to divide parishes. However, while the latter could only assign new parishes to new churches, the Ecclesiastical Commissioners could assign new districts to incumbents, and require the latter to hold services in licensed places until the church was built.

In the populous diocese of Llandaff the new bishop of 1850 did not repeat the mistakes of his predecessors and wait until a complete church was built in a given area before beginning services there. His register shows that he licensed temporary buildings for worship. Between 1849 and 1870 he licensed about sixty rooms and buildings for public services: the inhabitants of Hirwaun worshipped in a damp schoolroom; while the people of Cwmaman and Aberdare used a wet British schoolroom. Temporary structures were often erected or premises rented in a frantic effort to accommodate the industrial immigrants. Bishop Lewis's registers from 1883–1905 exhibited the same patterns as those displayed in Ollivant's. Lewis's episcopate coincided with the opening-up of the Rhondda valleys and the great developments in deep coal-mining. When he commenced his episcopate in 1883 the funds of the Llandaff Diocesan Church Extension Society were almost exhausted, and one of his first acts was to inaugurate the 'Bishop of Llandaff's Fund'. By 1893, £38,022 had been received or promised and, by the end of Lewis's episcopate in 1905, 201 projects had been started. Again, only a small proportion of the expenditure on new buildings emanated from the Llandaff Diocesan Church Extension Society. Much of the money was raised locally in the parishes.

The size of the ancient parishes and the distance of their churches from the new centres of population were not the only difficulties faced by the Established Church. The primary problem to be surmounted was the poverty of the mass of the population in a social structure which contained few powerful rich and resident gentry families. If the parishes lacked wealthy gentry families they were forced to adopt other methods of raising the necessary funds, such as levying the church rates. In the industrial areas such recourse was to the local industrialists. Monmouthshire had fared better from the ironmasters than Glamorgan, but, in the second half of the nineteenth century, the coalowners did more for Glamorgan than for Monmouth-shire.

Another difficulty confronting the Church was the number and the quality of the clergy. In 1850 there were about 700 clergy in Wales; by 1910 there were 1,543 clergy ministering in 1,014 parishes with 1,527 churches. Church historians have tended to argue that the Church faced its worst problems in the coalfield of south Wales and in the diocese of Bangor, where the language difficulty was most pronounced. The provision of competent clergy was, therefore, related to the question of language. The Established Church had to find clergy to serve the Welsh population of the new parishes; whereas the Non-conformists had the reverse problem of having to make provision for an Anglicized population. In the diocese of Llandaff, the Diocesan Church Extension Society more than doubled the number of clergy ministering in the industrial parishes to 201 in the two decades after 1850. This was achieved largely as a result of improvements in the provision for clerical education. There was no lack of candidates for the ministry, as Bishop Ollivant made clear in his first visitation charge in 1851. One of the serious problems was that they were too poor to bear the expenses of education. Since the eighteenth century most of the candidates for holy Orders had gone either to Oxford or Cambridge, or to divinity schools attached to the old grammar schools at Usk, Abergavenny and Cowbridge. Ollivant felt that the scheme was inadequate, as was also the provision made by St David's College, Lampeter, in the case of ordinands who were given a three-year course without a grammar-school training. Ollivant insisted increasingly on a pre-college training for the less academically gifted, followed by a period of residence in St David's College, Lampeter. The north Wales dioceses had depended on Ruthin School, St Aidan's College, Birkenhead, and St Bee's College, Cumberland, and Lampeter ordinands did not establish a firm footing in north Wales until a generation or so after they were manning the south Wales parishes.

Non-resident clergy, like G.W. Mabers who had been the non-resident Rector of Merthyr Tydfil, slowly began to give way to a different type of parish priest. John Griffith was sent to Aberdare in 1846, and thence to Merthyr Tydfil, and Henry Thomas Edwards went to Aberdare, Caernarfon, and thence became Dean of Bangor. These two clergymen injected new life into their parishes and represented, respectively, the evangelical and high-church wings of the Church. In the south Wales parishes the clergy began to take an active role in the community from the 1850s onwards. The first phase of change in the industrial districts had been from about 1838 to 1855, when the agencies of the Church were gradually being transformed. A second phase from 1856 to about 1866 saw the functions of the Church broadened to encompass a strong evangelical commitment to social and pastoral work in the community. One of the first symptoms of the active involvement and leadership of the clergy in the social life of the industrial parishes of south Wales was the increased number of clergy who sat regularly on the magistrates' benches from the 1840s onwards. At one time as many as 20 per cent of the magistrates in south Wales were clergymen. They were never popular with the Nonconformists, but they saw for themselves at first hand the crime, squalor and poverty of the industrial and rural communities.

The clergy performed other pastoral and social functions. In the severe winter of 1860, when thousands were unemployed and the future of the great iron-producing complex of Cyfarthfa, Dowlais, Penydarren and the growing ports of Cardiff and Newport, seemed in jeopardy, John Griffith, Rector of Merthyr Tydfil, and Canon Leigh Morgan of St Mary's, Cardiff, organized soup kitchens and clothing clubs for the poor. During the cholera outbreaks of 1849, 1854 and 1866 some clergy gave outstanding service to their communities. When there were colliery disasters local clergy often organized relief funds, for example, after the Cymmer disaster of 1856 when 114 men lost their lives and in 1861 when 138 were killed. The clergy were also actively involved in the movement to provide schools and to spread literacy throughout the industrial settlements. The Sunday school in the 1850s and 1860s became an important part of church life, and by 1870 the Church in south Wales claimed to have 15,000 Sunday scholars enrolled. In addition, they organized adult classes and, by 1866, there were as many as 1,500 adults enrolled by the Church in Llandaff in night classes.

By 1865 not only had the role and functions of the clergy changed, but so had their social status. In 1870 one-third of the clergy in the south Wales dioceses had been ordained as literates and had received no formal training; a further one-third were the products of St David's College, Lampeter. In 1850 the clergy could be regarded as an extension of the county and social order, and many had given evidence to the 1847 Education Commissioners. By 1860 there were signs of a change in outlook as some of the clergy became more sympathetic to the plight of the workers and their families. By the depressed years of the early 1870s many of the clergy were more firmly on the side of the miners and ironworkers. In 1875 the Revd John Griffith, Rector of Merthyr, was firmly in support of the parishioners when the South Wales Coal Owners' Association attempted to destroy the newly-formed Amalgamated Association of Miners in a prolonged strike over a reduction in wages. By 1870 a whole generation of clergy had collected a wealth of experience from their pastoral work in the front-line of the coalfield.

By the 1870s, however, the evangelical crusade was beginning to lose its sense of purpose and much of its impact. The deaths of E.P. Richards and Sir Thomas Phillips in 1867, and the involvement of H.A. Bruce in national politics, robbed the Llandaff Diocesan Church Extension Society of its most able members. The conversion of the Marquis of Bute to Roman Catholicism deprived the Church of one of its richest benefactors. In the late 1860s Bishop Ollivant of Llandaff, the zealous and vigorous pioneer of reform, was moving in a more conservative direction and even became opposed to the licensing of lay readers. By 1868 he was an aged and reactionary Tory. Ritualism had produced an uproar in the diocese of Llandaff in the late 1860s and Ollivant had compromised on the issue. In addition, some clerics like the indefatigable Rector of Merthyr, John Griffith, had begun to challenge the episcopal administration on such matters as ritualism, clerical standards, and the education and appointment of the clergy. Finally, the evangelical movement in the Church was being challenged by a whole cluster of secular forces, including the rise of unions and the diffusion of democratic ideals.

Revivals and Popular Religion

A revival which broke out along the American frontier in 1857 soon spread to Welsh settlements, and news of this reached the homeland by 1858. The revival began at Yr Hen Gapel, Tre'r-ddôl in Cardiganshire in that year and it soon spread to south Wales. The temperance campaigners had paved the way for a spiritual renewal and, in 1858, Aberystwyth had received a visit from J.B. Gough, the American temperance lecturer. In Bethesda, Caernarfonshire, no less than twelve pubs had been closed because of lack of custom, and at Tregaron a large quantity of home-brewed beer was thrown unceremoniously into the river. The revival was warmly received in the slate and colliery districts of the south, and in the lead-mining districts of mid Wales, where men worked under a common sense of danger. In the industrial township of Aberdare nineteen chapels were built or enlarged in the parish in the period from 1859 to 1862 and the revival was often regarded as a powerful visitation: 'Something like a heavy shower fell upon us. The large congregation was bathed in tears. Many a hard sinner was melted even to bitter weeping for his sad condition.' In Aberdare there were indubitably a number of social sources of revival: the harsh realities of underground work and the perpetual fear of death and injury were potent factors; there were rumours of an impending cholera epidemic in 1859; a trade depression following the end of the Crimean War in 1856 had serious repercussions on industry in the town; a 20 per cent fall in wages in the Crawshay Ironworks and a 15 per cent fall in colliers' wages made the situation much worse; and finally, in 1859 a series of strikes broke out in the Aberdare Valley, which were criticized by the Nonconformist ministers. The strikers were disillusioned by the open support given to the employers by these ministers who, in turn, were worried by the strike leaders' appeals to ignore the forces of religion. It probably occurred to the clergy that one way of nullifying working-class antipathy was by means of a religious revival.

There had been revival meetings in the Aberdare area early in 1858, before there were stirrings in Cardiganshire, and one of the chief protagonists of this was the coalowner, David Davies, Maesyffynnon, who employed several thousand men at his Blaengwawr and Aberaman pits. He had personally organized a number of underground and chapel prayer meetings which he and his workmen attended. Davies was an active Wesleyan and he had helped to finance and build a number of chapels. The period from 1858 to 1860 saw other attempts by Nonconformist leaders and local employers to influence working-class opinion. During the depression in the 1860s J.B. Gough made a number of lecture tours of the area. At Aberdare, colliery owners were almost universally Nonconformist and prominent men in their denominations, and they encouraged the spread of the revival, as did the emerging middle classes of the neighbourhood, as a way of preserving social stability. At Aberdare, as in many of the industrial communities, the revival was a force for religious conservatism, and its appeal lay not in its radicalism but in its ability to recreate the religion of the past.

The year 1859 had marked a climax in the tradition of popular religion. After the 1870s there emerged an organized evangelical mission with charismatic leaders and an enlarged scale of operations. Moody and Sankey are associated with this phase and visited Wales in the years after 1875. The Salvation Army organized its groups of 'Halleluyah lasses' to tour south Wales, and Welsh-speaking members of the Army were selected for these special operations. In February 1879, one of the Army's enthusiastic 'lasses', Kate Shepherd, organized special meetings for night workmen, and the revival spread to Mountain Ash, Dowlais, Merthyr, Nant-y-glo and Tredegar. After 1859 there was a distinct change from revivals to revivalism, as new, professional revivalists captured the heart of the movement. Modern revivalists were forced to appeal to the middle and upper classes for financial support and this coloured their approach to the lower classes. Denominations came to reflect, either in their authority systems or in their physical appearance, the wishes of the stable and rising economic and social groups. Religion itself was becoming institutionalized as the self-help philosophy and the concepts of industriousness and social progress took a firm grip of the religious denominations.

The last great revival was that of 1904–5. In 1903 the Calvinistic Methodists of south Cardiganshire had set out to recapture the spiritual feelings of 1859 and a number of meetings were subsequently arranged in Cardiganshire in which young people's meetings were promoted. One of those to be affected was Evan Roberts, a young man studying at Newcastle Emlyn Grammar School. In October 1904 he returned to Loughor to initiate a series of young people's meetings at Moriah Calvinistic Methodist Chapel. From there he travelled all over south Wales to Aberdare, Bridgend, Mountain Ash, and the Swansea and Neath valleys. He stayed at Merthyr for three weeks, and the number of converts in south Wales were estimated at 34,000 by January 1905. The 1904–5 revival was largely a young people's revival: there was an emphasis on prayer and on the beauty of congregational singing; there was to be no formalism in church services and short addresses instead of long sermons; and the overall theological emphasis was on the love of God and a total commitment to Christ. The revivalist, Evan Roberts, visited north Wales and Liverpool, but with little success. It is estimated that he made 7,370 converts in the north, whereas the south had proved to be more fertile ground with 76,566 converts by March 1905. Many areas remained untouched by the revival, such as Flintshire and Montgomeryshire in the north, and Monmouthshire and Pembrokeshire in the south. The chapel leaders in many areas were often positively hostile to the awakening; and, in Roberts's own chapel, the minister resigned. By the midsummer of 1905 the revival was waning, and criticisms were mounting, especially from among those who emphasized the primacy of education. The Revd Peter Price of Dowlais, BA (Hons.) Cambridge to boot, lampooned the revival and urged a gospel of modernism.

In a sense the 1904–5 revival had been a clear attempt to reverse the structure of chapel authority, to ignore ministerial guidance and break with tradition. It was an attempt to put the laity, and especially the young people, in charge of the spiritual renaissance. But it reflected also the social conditions of 1904–5 and a winter of discontent: by December 1904, the average wage of the south Wales miner was 15 per cent below that of 1900; non-unionism was divisive and at Llwydcoed the colliery office was blown up during a dispute among workmen over this issue; disease had struck yet another devastating blow with cholera deaths at Aberdare in 1904, and 300 cases of typhoid at Trealaw and Ystrad. The revival was the last of its kind, and it heralded the decline of organized religion in the Principality.

Challenges to Organized Religion

In the new industrial communities all the denominations, church and chapel, faced the same basic social difficulties, even though they differed from one another in their apprehension of the problems. The denominations had been one instrument in the hands of a people desperately trying to adapt to their environment. But as the century advanced, and as the church and the chapel faced rapid changes towards its end, so they were found wanting and inadequate in many ways. Nonconformity had been antagonistic to the early workers' unions and benefit societies, and in 1840 the Methodists condemned trade unions at their Tredegar Sasiwn (association). Welsh Nonconformity would not involve itself in the working-class movements in the industrial society and, although there was an uneasy peace between organized religion and such union leaders as Mabon (William Abraham) in the 1870s and 1880s, after 1898, when the new unionism appeared, a further breach opened between the two parties.

An additional challenge arose with the linguistic changes. Welshmen had believed that the success of religion among the common people could be explained by the continued existence of the Welsh language. The structure, morality and theology of Welsh religion all appeared to depend upon the existence of the language, and it is not hard to accept that many of those industrial and rural communities seemed to believe that Welsh was the language of heaven. But the language frontier was on the move continuously throughout the century, and largely as a result of industrialization. The latter involved not only the obvious introduction of industry, with concomitant changes in population levels; but it entailed also changes in the modes of production, in attitudes of mind and in values. English was the language of business, management and commercial transactions. Welsh was the language of labour, religion and the arts. In the decades after 1871, immigration into Glamorgan and Monmouthshire continued unabated, but with increasing numbers coming from the English counties: in Glamorgan, of the net absorption during the ten years from 1881 to 1891 of 76,200, 63 per cent came from the non-border English counties, and this percentage increased during 1901–11. The changing patterns of migration into the industrial areas of Glamorgan and Monmouthshire led to a decline in the numbers of those who spoke Welsh. In 1901, 59 per cent of the Aberdare district was Welsh speaking, whereas by 1911 the figure had fallen to 55 per cent. Ebbw Vale experienced an even greater fall from 21 per cent to 12 per cent, while the Rhondda valleys witnessed a reduction from 64 per cent to 55 per cent in the number of Welsh speakers. Undeniably, this process attacked the social basis of organized religion in the last quarter of the century.

The challenge of natural science and the impact of historical criticism on the Bible became far more significant towards the second half of the century. But the content of Welsh Calvinistic theology remained unchanged in the face of these challenges. Welsh preachers drew their theology from another age and tried to retain their biblical exegesis intact. Most of the leaders of Welsh Nonconformity, with notable exceptions such as Dr Lewis Edwards, remained blissfully unaware of, or indifferent to, the new learning that was emerging from continental Europe. A different story evolves in the late 1880s when Dr Thomas Charles Edwards, the first principal of the University College of Wales, Aberystwyth, and the son of Dr Lewis Edwards, gave an address on, 'Religious Thought in Wales'

(1888), to the Pan-Presbyterian Council in London. He believed that, at last, religious thought in Wales was adumbrating the new theology circulating in England, Scotland and on the Continent. Those who had been rescued from the groove of narrow fundamentalism had been saved by literature, according to Dr Edwards. He displayed the way in which a journal such as *Y Traethodydd*, which had been founded by his father, had introduced younger readers to the works of Coleridge, Augustine, Kant and Hegel. By the 1880s there were clear indications of the conceptual and theological challenges that organized religion would have to meet.

Nonconformity had triumphed in the early and middle part of the century largely for the reason that it was not 'wholly' religious. It had brought all kinds of activities, cultural, theological and recreational under the umbrella of religion, and under the chapel and vestry roof. Music, drama, poetry, and even sport, had no separate existence as the chapels assumed an ever-growing cultural role. After 1850 the chapels regarded themselves as the custodians of Welsh life, and Welsh culture was reshaped in the mould of denominationalism. Between 1850 and 1900 the chapels developed their choirs, orchestras, drama groups, literary societies, temperance groups, bands of hope, and innumerable eisteddfodau. This enormous expansion in the cultural role of the chapel seemed to create a spiritual and intellectual confusion of aims and purposes; and from the 1870s onwards there were doubts and confusions in the soul of Welsh Nonconformity over theology, and over its relationship with the secular world. As the chapels experienced their crisis of confidence, so the new secularism became more self-conscious and militant. After the 1870s, with the expansion of the so-called secular state, education was gradually wrenched out of the chapels' grip, as were many of the cultural activities which they had so proudly fostered. The eisteddfodau, brass bands and orchestras were no longer meeting in the chapels, as civic buildings, public institutes, and working men's halls were set up in open competition.

In the second half of the century the leadership of Welsh Nonconformity gradually underwent a change. The transition from the iron to the coal industry had a marked effect on the chapels. A new breed of men assumed the leadership of the pits and the chapels. They were men who had often begun as miners, worked their way up the colliery ladder, and had ultimately become colliery managers. Beneath them were the under-managers, foremen, subcontractors, colliery winders and firemen; and it was these who gradually permeated the *sêt fawr* (the deacons' 'big seat') from the 1860s onwards and who, together with the tradesmen and shopkeepers, dominated the social hierarchy of the chapels. This process weakened the community feeling and the social cohesion that had existed within the denominations. There was an erosion of contact between the chapels and their communities, and between the middle-class big seat and the ordinary member.

This cleavage had serious repercussions from the 1880s onwards as organized religion failed to give a social leadership in the new coal communities. The new middle-class leaders of the denominations were quite insensitive to the social problems of the period and adhered to the old issues of rural Wales. Nonconformity seemed far more concerned with its civil and political rights *vis-à-vis* the Church, than it did with the rights of an industrial work-force. During the closing decades of the century Welsh Nonconformity through its political agency, the Liberal Party, paid more attention to the question of dis-establishment than to the pains and problems of industrial society. But the industrial communities were fast-changing and becoming radicalized and Anglicized, as the new wave of immigrants swept into the coalfield. Trade unions made great advances in the coalfields in the years after 1890, and mainly under English leadership. Political and industrial leadership was passing into the hands of Keir Hardie, William Brace, Vernon Hartshorn and Frank Hodges and, by the turn of the century, the political meetings and miners' lodges were being conducted almost wholly in English.

SUGGESTED READING

E.T. Davies, *Religion in the Industrial Revolution in South Wales* (Cardiff, 1965).

E.T. Davies, *Religion and Society in the Nineteenth Century* (Llandybie, 1981).

H.T. Edwards, *Gŵyl Gwalia: Yr Eisteddfod Genedlaethol yn Oes Aur Victoria, 1858–1868* (Llandysul, 1981).

R. Brinley Jones (ed.), *Anatomy of Wales* (Glamorgan, 1971).

I.G. Jones, *Explorations and Explanations* (Llandysul, 1981).

I.G. Jones, *Communities* (Llandysul, 1987).

W.R. Lambert, *Drink and Sobriety in Victorian Wales, c.1820–c.1895* (Cardiff, 1984).

P. Morgan and D. Thomas, *Wales: The Shaping of a Nation* (London, 1984).

T.J. Morgan, *Diwylliant Gwerin* (Llandysul, 1972).

Articles:

G.P. Ambrose, 'The Aberdare Background to the South Wales Choral Union'; *Glamorgan Historian*, 9 (1973).

E.T. Davies, 'The Education of the Clergy in the Diocese of Llandaff, 1750–1866', *J.H.S. Ch. in W.*, XXVI (1979).

W.R. Lambert, 'Some Working Class Attitudes towards Organized Religion in Nineteenth-Century Wales', *Llafur*, 2, no. 1 (1976).

W.R. Lambert, 'Drink and Work-Discipline in Industrial South Wales, c.1800–1870', *W.H.R.*, 7(1974–5).

W.D. Wills, 'The Clergy in Society in Mid-Victorian South Wales', *J.H.S. Ch. in W.*, XXIV (1974).

W.D. Wills, 'The Established Church in the Diocese of Llandaff, 1850–1870', *W.H.R.*, 4 (1968–9).

11. Education and Society 1850–1880

THE years from 1847 to 1880 formed a period of transition, activity and achievements in the field of elementary education. There was a gradual transformation from a state of educational, political and social destitution to a new epoch of national confidence. Graham's Factory Bill of 1843 was a landmark in Welsh educational life, and its clauses had angered the Nonconformist denominations throughout England and Wales. It had promoted the growth of a Voluntaryist and anti-State-aid stance among the Dissenters and Nonconformist congregations. The Blue Books of 1847 had roused the Nonconformists from their political slumbers and gone a long way towards removing the denominational barriers. Of the many factors which would determine the future pattern of education, the influence of religion was probably one of the most powerful. The 1840s had effectively cemented and consolidated the relationship between religion and education, and this marriage would be one of the determinants of modern educational theory and practice. In this chapter we shall continue to examine that relationship and consider the contributions of the educational societies, the work of the religious denominations, the activities of the employers, the impact of the 1870 Education Act, and the changes in higher education.

The British Schools

Although a few British schools had been established in south Wales during the first half of the nineteenth century, the significant expansion had occurred in north Wales, especially in the 1840s. In the south, attempts to set up schools had been hampered by the Voluntaryists who refused to accept State aid. The committee of the British and Foreign School Society had steered well away from the Voluntaryists and had taken no steps to appoint an agent in the south. In 1853 there were only fourteen British schools in south Wales, with approximately 1,500 children receiving instruction. The Nonconformists had been quite busy setting up small schools along voluntary principles in the years immediately after the 1847 Reports. But these schools, which were largely under the supervision of the recently-formed South Wales Education Committee, were dying out by 1853. One important reason for this was that Voluntaryism was gradually losing its initial vigour, and the violent reactions to the 1847 Reports were dying down. Many Nonconformists were beginning to appreciate that the British schools offered unsectarian schooling. The collapse of the Voluntary Normal School at Swansea in 1851 sealed the gradual demise of Voluntaryism as an educational movement in the southern counties.

It was at this time that a number of prominent Nonconformists urged the British Society to take more positive action, especially in the industrial valleys of the south. The Society in its Annual Report of 1853 responded to these overtures and, on the recommendation of the indefatigable Hugh Owen, it appointed Revd William Roberts (Nefydd) of Blaina, Monmouthshire, as the agent for south Wales for an experimental period of twelve months, from 1 December 1853 at a salary of £60 per annum. Nefydd devoted himself to the Society's work for sixteen days each month, and he remained agent for ten years. During his period of office he kept a journal of his work and this has provided researchers with a fascinating account of school provision and educational details in mid-century.

During his period as agent for the British Society, Nefydd built up a close working relationship with Hugh Owen, and with one of the best school inspectors of the era, Joseph Bowstead. Owen, in particular, encouraged and advised Nefydd in his new job, and organized training sessions for him in the Society's school at Borough Road, London. Nefydd proved to be a receptive student and set about establishing work committees in each of the south Wales counties. He concentrated his campaign in the counties of Glamorgan and Monmouth, and thence pushed westwards into Carmarthen, Pembroke and Cardiganshire. Within a week of returning home from London, Nefydd had despatched thirty-two letters to various parts of the south.

Over the years he convened meetings and committees all over the southern counties, but perhaps none was as important as the first which was attended by Nonconformists from all parts of south Wales. The Nonconformist leaders seemed intent on making up for lost time and the delegates agreed that the newly-appointed secretary should make every effort to ensure that a pamphlet be produced, containing information in English and Welsh on the Society's activities and the government funds available. Hugh Owen came down to south Wales in the first year of Nefydd's agency, and they journeyed from village to village in the southern counties. On their perambulations they encountered delays and frustrations in many areas. At Llwyndafydd, Cardiganshire, they discovered a school which had been started six or seven years earlier under the auspices of the Cambrian Education Society, and with which Hugh Owen had been associated. The supporters of the school had waited from 1847 to 1855 for Hugh Owen to open the building and, in so doing, they had sacrificed their children's schooling. Incidents such as this were typical of the period and they were sharp reminders to Owen and Nefydd of the sort of problems which militated against their Society's success.

On 1 December 1854, Hugh Owen attended an important conference at the Temperance Hall, Merthyr Tydfil, to establish a society that would act as an auxiliary of the British and Foreign School Society in south Wales. The Society became known as the South Wales British Schools' Association, and the conference was again well attended by ministers and laymen from Monmouth, Brecon and Glamorgan. Owen stressed the urgent need for elementary education in the industrial valleys and he presented a statistical picture of school provision in Wales. He estimated that the number of children in Wales attending schools of all descriptions was 103,247; whereas at least 145,392 ought to have been receiving instruction in day schools, according to his calculations based on the recent census. Armed with these figures he urged his audience to apply for the government grants, which were now available.

In the years after 1853 the British school movement and its advocates found an enthusiastic supporter in Joseph Bowstead. In 1855 he completed a report on the state of education in south Wales. He focused on Glamorgan and Monmouth and observed a deplorable lack of non-denominational schools in a strongly Nonconformist region. He was convinced that the British schools were the best possible institutions to fill this gap and he urged Welshmen to grasp the nettle and set up such schools. There were some churchmen who bitterly resented these exhortations and Bishop Connop Thirlwall of St David's diocese voiced his criticisms in no uncertain terms. The ensuing correspondence between Bowstead and Bishop Thirlwall lasted for many years.

Denominational rivalry of this kind was one test of Nefydd's abilities as an agent of school provision. The Voluntaryist, anti-State-aid cause was a further hindrance to the development of the British school movement. Even though Voluntaryism had lost much of its edge by the middle 1850s, it could still thwart the Society's supporters. At Penmain in Monmouthshire a voluntary school had been closed so as to prevent it from accepting government grants. At Mynyddislwyn the objections to government aid were robust enough to ensure that government inspectors and the like would not be admitted to the school, and this inscription was placed on the outside of the school: NON DELIGATUS ADMITITUR!

After the Revd David Rees, Llanelli, set aside his objections to State aid in 1853, there was a steady flow of supporters away from the Voluntaryist cause. The British schools became more familiar in the south, and many of the works' schools also adopted their non-sectarian principles. H.A. Bruce, MP for Merthyr Tydfil from 1852 to 1868, and a devout churchman, decided that his schools should sever their connections with the National Society and transfer their allegiance to the British and Foreign School Society.

Nefydd faced many other problems during his period as agent for the Society: finding suitable freehold sites for the schools was frequently difficult, for many of the Anglican landowners were reluctant to render assistance to the Nonconformists; another major problem was the shortage of qualified teachers, and as the number of schools multiplied, so the dearth of manpower became more acute; non-attendance and irregular attendance at schools were perennial evils throughout England and Wales.

After a number of very successful years in the post, Nefydd began to tire as some of these problems seemed intractable in some areas. From 1853 to 1860, 102 British schools had been set up in the southern counties, with provision for 24,000 children. But as the 1860s dawned, the pace of improvement slackened, and from 1861 to 1862 only five new schools were opened. Nefydd was aware of the problem and responded to the Society's concern by outlining his successes as part-time agent for ten years. Eventually he was compelled to relinquish his post to David Williams, Headmaster of the Copperworks' School, Llanelli.

Church Schools

If the Nonconformists could be accused of building too many chapels in the nineteenth century, the Church could probably claim that it had built too many schools in Wales. The Church had provided 230 primary schools by the year 1826, and 336 by 1831. In the year of the famous Education Report there were 1,009 church schools in Wales, and there are those who would argue that the Church has not been given sufficient credit for its contribution to primary and elementary education. Social and economic discontent, in the form of Chartism and the Rebecca Riots, triggered the mechanism by which the Church began to campaign for enhanced school provision in the years after 1838. The 1851 census (Education) showed the remarkable fruits of those labours and Anglican schools provided instruction for 11,000 children between the ages of three and ten years within Wales. This meant that the Church was providing for one-third of the total number of children. The Sunday schools were just as important in the educational armoury of the Anglican Church, as is illustrated by the 1851 census figures given in Table 11.1.

The years after 1850 witnessed a revival in the fortunes of the Established Church, and nowhere was this more apparent than in the diocese of Llandaff. The governing classes in the south Wales coalfield began to assert themselves in this mid-century period, and a number of factors would explain their sudden burst of activity: the Education Report of 1847 had spurred them into action; the Chartist crisis had made a deep impression on the Church and the governing groups; the 1848 revolutions in Europe sent shock-waves across the Principality; as did the horrific effects of a cholera epidemic in 1849–50; there were

Education and Society

Table 11.1   Sunday School Attendance in 1851
(South Wales)

Registration district	Church of England		All other denominations	
	No. of schools	*Attendance*	*No. of schools*	*Attendance*
Chepstow	19	946	13	762
Monmouth	27	1,899	19	1,207
Abergavenny	19	854	75	11,047
Pontypool	11	931	43	4,833
Newport	16	1,072	61	5,331
Cardiff	22	1,189	53	4,606
Merthyr Tydfil	13	1,279	84	14,437
Bridgend	7	297	63	4,643
Neath	13	920	95	10,215
Swansea	19	1,326	62	6,651
TOTALS:	166	10,713	568	63,732

strikes in various centres across the south Wales coalfield; and
the appointment of new, energetic leaders in the Church was felt
in most of the Welsh dioceses. Alfred Ollivant was entrusted
with the diocese of Llandaff in 1849, and this scholarly and able
administrator soon set about forming the Diocesan Church
Extension Society. This was the embryo from which the
Llandaff Diocesan Board of Education grew, and this latter
association provided additional schools and teachers in the
1850s and 1860s, as the following figures show:

	GLAMORGAN	MONMOUTHSHIRE
	Number of schools	*Number of schools*
1851	48	56
1868	112	97

Under Ollivant, the church's educational policy became
broader, and almost non-denominational.

The Church also tried to provide leisure-time activities for the
working classes. A policy of adult education gradually evolved
and night-schools were set up in the industrial zones. In 1851
there were twenty-three schools in Llandaff with 641 adults
enrolled; and by 1866 the Church claimed that 1,457 adults

were registered for night classes. During the 1850s there seemed to be few disputes of any real importance between the Established Church and the Nonconformists, as both endeavoured to restore order to the industrial areas and co-operated on such matters as temperance and education. All the denominations were sensitive to the problems of the new and rapidly expanding society, and a close and harmonious relationship emerged among them as they attempted to solve these problems. In a sense, religion in these years became social, educational, and almost non-doctrinal. The dominant theme seemed to be the Victorian, evangelical desire to improve society.

The Works' Schools

The Ironworks' Schools

It was in the twenty-year period after 1840 that the greatest expansion of these schools occurred. Over thirty were established by the large iron companies in the period from 1840 to 1860. Some were set up in the highly populated industrial districts of Monmouthshire, and the school promoted by the Rhymney Iron Company in 1843 was envisaged as part of a much more elaborate scheme for the whole town. This particular school, affiliated to the National Society, was considered superior to the British schools in the area. In 1858 a new National school was built at a cost of over £3,000, and part of the building accommodated a library and a scientific institution. In the Sirhowy Valley, Samuel Homfray had operated schools in the Town Hall at Tredegar in 1838, and in 1841 the schools were under the guidance of the National Society. The Tredegar Ironworks' Schools were regarded as some of the best in the industrial districts of Monmouthshire. They were well equipped and sectioned into departments for boys, girls, and infants.

In the old parish of Aberystruth, on the border of Monmouthshire and Breconshire, were the large iron-smelting centres of Blaina and Nant-y-glo. By 1846 the parish population had increased to 12,000, with ten day schools and eighteen Sunday schools in operation. But the largest schools were the Nantyglo and Blaina Ironworks' schools. Blaina was the home of the Revd William Roberts, (Nefydd), the first part-time agent of the

British and Foreign School Society in south Wales. There were two ironworks' schools in Blaina and both were associated with the British Society. These schools ranked alongside the Hafod and Llanelli copperworks' schools, and they provided training for pupil-teachers in Monmouthshire.

In Glamorgan, the schools were likewise confined to the main industrial regions. Most of these industrial areas had few educational facilities in the year of the great Report of 1847. In Merthyr Tydfil no provision would seem to have been made for the children of those men employed at the Cyfarthfa, Plymouth and Penydarren works. In 1849 another report highlighted the educational deficiencies of the area and noted the urgent need for more schools in the iron metropolis. By 1848 Crawshay had kept his promise to the Assistant Commissioner of 1846 and erected the Cyfarthfa Works' School on the principles of the National Society. The Plymouth Ironworks' School was probably opened in 1850, and the Penydarren in 1852; but little is actually known about these.

Meanwhile, Sir Josiah John Guest's schools at Dowlais were making remarkable progress and were becoming the best of their kind in Wales, if not in the whole of Britain. It was during the second phase of the development of the Dowlais schools, from 1844 to 1855, that the ambitious 'educational scheme' was evolved. Although Sir John Guest was the instigator of the movement to establish day schools in Dowlais, it was his wife, Lady Charlotte Guest, who eventually took the initiative in promoting the enlargement of the schools, and creating a more liberal and balanced curriculum within the Dowlais schools. She aimed at establishing an educational ladder, a progressive system from the infant to the adult stage. The Guest educational scheme had a carefully devised fourfold graduation: infants' schools, junior and senior day schools, adolescent evening schools, and adult day and evening schools. The average daily attendances for each department in this remarkable scheme on 12 February 1849 are shown in Table 11.2.

In October 1850, the Revd H. Longueville Jones, HMI, compiled a complete list of attendances for all the schools in the scheme, and the highest total attendance was 1,141 on 15 October. The lowest was 647 on 28 October, but this excluded evening schools. In 1865, the total attendances, excluding

Table 11.2

Adult and adolescent		
Male upper evening school	23	
Male lower evening school	93	
Female lower evening school	127	243
Junior and senior		
Boys' upper school	45	
Boys' lower school	142	
Girls' day school	112	299
Infants'		
Dowlais infants	140	
Gwernllwyn infants	145	
Gellifaelog infants	131	
Banwen infants	51	467
	TOTAL:	1,009

evening schools, had reached 2,156. The Inspectors' Reports for 1850 and subsequent years eulogize the Dowlais schools for their resources, teaching commitment and liberal curricula. Criticisms, sometimes quite severe, were reserved for the worsening accommodation problems. By 1854 it had become obvious that new extensions were required for the boys' and girls' departments.

Sir John died in 1852, but Lady Charlotte continued with her work and she found that her new works' manager, George T. Clark, shared her enthusiasm for, and commitment to, the schools. By 1855 new schools had been prepared, and these launched the third, and possibly the most successful stage of the Dowlais schools, which lasted until 1892. The costs of the new schools amounted to £20,000, and were borne by the Dowlais Iron Company. After 1855 the schools were officially placed under government inspection and they became eligible for grants. Also, the schools were transferred from the National system to the British and Foreign School Society's care. During this third, unsectarian phase, the schools at Dowlais reached the apogee of their success. By 1858 there were over 500 infants attending the schools, and the evening classes were reported as having an average attendance of 443 during the winter session of 1856. In 1862, although the headmaster deplored the early age at which many of the boys were withdrawn from school, he claimed that most of these could read and write fairly competently at ten years of age.

These model schools at Dowlais were successful for a variety of reasons: the schools had accepted a system of government inspection; grants were received to augment the teachers' salaries; the zeal and dedication of the Guests was, undoubtedly, the driving-force; but the principal reason for their success was the quality of their teaching staff, all of whom were trained teachers. The Dowlais schools also evolved as a training-ground for apprentice teachers and many schools in south Wales could claim that their teachers were the products of the Merthyr academies. By 1865 they had attained the pinnacle of success and, when they were transferred to the Merthyr School Board in 1892, the total number of scholars in attendance was 2,492.

Finally, we should not forget those schools on the western rim of the coalfield. At Ystalyfera in the Swansea Valley, the Budd family had promoted two schools: the Wern School for Girls, begun in 1842; and the Tinworks School opened in 1852. In nearby Carmarthenshire, the Amman Ironworks had set up a British school at Brynamman, which experienced two periods of life: the first as the Ironworks' School from 1848 to 1868; and the second as the Brynamman Tinworks' School from 1868 to 1898.

Copperworks' Schools

Two schools are worthy of mention after 1847, the Hafod Copperworks' schools at Swansea, and Nevill's schools at Llanelli. The former were erected in 1847 by the Vivian family, the copper tsars of the south. The schools were conducted on an undenominational basis and they were regularly inspected by the British and Foreign School Society. Each school was divided into three sections, a boys' school, girls' school, and an infants' schoolroom. Pupils were attracted from the outlying districts of Swansea, from as far afield as Llangyfelach, Birchgrove, Sketty, and Pontarddulais. From 1847 to 1854 the Hafod schools received no grants, and the school pence covered the cost. The teachers' salaries, payments to pupil-teachers and building maintenance were all paid by the Vivians.

When the Hafod schools were opened in 1847 there were 350 pupils enrolled. This number had risen to 521 in 1865, and by

1893 there were 1,114 pupils, with an average attendance of 889. Inspectors frequently praised the schools for their efficiency and the Vivian family for their foresight and benevolence. The Vivians went so far as to set up evening classes, and hoped that this measure would counteract the endemic problem of early withdrawal from school. The classes were not, however, as successful as those at Dowlais.

At Llanelli, also, there were indications that the industrial entrepreneurs were taking an interest in education by the 1840s. In 1840 there was no National nor British school at Llanelli and R.J. Nevill, the prominent industrialist, began to press for increased school provision. By 1846 he was busily preparing the way for new schools in association with his company. At the end of that year, school buildings for boys and infants were started, and these came into operation in 1847. In January 1852, a girls' department was added to the schools. The whole educational complex was intended to serve the needs of children whose parents were employed by the Copperworks Company. Workmen were expected to make contributions from their wages and children were required to pay the school pence.

The schools at Llanelli prospered under the stewardship of David Williams, who was headmaster from 1847 to 1863. In that year he left to succeed Nefydd as agent for the British and Foreign School Society in south Wales. He was succeeded by J.E. Jones, who led the schools from 1863 to 1894. Jones's scientific and technical interests soon began to influence the curriculum at Llanelli and, by 1867, pupils were being awarded certificates in plane and solid geometry, and mechanical and machine drawing. By 1874 practical and organic chemistry had been introduced to the upper school curriculum. Jones Heolfawr, as he was often called, also held navigation classes for local sailors, and steered the Llanelli schools through storms and tempests to a safe haven in 1894.

Tinworks' Schools
From 1850 to 1870 many tin-plate works were established in the Llanelli and Swansea areas. But no real tinworks' school was opened in Llanelli, the tin-plate metropolis. The Morfa Tinplate Works were erected in 1851, and others followed in rapid succession, but it is not clear whether a local school was

connected to these. In the Amman Valley, the Amman Iron Company built a three-mill tinworks in 1872, and in the same year the Brynamman Tinworks' School was opened. The school committee advertised for a master, and a young student was appointed. Henry Jones had come directly from Bangor Normal College, and he would soon leave Brynamman to pursue his academic studies at university. After a brilliant career he became Professor of Moral Philosophy at Glasgow University, and was subsequently knighted for his services. Although the Brynamman Tinworks' School lasted to 1893, it would never again be led by as eminent a figure as Sir Henry Jones.

There were other tinworks' schools at Glais, in the Swansea Valley; at Melincrythan; and at Hendy, near Pontarddulais. The Hendy Higher Grade Elementary School erected in 1885 was the last of this type.

Colliery Schools

In 1839 the Committee of the Privy Council on Education was set up, and in its first year of existence the Minutes of the Council contained a gloomy report by H.S. Tremenheere on the mining districts. On 25 March 1840, the Committee of Council sent a circular letter to the twenty-nine mining owners in Monmouthshire, deploring the lack of educational facilities in the county. The Committee offered to help build schools in the area provided that their promoters appointed teachers trained by the National or British Society. The first works' school in Wales to be aided by a parliamentary grant was the Courtybella Colliery School in the parish of Mynyddislwyn, Monmouthshire, opened in 1842.

Colliery schools were also established in the Swansea Valley in the 1840s. One was a small school at Llansamlet, started by the coal proprietor, C.H. Smith, in 1841. This was enlarged into a new National colliery school in 1845. In the upper Swansea Valley, Messrs James and Aubrey sponsored the Cwmllynfell School, and M. Crane the Cwmtwrch School. The Marquis of Bute supported Church schools in those areas of Glamorgan where the family had significant industrial interests, but the Bute family never established a colliery school.

The real expansion of the colliery schools in east Glamorgan and, in particular, in the Rhondda valleys, occurred in the years after 1860. As the Rhondda coal industry grew, so the new colliery schools appeared; and the Voluntary societies spread their wings across the eastern rim of the coalfield. The Treherbert and Pentre National Schools opened in 1862 and 1864 respectively, and the Tonypandy National School in 1870. The British Society established schools at Llwynypia in 1865; Treorchy, 1866; Dunraven and Blaen-y-cwm, 1863; Pentre, 1875; Ton, Ystrad, 1869; Pen-y-graig, 1869; Ferndale, 1869; Cwm-parc, 1871; and Clydach Vale, 1872.

One of the most exciting educational developments took place, not in the Rhondda, but in the Aberdare Valley, where the Duffryn colliery schools were launched in 1857. They were promoted by a group of colliery owners, among whom was the enthusiastic figure of Henry Austin Bruce, later Lord Aberdare. The original schools were built for boys, girls and infants, but as the population grew, so additional schools were set up at Mountain Ash. The schools were managed with Lord Aberdare as chairman. The Duffryn schools resembled the education scheme operating at Dowlais under the aegis of the Guests. There was an intricate system of feeder schools, and evening schools were provided for adults and adolescents who were unable to enjoy the benefits of the day classes. The management panel permitted pauper children from the parish of Llanwonno to attend the schools on payment of a special fee from the parish clerk.

It would seem that no colliery schools were established in Carmarthenshire and Pembrokeshire, and there was only a scattering of schools in the western region of the coalfield. Two reasons probably accounted for their absence: first, the anthracite areas were not fully exploited until the 1890s; and by the 1890s there was a network of local school boards serving the area. There were isolated examples of colliery schools, as we have already seen, but they were neither as widespread nor as significant as their counterparts in the eastern parts of south Wales.

The works' schools compared favourably with the day schools and, in most cases, were actual improvements on the elementary schools. Many of the works' schools organized themselves into separate departments, consisting of infants, boys, girls, and evening classes. Their schemes of work and curricula could often be broad, balanced and comprehensive in nature. In the large and more opulent works' schools a curriculum could include subjects such as history, geography, music, and technical subjects. In the large schools at Cwmafan, Dowlais, Hafod, Swansea and Llanelli, more advanced subjects were offered, such as algebra, geometry, and astronomy. Dowlais was the only elementary school in Wales where a modern language was introduced. In 1869 a teacher was appointed to teach French and drawing to the Boys' and Girls' Schools. By 1874, however, the master had miserably failed to inculcate into the children the principles of the Gallic tongue and he was dismissed. The degree of financial independence in the works' schools often enabled them to offer a more varied curriculum. Many of them did not accept government grants and the much-despised Revised Code of 1861, which introduced a system of 'payment by results', had little impact on the works' schools.

The reports of the Committee of Council after 1850 show that all the larger works' schools were organized in classes and trained teachers were responsible for each class. The teachers were usually quite well paid, since the schools often received the support of the employers, the education societies, the Government, and the workmen themselves. The most distinctive feature of the works' schools was the educational tax levied on the workmen for the support of the schools. The levy was not uniform but varied from school to school, and from area to area. The 'stoppage' was compulsory and imposed on all persons employed in the works. Young and unmarried men and boys were required to pay for the upkeep of the schools. The schools were maintained in a variety of ways: some proprietors merely built schools for their employees, and all the maintenance costs fell on the workmen. This was the system in ironworks' schools at Llynfi, Maesteg, Tredegar, Rhymney, Blaenavon and Cwmafan. There were instances where the proprietors provided the school buildings and maintained them — Lord Penrhyn's schools at Llandygái and Mrs Oakeley's National School at Llan Ffestiniog were examples of these. Some proprietors deducted no stoppages from workmen's wages, but insisted that the children should pay the school pence. This happened in most of the slate quarry schools of north Wales. The large schools at Dowlais, Hafod,

Llanelli, Margam and Aberafan combined both the school pence and the poundage.

In some places the work-force built and maintained their own schools. The workmen in the upper reaches of the Swansea Valley bitterly resented having to send their children to the works' National schools and they established their own British schools. In the colliery schools the stoppages on wages were carefully graded so as not to upset the workmen and to ensure that different categories of employees paid different rates. The school fund of a typical colliery could be operated in the following way: every adult workman paid 4*d*. per month; all boys working underground and earning 6*s*. to 8*s*. per week paid 2*d*. per month; all boys working above ground and earning 1*s*.6*d*. per day paid 4*d*. per month; other boys engaged in occupations such as doorkeeping paid nothing. But the works' schools were almost exclusively under the control of the companies and the proprietors and, prior to 1870, the workmen were usually unrepresented on the management committees. In later years the majority of school management committees included workmen's representatives.

Educational Problems and Government Legislation in the Years, 1850–1880

In the years before 1870 the elementary day schools faced the twin handicaps of the early withdrawal of children from schools and irregular attendance. They were faced with the almost insuperable problem of persuading children to attend them. Sunday schools were overflowing and had no major problems. But the day schools and the works' schools had to contend with these twin drawbacks. Annual inspectors' reports and government reports dealing with the industrial regions of Wales before 1870 show that the possibility of early employment in the works was the greatest problem facing the schools. The same publications, however, loudly proclaim the appeal of the Sunday schools.

The causes of the early withdrawal from school are not difficult to find: parents often withdrew their children because they were unable to make the necessary financial contributions to the school; child labour was needed to supplement family incomes; but the significant factor which seemed to be common to all the industrial districts, was the lack of appreciation by parents of the importance of education for their children. Parents believed that it was their right to withdraw their children from school at an early age so that they would lose no time in finding a suitable source of livelihood. When works' schools were available in the industrial districts, parents often believed that the better the school the earlier the age at which their children could leave. The Sunday schools could always provide any additional instruction that was felt necessary, as could the evening classes. In some industrial districts children were withdrawn from school after only a year's attendance. The practice was rampant at many of the works' schools, and the Cyfarthfa School at Merthyr Tydfil was one of the more obvious examples of early withdrawal. In 1854 the school registers furnish the following revealing details:

(a)　　*Children in school*
　　　　Number in school under　6 years old　　　45
　　　　Number in school under 10 years old　　　45
　　　　Number in school over　10 years old　　　17

　　　　　　　　　　　　　　　　　　　Total:　107

(b)　　*Children who attended school*
　　　　For less than one year　　　　　　　　　95
　　　　For more than one year　　　　　　　　　6
　　　　For more than two years　　　　　　　　3
　　　　For more than three years　　　　　　　3

　　　　　　　　　　　　　　　　　　　Total:　107

The position seems to have been a little better in the copper-smelting districts than in the iron and coal areas, and most of the boys employed at Vivian's copperworks had attended school for more than three years in 1862. In the 1860s, however, early withdrawal was rapidly on the increase and it threatened to abort all efforts to educate the working classes. One particularly disturbing feature of the process was the high percentage of illiteracy among young men from eighteen to twenty-two years of age. Most of these young people had been taught the rudiments of reading and writing in the Sunday schools, but the results were often quite inadequate.

The other intractable problem facing the schools was irregular attendance. Schools were regarded as an interference which prevented children from attending to their work. In the industrial districts children were kept at home to look after smaller children, or to carry food to other members of their family who were employed in the local works. In the rural counties irregular attendance assumed a seasonal pattern, and it was often worst at harvesting. At least the withdrawal took a more systematic form over longer periods. A child would often be withdrawn from school for a specific period of two or three months in a year, and teachers could plan their lessons accordingly. In the industrial sectors most of the pupils were absent for the greater part of the year, as Table 11.3 illustrates.

Table 11.3

Poor Law Union	No. of schools giving Returns	Total scholars	Proportion per cent attending school during year 1857–8				
			Less than 50 days	50 to 100 days	100 to 150 days	150 to 200 days	Over 200 days
Dolgellau	15	908	9.7	8.7	18.6	27.1	27.0
Ffestiniog	15	1,147	19.2	27.7	19.9	19.8	17.7
Neath	20	1,910	25.0	21.6	23.2	20.3	10.1
Merthyr Tydfil	22	4,153	35.1	15.8	15.5	23.4	16.9

Many methods were adopted to try to combat the problems of early withdrawal and irregular attendance. In many areas a child's education was started earlier in infants' schools as part of the drive to overcome early school-leaving. Many of the works proprietors paid particular attention to these schools, for example, the ironmasters at Dowlais, Cwmafan and Neath Abbey; the copperowners at Llanelli, Hafod and Kilvey; and some of the slate quarry schools at Ffestiniog. In other areas the more able pupils were often offered better posts at the works in the hope that the prospect of promotion would deter them from leaving school too early. Although the number of posts available was limited, the method of combating early withdrawal was quite effective in a number of areas. The plan operated at some of the large works at Dowlais, Swansea and Llanelli. At

Cwmafan, the Gilbertsons often accepted boys directly into the works' office from the school.

Some schools apprenticed promising pupils to special trades or processes in the works and provided opportunities for them to train as pupil-teachers. Employers would often introduce an educational test as a condition of employment for children from ten to twelve years of age. Certificates of merit in reading and writing were required before children were accepted, but the prescribed standards were quite low and children found them easily attainable. Several industrialists discovered that, once the children had left the day schools, they had forgotten almost all they had learnt. Enterprising works' owners sometimes established refresher classes for boys between twelve and sixteen years of age so that they were able to return to school for short periods.

One of the most exciting methods developed to combat the evils of early withdrawal and irregular attendance was the Prize Scheme or Association. These schemes had been initiated in Staffordshire, Shropshire, Northumberland and Durham in the early 1850s. In 1856 H.S. Tremenheere, an Inspector of Schools, in conjunction with Sir Thomas Phillips, the celebrated Mayor of Newport during the Chartist disturbances, launched the South Wales Iron and Coal Masters' Association. This consisted of three regions: the eastern region, from the Pontypool Valley to the Rhymney Valley; the central region, from the Dowlais Ironworks to the Rhondda valleys; and the western region, from the Llynfi Valley to Llanelli. The Association hoped to persuade parents to keep their children at school for a longer period and to attend more regularly. It awarded prizes to those who were successful in an annual competitive examination. Children entering for the examination were required to attend an elementary school approved by the Association for a period of at least two years; secondly, pupils should be at least ten years of age; and each child was expected to produce a certificate to show that he or she had attended the day school for at least 176 days during the preceding year.

The first of these examinations for the eastern region was held at the National School, Newport, in June 1857. Twenty schools participated and 219 pupils competed for the prizes. The tenth and final distribution of prizes was conducted in 1866 when nineteen schools, with a pupil population of 324, competed in the examination. After 1866 the Association terminated its prize schemes, largely on account of the effects of the Revised Code, which had been introduced in 1861.

Evening schools were established in many of the industrial regions as centres of further education. Their aims were fourfold: to militate against early withdrawal and erratic attendance; to promote technical instruction for the adult and adolescent workman; to provide advanced courses and tuition for the examinations of the Department of Science and Art; and finally, to encourage leisure-time activities for the workmen. Evening classes for elementary instruction were held at Llanelli Copperworks' School, at the Hafod and Kilvey Copperworks' Schools, and in the colliery districts of the Rhondda and Aberdare valleys. But the schools were generally unpopular and the labouring classes showed little enthusiasm for them. One reason for this was that most people were too exhausted to think of attending classes after a hard day's labour in the mines. The lectures were also on topics of a scientific or a technological nature and most people lacked the necessary background to understand them. A full review of the state of evening classes was made in 1860 after the Assistant Commissioner had visited south Wales. He observed that the ordinary working man was totally indifferent to the schools. The exceptions were the evening technical classes which led to some qualification.

Factory and mines legislation seems to have had a minimal impact on Wales in the years before 1850. The Collieries Act of 1861 did affect south Wales for, under its provisions, children under ten years of age were to be excluded from employment as before. A significant change was that the employment of children between the ages of ten and twelve was to be restricted to those who were certified as being capable of reading and writing. The log-books of some of the colliery schools showed that schoolmasters assisted the implementation of the Act by ensuring that managers and owners were mindful of their duties.

The Factory Act which was to make the deepest impression on south Wales was the Factory Acts Extension Act of 1867. This stipulated that half-time attendance at school was to be compulsory for all children between the ages of eight and thirteen. The Act further prohibited night work. There were loud protestations from the employers against this measure, and particularly from the tinmasters, who employed child labour extensively. The Act did not come into full operation until 1 July 1870.

That year also saw the implementation of Forster's Education Act, introduced 'to fill the gaps', and to try to provide the country with good schools and encourage parents to send their children to them. The Act divided the country into school districts, and School Boards were set up to manage the board schools, to decide the form of religious instruction, and to pass by-laws for the compulsory attendance of children between certain stipulated ages. The Act did not abolish the voluntary schools but, where the voluntary effort had faded, School Boards were to be formed.

The Act of 1870 evoked a wave of protest from the Nonconformist communities. The centre of opposition was Birmingham, where Joseph Chamberlain and John Morley made the National Education League the spearhead of political dissent. In Wales the position of the Church was particularly resented, for the Church National schools had penetrated into many industrial and rural areas. By 1880 there were 223 Church schools in St David's diocese alone, with an average attendance of 19,000 pupils per year. Of the twenty-seven grammar schools endowed under the Endowed Schools Act of 1869, two-thirds of the pupils were Anglican. The grant aid awarded to the National schools by Forster's Act was, therefore, keenly felt in Wales.

Another issue raised by the 1870 Act was that of religious instruction in schools. This actually splintered the Nonconformist camp. A conference of Welsh Nonconformist leaders at Aberystwyth in January 1870 decided in favour of permissive biblical instruction, with denominational teaching outside school hours. Among the Independents, however, there was a strong feeling that all religious teaching should be removed from the schools. Their views were voiced by Henry Richard during the second reading of the Bill. The inclusion of the Cowper-Temple conscience clause in the Act enabled Nonconformists to withdraw their children from religious instruction classes, if they so wished.

Once the Act was passed a dual system of Church and Board School education was effectively created. The School Boards and the ensuing elections became trials of strength between the various denominations. The Boards began to reflect the religious complexity of Wales and, by 1886, it was estimated that there were no less than fifty secular School Boards in the Principality. In 1899 a Church spokesman presented the following figures: that, of 320 Schools Boards in Wales, 62 had no religious instruction, 118 taught the Bible without comment, and almost all had no religious examination.

In the years after 1870 a number of changes affected the state of elementary education. In 1876 Lord Sandon's Education Act declared that it was the duty of a parent to ensure that every child should receive instruction in reading, writing and arithmetic. The Act prescribed that no child under ten years of age was to be employed, and no child between ten and fourteen unless he had passed Standard IV or had attended not more than two schools in each year at least 250 times for a period of five years. Universal compulsory education was achieved eventually in 1880 under the provisions of Mundella's Act.

Sir Hugh Owen and the Development of Intermediate and Higher Education

Hugh Owen (1804–81) was undoubtedly one of the great pioneers of education in the last century. Born of fairly comfortable farming stock in south-west Anglesey, he attended a private school in Caernarfon and, in March 1825, he left his native Anglesey for London. After a series of clerical posts in the city, he was appointed as a civil servant in the Poor Law Commission in 1836. He moved rapidly through the ranks and became the Chief Clerk of the Local Government Board, a post which would be almost similar to that of Permanent Secretary in today's Civil Service. From the 1830s onwards Hugh Owen turned his attention to the problems of education in Wales and devoted the rest of his life to this one major important issue. In 1843 he published his famous letter on day schools and campaigned vigorously for the British and Foreign School Society. As a strong advocate of State aid in education, he hoped to persuade the Nonconformists to bury their Voluntaryist principles and to accept government help in establishing elementary schools. Throughout the 1840s and 1850s, as we have seen, he actively encouraged the Welsh people to set up British schools, and energetically supported the Society's agents in their task.

The campaign to establish British schools had been hampered by a variety of difficulties, not the least of which was the desperate lack of trained schoolmasters: Hugh Owen had suggested in the 1840s that young men should be sent to Borough Road College in London for their training, and young Nonconformists soon began trekking there. In a policy declaration in 1847, the British Society had announced its intention of building new training colleges in selected centres outside London. It was strongly suggested that students from north Wales should attend a college in Cheshire or Lancashire, and those from the south should proceed to Gloucestershire or Somerset. Owen did not oppose these proposals at that juncture.

He was worried, however, that the Church authorities would soon steal a march on the Nonconformists and build their own college. In 1848, when a training college for men was opened at Carmarthen, Owen's fears were realized. A year later a similar college was opened at Caernarfon. Owen's reluctance to set up a college in Wales, and the outbreak of the Crimean War in 1856, put paid to some of his plans in the early 1850s. From 1855 onwards he and his colleagues presented a united front in campaigning for the establishment of a training college at Bangor. The large number of British schools in the north tilted the balance in favour of the northern location. Owen, and his untiring British Society agent in the north, the Revd John Phillips, campaigned endlessly for funds. On 26 January 1858, the Bangor Normal College was opened in temporary buildings with twelve students. The Government allocated a grant of £2,000 towards the cost of the permanent buildings, which were opened in August 1862. By the late 1850s, therefore, there were three training colleges with accommodation for over 150 men students within the Principality; but there was still no college for women. This was eventually opened at Swansea, and Owen had taken positive steps to ensure that there was a regular supply of schoolmasters and mistresses in Wales during the last few decades of the century.

Sir Hugh Owen's boldest scheme centred on the concept of a Welsh university. University College, London, had been founded in 1826, a year after he arrived to seek employment in the city. St David's College, Lampeter, had been founded in 1827, and King's College in London had been set up in 1829. The University of Durham followed in 1832, Queen's College in Ireland in 1849, and Owen's College in Manchester in 1851. There had been much activity in Wales in the 1840s and 1850s, and many references to the lack of colleges of higher education appeared in journals, newspapers and denominational circles. It was in 1854 that Hugh Owen convened a private meeting in London at the home of Thomas Charles. Owen read a paper proposing the establishment of colleges in Wales, and he launched the so-called university movement. In the period from 1856 to 1862 Welsh Nonconformist energies were channelled into such projects as founding the Normal College, Bangor, and congregational colleges at Carmarthen, Brecon and Bala.

Throughout the 1860s a number of prominent Nonconformist figures began to campaign for a university in Wales. In 1862 Dr David Thomas, a Congregational minister of Stockwell in London, wrote a letter on the need for a university to the *Cambrian Daily Leader*, a Welsh daily newspaper owned by his son. Dr Thomas Nicholas wrote a series of letters in the *Cambrian Daily Leader* and the *Caernarvon Herald* on the same issue. Hugh Owen was impressed by these moves and a series of meetings were held at the Freemason's Tavern, Great Queen Street, London. Hugh Owen became one of the honorary secretaries of the Provisional Committee which was subsequently formed. The Provisional Committee, which was largely sponsored by London Welshmen, soon pressed ahead with the tasks of raising funds and finding sites for the prospective college.

The Castle Hotel at Aberystwyth came on the market in 1867 at a reasonable price and the Committee acquired it for £10,000. Hugh Owen actively involved himself in the movement to establish a university college and participated in all the complicated administrative and legal activities. In 1868 the Committee approached the Government for help, but they were rejected by Disraeli. In the meantime thousands of pounds had been subscribed in a national appeal, and a site had been obtained at Aberystwyth. In 1870 approaches were made to Gladstone for financial support. He was sympathetic to the cause, but he seemed unwilling to furnish grant aid. He was obviously afraid that this would rake up the religious issue and the request was turned down.

Under considerable financial pressure, and with no money forthcoming from the Government, the promoters of the movement seemed to be under a cloud of despondency. In the autumn of 1871, however, various local committees in Wales, Manchester and Liverpool pressed harder to realize their dream and careful plans were laid to collect adequate funds to maintain the college. With a debt of over £7,000 outstanding on the purchase account of the Castle Hotel, the college was formally opened on 15 October 1872, with twenty-five students. That number increased to over sixty by 1873, and to seventy-five during the 1876 session. But the financial problems were not over yet and, when Dr David Charles resigned from the post of college secretary in 1871, Hugh Owen became the honorary secretary. He retired from his full-time post at the Poor Law office and, for six years, he devoted himself to the task of building up the college finances. He organized an annual 'University Sunday' throughout Wales so that all the churches and chapels would have a chance of subscribing money to the college. In addition, he arranged house-to-house collections throughout Wales. He visited almost every important town in Glamorgan and Monmouthshire, before embracing the whole of north Wales. It has often been claimed that the contributions of the quarrymen from Bethesda, Llanberis, Nantlle and Blaenau Ffestiniog are without parallel in the history of education.

The future of the college was perhaps made more uncertain by the absence of any organized schooling above the elementary level. With the change of Government of 1880, Hugh Owen decided to seek the support of Lord Aberdare, the College President, to persuade Gladstone to appoint a committee to inquire into the state of higher and intermediate education in Wales. On 10 May, Hugh Owen sent another famous letter, this time to Gladstone. The letter, with the support of Lord Aberdare, urged the Liberal Prime Minister to set up the inquiry. Gladstone acceded to the request and in July 1880 the Committee was established. The Committee was to concern itself with higher education, and with intermediate, secondary schooling.

The Aberdare Committee acted with considerable speed and efficiency, and its Report appeared in August 1881. It was totally unlike its predecessor of 1847, with the preamble sympathetically acknowledging the distinct nationality of Wales. The Report recommended the creation of a new system of intermediate schools, run by elected governing bodies. The new schools were to be supported by a $\frac{1}{2}d$. rate and a parliamentary grant on a pound-for-pound basis. The Committee agreed that Wales did not have adequate provision for higher education and recommended that two colleges be set up, one in north Wales, and the other in the south. The Government started to act on the latter proposal. In 1882, a year after Hugh Owen's death, Aberystwyth received its first grant of £2,000 from the State. It was the first State grant ever made to a Welsh university college. Negotiations also began over the sites of the proposed new colleges. In south Wales the adjudicators preferred the Cardiff site to Swansea, possibly on account of the grant of £10,000 from the Marquis of Bute. The new university college was opened in October 1883. By 1884 it had 152 students. In north Wales thirteen towns were canvassed as possible sites for the new university college. In August 1883, the adjudicators settled on Bangor and the University College of North Wales was opened in 1884. The Charter constituting the University of Wales finally received the Royal seal of approval in 1893.

In the meantime the proposal to create a network of intermediate schools was not allowed to slumber, and the Welsh Intermediate Education Act of 1889 inaugurated a new era in Welsh education. The new secondary schools were to be based on the Local Government Act of 1888. Many of the old grammar schools were soon adopted as county schools under the new scheme, and it was at Caernarfon town that the first purpose-built school in Wales was opened in 1894. The school was appropriately called the Sir Hugh Owen School. By the time of the 1902 Education Act, there were ninety county schools in Wales. The Welsh Intermediate Education Act of 1889 was yet another precedent for separate legislation for Wales, and it was a fitting characteristic of the political awakening of Wales.

SUGGESTED READING

B.L. Davies, *Hugh Owen, 1804–1881* (Cardiff, 1977).

E.T. Davies, *Monmouthshire Schools and Education to 1870* (Newport, 1957).

L.W. Evans, *Education in Industrial Wales, 1700–1900* (Cardiff, 1971).

G.E. Jones, *Modern Wales* (Cambridge, 1984).

P. Morgan and D. Thomas, *Wales: The Shaping of a Nation* (London, 1984).

Articles:

B.L. Davies, 'British Schools in South Wales', *N.L.W.J.*, XVIII (1973–4).

L.W. Evans, 'School Boards and the Works School System after the Education Act of 1870', *N.L.W.J.*, XV (1967–8).

G.W. Roderick, 'Education, Culture and Industry in Wales in the Nineteenth Century', *W.H.R.*, 13 (1987).

12. Political Awakening 1850–1880

The System of Parliamentary Representation in 1850

THE system of parliamentary representation had survived since the Act of Union and had been amended by the Reform Act of 1832. The Act of Union had given Wales twenty-seven members, and the Reform Act had raised this to thirty-two with the additional seats going to the counties with the largest population, namely, Glamorgan, Carmarthenshire, and Denbighshire. The Glamorgan boroughs had also been divided into two groups, and the town of Merthyr enfranchised for the first time. The total Welsh electorate was increased to almost 49,000 in 1832, or 5.5 per cent of the population. The Act had established the principle that the suffrage was a privilege vested in holders of property, and the system heavily favoured the rural areas. The ratio of members to population within the constituencies varied considerably in 1832, but it was the industrial regions which suffered most. In Radnorshire the ratio was one member to 18,000 people, in Monmouthshire it was one to 85,000. In the boroughs the pattern was the same, with Brecon having one member to 5,000, and Swansea one to 27,000 people in 1832. By 1850 there were thirty-two members representing a population of 1,163,139 in Wales, or one member per 36,000 persons. There were considerable variations in the ratios: Radnorshire had one member for 12,000 people and Monmouthshire one for 52,000. By 1866 the ratio for Monmouthshire had increased to one to 130,000. What changed the ratios was the movement of population in response to economic changes. The counties with relatively unfavourable ratios were those in which industrialization was advanced.

The county and borough constituencies differed quite significantly. There were seventeen county constituencies in 1850 with an aggregate population of nearly 850,000, so that each county member represented on average around 50,000 people. Again there were variations in the ratios, and the counties whose industrial economies were attracting population were in the least favourable position. The member for Radnorshire represented 18,000 people, and the member for Caernarfonshire 66,000. There were fifteen borough constituencies, five in north Wales and ten in the south. The borough representation in Wales was unique, for the reformers of 1832 had not abolished the system of enfranchisement of contributory boroughs. The fifteen borough members represented not fifteen boroughs, but sixty spread over the whole country. There were only two single-town constituencies — Brecon and Merthyr, and the latter consisted of all the towns and townships in the parishes of Merthyr and Aberdare. This system of enfranchisement of contributory boroughs had the effect of giving the vote to certain of the inhabitants of virtually all the main urban centres in Wales. In the north, four towns in Anglesey were enfranchised, six in Caernarfonshire, four in Denbighshire, eight in Flintshire and six in Montgomeryshire; while in south Wales, three of the main towns in Monmouthshire, nine in Glamorgan, seven in Pembrokeshire, and six in Radnorshire.

There was considerable variation in the size of the borough constituencies. The average ratio was one member to 19,000 people, but Brecon had a ratio of one member to 6,000, while Merthyr was one to 63,000. Radnor had one for 7,000, and Swansea one for 45,000. No one in 1832 could have foreseen the scale of the population shift which would occur in the next twenty years. But the system in 1850, as in 1832, was heavily weighted in favour of the landed gentry. The distinction between the county and borough seat in Wales was a theoretical and political one, for the Welsh towns had been too small to create economies which were different from their hinterlands.

The Members of Parliament representing the county constituencies were all of ancient lineage, very wealthy, and all resident as proprietors in the counties they represented. In 1850 the Wynns of Wynnstay, the Bulkeleys, the Pennants of Penrhyn, the Mostyns, the Rices of Dynevor, the Talbots, the Powells, and others dominated the county and parliamentary scenes. The same was invariably true of the boroughs, and the members they returned came almost exclusively from the same aristocratic class. The exceptions in 1850 were few, and perhaps the outstanding ones were the two Glamorgan borough representatives, Sir Josiah John Guest, member for Merthyr, and Henry Vivian, sitting for Swansea. Both were leading industrialists, technocrats and owners of two large industrial concerns. But they were landowners as well as industrialists, for Vivian owned Singleton Park in Swansea, and Sir John possessed wide estates in Berkshire. By the 1850s, therefore, there had been a convergence of the two kinds of wealth, landed and industrial. The industrialists bought landed property, and the landed gentry moved into commerce and industry.

The electors were those whose property gave them a stake in the country, and the enfranchised portion of the population was small. On average, about 4.9 per cent of the population had the vote, or roughly one in twenty. The counties were slightly better off than the boroughs with one in eighteen as against one in twenty-three. In the counties there were no great variations in the ratio, whereas in the borough constituencies, the variations were quite staggering. Merthyr Tydfil with its population of 63,080 had only 1,102 voters, or one in fifty-seven. Swansea, with over 45,000 inhabitants, had only 1,698 voters, or one in twenty-six. Most of the borough constituencies embraced industrial activity, and the greater the extent of industrialization, the greater the political inequalities. The right to vote had been attached to the possession of property and, in the counties, this right was restricted to certain types of freeholders, leaseholders of specified kinds, and to the tenants of properties with £50 or more per annum. The borough franchise depended upon the occupation of a house or premises of an annual value of not less than £10. These property qualifications carried certain restrictions: in the boroughs, all local rates due during the previous year must have been paid; and the receipt of any assistance from the rates during the year brought automatic disqualification.

In the period from 1850 to 1868 there were few contested elections in Wales; if by-elections are excluded, there were only about thirty contested elections out of a possible 158. One reason for this was the congruence between the two types of constituency and their social composition, the rural and the urban. Urban people existed in rural constituencies and rural people in urban constituencies, and this decreased the possibility of tensions being expressed. Contested elections were certainly rarer in rural constituencies than in urban constituencies, and almost non-existent in those rural constituencies where there was scarcely any industrial development. There were no contests between 1852 and 1868 in Anglesey, Montgomeryshire, Breconshire and Radnorshire. The exceptions were Cardiganshire, where there were three contested elections, and Merionethshire, where there were two. We shall be examining one of these, Merioneth, in a little more detail at a later stage. Suffice it to say that there were important social changes taking place in both these constituencies. In all the borough constituencies, with the exception of Radnor, there were contested elections.

The reason why these constituencies should have differed in the levels of political activity is that they contained differing social structures. The rural constituencies were pre-industrial societies stratified hierarchically into estates and with a strict correlation between status and the ownership of land. They were communities in which deference operated, where custom, rights and duties were observed throughout the community. The communities were organic, held together by the complex of kith and kin relationships and by communal work patterns. Not so in the borough constituencies and the industrial communities, which were functional and worked according to the impersonal demands of the industries which dominated them. The relationships of the inhabitants of the towns to the industries were mainly economic and contractual and brief. They were stratified by 'class' and the upper class was manifest to all — the ironmaster, coal-owner and copper king. His power was probably greater and more widespread than the rural landlord's; and within these industrial communities the conditions necessary for political activity and contest, and for eventual class conflict, were being established. In the next section we shall examine those conditions and their relationships to the development of political activity in the years leading up to 1868.

Health, Wealth and Politics

There were many threats to the industrial communities in the nineteenth century, and one obvious, recurring possibility, with almost each downward turn in the trade cycle, was the collapse of their industrial bases. Political activity engendered by the concern with public health was another potent threat. The concern with public health, and the association of dirt, disease and urbanization, really began in the early 1840s with the work of Edwin Chadwick and the General Report on the Sanitary Condition of the Labouring Population of Great Britain of 1842; the Reports of the Royal Commission on the State of Large Towns of 1843–5, and the passing of the first Public Health Act of 1848. But it was the terrifying visitation of cholera in 1849 which concentrated the minds of those who governed and led to the first sanitary reforms. Cholera killed 53,000 people in Britain, and none of the main urban centres in Wales escaped its fury and ravaging effects. In Merthyr Tydfil, the largest town in Wales, 1,683 died in 1849 and another 455 during the 1854 outbreak.

The cholera epidemics highlighted the desperate needs of the urban places: towns were largely unpaved, sewers were open and on the surface of roads, there were no arrangements for the removal of human effluvia, and the cesspool was the common repository. Running water was very scarce, and rivers were the common source of supply. But these were also dumping-grounds for industrial and human waste. Water for human consumption was therefore always, and in towns heavily, polluted. Sanitary needs were threefold: first, to clean the towns; secondly, to arrange for sewage removal; and lastly, to provide a supply of piped water. As a result of these conditions, and the passage of the 1848 Public Health Act, about twenty-five urban and urban-rural places in Wales (and seventeen of these were in south Wales) decided to petition to adopt the new Act. By the time of the 1858 Act some more places had been added, and at the time of the Local Government Act of 1872, some seventy places had adopted the Act. But, until the passing of the Sanitary Act of 1866 and the Public Health Act of 1875 most of the legislation was permissive. There was lack of central direction and control and of powers of compulsion, and the voluntary nature of the legislation delayed effective sanitary reform.

The mortality rates in Wales illustrate this dreadful delay. In 1841 the death-rate per 1,000 population in Wales was 20.2. In

1848 it had risen to 22.0. In the year of the cholera epidemic, the overall death-rate had increased to 25.8. Merthyr was a disease-ridden town: typhus, smallpox, and scarlet fever were endemic; and the crude mortality figures confirmed these melancholy facts. The death-rate from all causes in the period 1846–55, before any sanitary works were in operation, was 332 per 10,000, and the average mortality for the years 1847–53 was twenty-nine per 1,000 without cholera. If cholera deaths are included, the figure rises to 34.7 per 1,000. The 1848 Act and that of 1854 could not be applied except on petition of two-thirds of the property owners and ratepayers or when mortality exceeded twenty-three per 1,000. Although the Commissioners turned to the rural areas from 1864 onwards and Dr Hunter presented reports on south-west Wales in the 1860s, the focus of attention was on the urban areas, for it was clear that it was to the industrial areas that the excess population of the countryside was moving. By the decade 1851–61 every county in Wales, with the exception of Denbighshire and Glamorgan, experienced a net outflow of people. These young migrants and their families left their rural hovels in search of new abodes. What they did not foresee was the unhealthy, insanitary and often precarious nature of life in the industrial townships.

Why was so little done to ameliorate the social and sanitary conditions of the people? G.T. Clark, the manager of the Dowlais Iron Company, was a keen observer and he offered one important answer to this question: 'the wretched civic economy of these districts'. T.W. Rammell visited Merthyr Tydfil in 1849 and published his report on the sanitary conditions of the town a year later. He was astonished to find a town of 50,000 inhabitants, 'as destitute of civic government as the smallest rural village of the empire'. The problem was that there was no sizeable middle class in the town. Those professional people who lived in the town were unorganized and generally apathetic, even pessimistic. The vast majority seemed to subscribe to the basic political philosophy of Anthony Hill of Penydarren that local government, or what existed of it, should be confined to two objects: to tax and to punish people.

There were existing models of town government to which observers often referred, and these were the municipal corporations. These were the governmental systems of the ancient chartered boroughs which had been reformed in 1835. Swansea was one example, with its mayor and twenty-four councillors, aldermen, recorder and seven JPs. They governed the town and most of the reaches of the Lower Tawe Valley. Cardiff, Newport and Neath had similar corporations. The possession of institutions of government never guaranteed good government. The boroughs were better off only if these institutions were put to good purpose. In the new industrial districts, however, the lack of an organized political life and of institutions meant that there was no way of putting pressure on those who were responsible for the delays in improving the towns. Merthyr Tydfil was the classic example of a ruling industrial oligarchy. The master, his family and agent were the rulers, the iron-despots, who had little time for social improvement and the like. The ironmasters dictated the terms and parameters of government, and usually preferred to reside outside their industrial empires. In those areas where the gentry had turned to industrial entrepreneurship, and the local landowners had led the way in industrial development, their presence was a determining factor in the shape of social developments, for example, Lord Bute and Lord Penrhyn entered into the minutest details of architectural and town planning.

The industrial boroughs also tended to possess a more variegated lower middle class. Swansea had an extensive and rich shopkeeping class, while the iron-towns possessed few professional men and the shopocracy there was small. Swansea was most certainly working class, with just under 5,000 male occupiers of houses (10,636 houses), of which just under a half were below the £10 rateable value. Merthyr had 8,000 occupiers of houses (16,114 houses) of which nine out of ten were below £10 rateable value. The determining factor was the relative diversification of industry: in places like Swansea and Neath there were industries of various kinds and, therefore, a greater variety of workers and of gradations of wealth. In the one-industry towns of the coalfield, there was a greater uniformity of class, which militated against the development of organized political activity.

But it was in the local communities, and at a local, parish level that Welshmen learned about politics. The greatest government interference came in legislation concerned with the poor and public health; and both the Poor Law Amendment Act of 1834 and the Public Health Act of 1848 brought fixed procedures into local government and created institutions based on democratic forms of government. These Acts were of great importance in the history of evolving democratic structure, for it was in the working of the local franchise that the ordinary ratepayer and householder learned the realities of political organization. Added to these, and supportive of them, were his experiences of chapel government, the Friendly Society meetings, the trade union, and the club. It was in local government that people first learned about politics, about the ideas and practices of representation.

It was at the local level also that the lower middle classes, and the shopocrats, the skilled craftsmen and artisans, and the aristocrats of labour had their first experiences of the difficulties and circumstances that conditioned their political activity. The major obstacle was the range of legal and constitutional constraints on action. The way in which the vote was distributed among the population was one factor in this process. Not everyone had the vote, and it was the possession of property or the occupation of someone else's property that conferred it. In the counties only about 4.45 per cent of the population possessed the vote, and there was a better chance of having the vote where there was no heavy industry. In the municipal boroughs, all ratepayers were given the vote in local elections provided that they had resided in the town for three years and paid the rates. Even in the municipal boroughs the franchise was distributed according to a system of classification by wealth — property rated at less than £50 gave one vote, £50 to £100 two votes, and so on to a maximum of six votes for property values of £250. The Public Health Act of 1848 and subsequent Acts up to 1872 adopted this system of plural voting. The parliamentary franchise was confined to the £10 householder up to 1867, and rather less than 4 per cent of the borough populations was enfranchised. Again, one had a better chance of a vote in the rural boroughs of Radnorshire, where one in seventeen had the vote, than in the industrial boroughs of Swansea, where in Neath one in thirty-nine had the vote, and in Swansea itself one in thirty.

The other notable constraint on political involvement and activity was that the vast majority seemed to accept the social structure as they experienced it. Some contemporaries attributed this to ignorance, apathy, or even a failure or refusal to perceive the reality of life. Others castigated the religious denominations for this readiness to accept life as it was. There were certainly two important factors which accounted for this political acquiescence. One was the nature of urbanization and the overwhelming power of the industrialists: they mastered men and women and societies; they owned all the means of production; they owned the raw materials, furnaces, mills, reservoirs, quarries, brickworks, the land on which workers' houses were built, the canals, the railways, and the banks. They were a ruling oligarchy, who repelled all challenges to their power and kept the Merthyr Tydfils of this world firmly in their grasp. The other factor was the nature of migration into the industrial communities from the countryside. As people moved from the countryside and created new settlements, so they carried their rural culture with them. The immigrant made life more comprehensible in the new regions by a transfer of values, and he transported familiar conceptions of order and degree, and of political behaviour. The new works and masters corresponded, therefore, to the old rural estates and the landlords. Merthyr Tydfil, Dowlais and Ystalyfera became, in a sense, the industrial analogues of rural estates. The immigrants thought of their industrial politics as replicas of their rural politics. In the country they had been accustomed to elections and electioneering based more on family and connection than on principle, and in the elections they did as they were told. Once they moved to the industrial districts they found a similar system in operation, and industrial magnates such as the Vivians or the Guests never seriously contemplated that their workers might not vote for them in the era before the Ballot Act of 1872.

Political Reform Societies, 1847–1880

The years from 1847 to 1868 were not uneventful in Victorian Britain. They were years during which the working classes were tutored in the organization and methodology of political activity. They were years of consolidation, the product of a variety of powerful forces: Chartism persisted resolutely for a considerable period; the 1867 Reform Act was itself the concluding episode of a long drawn-out public debate; in 1855 and 1861 the taxes on knowledge were repealed, thereby releasing the newspapers and journals into the provinces, and into the hands of ordinary working people; activists espoused a spectrum of other causes, like temperance, anti-slavery, and social and economic reform; there was the extension of free trade and the beginnings of Civil Service reform; there was the growth and development of the Liberation Society, one of the political agencies which created a new public opinion in Wales in the generations before the elections of 1868; working-class organizations, both industrial and political, evolved; and there was the establishment of Welsh Nonconformity as a formidable ecclesiastical, social and political force.

In the years 1847–8 economic crises at home and revolution abroad were most potent factors, stirring the revival of Chartism as a mass political movement. Though no serious Chartist outbreaks occurred in Wales, there was considerable tension and Merthyr once more forced itself to the forefront of the Welsh movement. In this mid-Victorian period Chartism was often confused with the other reform movements, and the Chartists themselves seemed more preoccupied with unity and survival than with the great political issues. Their survival was visible at parliamentary elections, where working-class representatives rose to demand manhood suffrage, the ballot, etc. Yet the working classes were not zealous campaigners in these years. Their demonstrations were usually tempered with restraint and discipline. Protest became more respectable, and the violence of earlier years was tamed.

Chartism was only one facet of the reform movement in mid-century. The electoral system in Wales in the post-1832 era was full of inconsistencies and irregularities, and conducive to further agitation. In the 1850s and 1860s political justice and the fairer representation of classes and interests were the recurrent themes of electoral reform movements. Many Welshmen were more enthusiastic over the ballot than other measures, and many editors of the religious press emphasized the uselessness of the 1832 Act which had omitted the ballot.

The reform movement of the late 1850s was almost completely taken over by middle-class Radicals, who needed the support of the working classes but were fearful of their motives. The working classes seem to have taken little part in local reform movements at this point; but there were definite signs of change, as the contested elections of 1859 reveal.

The Reform League was one agent which endeavoured to create an intelligent and educated public opinion in Wales on the question of parliamentary reform. The League set up thirteen branches throughout Wales, and most of these were scattered in the industrial districts. Brecon Reform League appeared in late 1865, but the majority of the Welsh branches surfaced in the late summer and autumn of 1866. At least two of the Welsh branches were formed through the efforts of local trade unions: the initiative for the Merthyr societies came from the Shoemakers' Union; while the Cardiff Society was inspired by the Trades' Council. The Reform League's tactics were wholly constitutional, and it would not consider any form of violent opposition. The social composition of the societies included shopkeepers, tradesmen and craftsmen rather than ordinary workers. An important group in the Welsh branches were the Nonconformist ministers.

Another reform body, the National Reform Union, also attracted considerable Nonconformist support in the Principality; and several of its vice-presidents were Welsh clergymen: the Revd Thomas Price, Aberdare, Revd Thomas Gee, Revd Thomas Levi, and at least six others were known to hold this distinguished rank. The Union held a number of meetings in Wales, and its major impact was reserved for the north-eastern part of the country. The movement was middle class, moderate, and Manchester-based and it succeeded in making only a limited impression in Wales.

The Liberation Society

But there was one society, perhaps more than any other agency, which was responsible for shaping the political and religious attitudes in Wales which produced the results of the 1868 elections. That society was the Anti-State-Church Association or, as it later became known, the Society for the

Liberation of Religion from State Patronage and Control. The man who was responsible for the creation of this Society was Edward Miall of Leicester who, in 1841, established *The Nonconformist* newspaper in London. He proposed that Church and State should be separated and that parliamentary reform was not only a necessary step in this process, but an important end in itself. In December 1843, seventy ministers from the Midlands met at Leicester and passed a resolution calling for the separation of the Church from the State. A conference was subsequently held in London to launch the movement on a national basis. Welsh representation at this was strong, with twenty-two delegates attending: eight from Monmouthshire, four from Glamorgan, four from Montgomeryshire, three from Carmarthenshire, two from Denbigh, and one from Merioneth. Edward Miall made his first public appearance in Wales in 1848 at Newport. He went on to speak at nine towns in south Wales, and it was in the south and the border counties that the Society made its initial impact. Liberation committees were set up in a host of Welsh towns in the 1840s and 1850s, and the bulk of Liberationist activity in these years was associated with visitations from Society lecturers. In south Wales the year of expansion was 1862–3 when the number of places making contributions rose from twenty-two to forty-five, and the growth was greatest in the towns and industrial belt of Glamorgan. In north Wales the expansion began in 1863–4 and continued in 1867–8. In 1863 ten places were contributing; in 1864, twenty-one; in 1867, thirty-two; and in 1868, fifty-five. More people in more places were making contributions and this indicates that the Liberation Society was establishing itself and growing at a steady pace throughout the 1850s and 1860s.

It was in the 1860s that the Society made some striking advances in Wales. The Welsh denominational magazines, *Y Diwygiwr* and *Seren Gomer*, printed abbreviated reports of the Society's annual meetings, and the editor of the former, Revd David Rees, Llanelli, welcomed articles on the theme of disestablishment. In the years before 1861 there was little local effort in Wales: the Society could only afford to send its lecturers infrequently to tour the Principality; no tracts appear to have been made available in Welsh; there were very few local committees; and subscriptions actually fell. At a national level, however, the association was becoming more influential in British politics, and it took an active role in organizing Dissenting opinion in each election after 1847. It was in the period after 1861 that the Society decided to pay particular attention to Wales, and by 1862 it had been decided to hold two conferences in Wales during the year, one in south Wales in May or June, and the other at a later date in the north.

The Swansea Conference of September 1862 lasted two days and was attended by 200 delegates. The speakers were all prominent Dissenting laymen or ministers, the exception being L. Ll. Dillwyn, the member for Swansea and a vigorous Liberationist. One result of the conference was that a committee for south Wales was established, and a district agent appointed. An electoral agent was appointed in south Wales and it was his task to nurse the Cardiganshire constituency for Henry Richard at a future election (post-1865). In the years after 1862 the Society launched a concerted attack on south Wales. It was not until September 1866 that it attempted a similar assault on north Wales, organizing a series of conferences throughout the northern counties. The success of the northern conferences was astonishing and the theme was the same, the political ineffectiveness of a majority religious movement. The conferences resulted in the setting up of a network of committees in the counties, and these were required not only to spread the gospel of disestablishment but to build up a political organization in readiness for the next general election. By August 1867, an agent for north Wales was also appointed at an eventual salary of £50 per annum. By 1867, therefore, there existed in Wales an organization, with a staff of agents and political experts, and a network of local committees and caucuses, which was to channel into political action the potentialities and enthusiasms of Welsh Nonconformity. The Liberation Society in Wales lent its support in July 1867 to the South Wales Liberal Registration Society, when that body was formed at Carmarthen. The Liberation Society was also behind the formation of a Welsh Reform Association in July 1868. It was the Liberation Society, more than any other reform association, which was responsible for the reform agitation of the period; and in Wales, parliamentary reform had a religious or ecclesiastical rather than a secular colouring.

Suffrage extension was a tremendous boost to the Liberationist cause everywhere and in the 1868 election the Society paid particular attention to Wales. The Society was most directly involved at Merthyr, and in Henry Richard's campaign; its activities extended also to the Welsh Representation Society, which was formed at Aberdare in 1867, to promote Welsh Nonconformist parliamentary representation. The role of the Society was significant in the two Denbighshire contests, where Thomas Gee was a prominent figure. Liberationists exerted some electoral influence through their control of the South Wales Liberal Registration Association, which claimed registration victories in Cardiganshire, Carmarthenshire, and in the Monmouthshire boroughs. In the ensuing 1868 general election, Wales returned twenty-three Liberals and ten Tories. The Liberation Society's role in the individual contests was not great and it could be accredited with no overwhelming success except at Merthyr. Yet 1868 did mark a break with tradition and the essential contribution of the Society lay in its educational work over the years, and in translating religious sentiment and Nonconformist enthusiasm into political activity.

After the 1868 election the Society intensified its exertions in Wales; and its activity mirrored the current controversies: Irish disestablishment was one theme, and another was public education. The Revd Thomas Levi was the Society's agent for south Wales in the years 1868–71 and it was then that Welsh-language publications were produced. The early 1870s were the point at which the Society began to make a determined effort to increase its appeal to the working classes, and to nurse public opinion in favour of disestablishment. The 1874 general election caught the Society by surprise and the contribution of the Liberationist registration bodies, the Welsh Reform Association and the South Wales Liberal Association was minimal. In the late 1870s and early 1880s the greatest Liberationist expansion occurred in industrial areas, in towns like Aberdare, Cardiff, Llanelli, Newport and Swansea. The Society also continued to court the favour of working-class leaders, and William Abraham (Mabon), the south Wales Miners' Leader, addressed many Liberation meetings.

Trade Unions and Politics Before 1880

Trade unions did not suddenly appear on the scene in the 1860s and 1870s, but it was then that they began to play a notable role as political pressure groups. Trade unions appeared in the early 1830s, when lodges of the National Association for the Protection of Labour (NAPL) were formed. Combinations of workers had existed earlier than this but in a disorganized and ineffective form. The opposition of employers and sections of Welsh Nonconformity undermined the work of NAPL. In the 1840s and 1850s there were hardly any permanent trade union organizations in the country. There is evidence to suggest that there were periods of temporary strength, as in 1841 when Lord Bute claimed that unions among the south Wales colliers were — 'as firm and unbroken as ever and that they are altogether above and beyond the control of their Employers'. This unity was transient, local, and usually confined to times of crisis.

Welsh trade unionism in the early 1830s was largely associated with the miners and colliers, though from the 1840s the trade union movement spread among the skilled artisans of the towns of Wales. *The United Kingdom First Annual Trades Union Directory* of 1861 listed fifty-one trade unions in Wales. Most of these were small, exclusive unions and they embraced a variety of trades — shoemakers, boilermakers, carpenters, and shipwrights were included — but the stonemasons (twenty-one societies) were preponderant. There was no clear distinction at this juncture between unions' industrial and political interests, and there was a widespread suspicion among these early unionists that involvement in Radical politics would damage their cause. During the 1840s and 1850s official trade unions steered clear of political activity: and the failure of Chartism as a political movement seemed to confirm the supremacy of industrial action. It was not until the 1860s that trade unions began to emerge as directly political organizations.

The early 1860s saw the gradual move towards political activity; and the main impulse came from the London Trades Council, founded in 1860. Its leaders worked to bring unionists into political agitation and launched a series of reform organizations in these years. Their objectives were to remove the legal restraints under which unionists operated, to safeguard their funds, and to conduct strikes without fear of criminal charge.

Reform League branches at Merthyr and Cardiff were initiated by trades' organizations. The Merthyr shoemakers formed a branch in January 1867; and the first trades' council in Wales operated in Cardiff in the 1860s. In Cardiff and Newport trade union leaders threw their weight behind the Liberal candidate in the 1868 election.

In Wales the most politically active section of labour was the miners, and the *Miner and Workman's Advocate* circulated widely throughout the valleys. In January 1865 it had sixteen agents in Wales, mostly distributed through the south Wales valleys. By 1869 the miners were beginning to integrate into a national organization, the newly-formed Amalgamated Association of Miners (AAM). In 1873 it had branches in eight Welsh counties and a membership of over 30,000 in south Wales alone. Its most direct political gesture was the support of Thomas Halliday at the Merthyr election in 1874. It was in the Merthyr area that the earliest incursions by labour into local politics occurred. In March 1874 Revd T.D. Mathias, a local Baptist minister, polled almost 4,000 votes as the working-men's candidate. William Gould, the Merthyr Chartist and ex-miner, sat on the Merthyr Board of Guardians as a respectable grocer. At Aberdare, Isaac Thomas was elected to the Board of Health in April 1875. These candidatures were signs of direct labour participation in local elections in the Merthyr area in the early 1870s.

In the mid and late 1870s trade union activity was hit by a trade depression, and membership of the unions declined. The south Wales unions reverted to district unions in the period, and by the late 1870s unionism had probably penetrated Wales to a greater degree than is usually appreciated. Branches of the large amalgamated English unions — carpenters, tailors, bricklayers, stonemasons, engineers and blacksmiths — all existed in a large number of Welsh towns. Unions were also growing up in the tin-plate and iron industries: a poorly administered tin-plate association operated in west Glamorgan and Carmarthenshire in the early 1870s, while iron and steel unions fluctuated in south Wales after 1872. Trade unionism in Wales before the 1880s was limited in influence, ill-organized, and ephemeral; and the unions themselves were numerically weak.

The *1868 Election*

In 1866, out of a total population of around 1,313,000 in
Wales there were just over 62,000 voters. The Reform Act of
1867 gave the vote to about another 59,000 Welshmen, thereby
raising the percentage of the population who voted from around
4.5 in 1866 to about 9.1 per cent in 1868. The Act also gave
Wales one extra member — Merthyr was given an extra seat —
and this brought the total number of seats to thirty-three. Half
the population was excluded because they were women, while
the Act wholly disregarded agricultural labourers. Thousands
of industrial workers living outside the borough boundaries
were also excluded. Even in the borough constituencies, as the
figures in Table 12.1 disclose, adult male suffrage was still a long
way off.

Table 12.1

Constituency	Population in		Electors	
	1871	1868	1871	1877
Brecon	6,308	701	808	819
Merthyr	97,020	14,577	14,097	15,340
All Welsh boroughs	465,593	55,360	55,532	71,743

The 1867 Act did, however, pave the way for the 1868
election, the *annus mirabilis* of nineteenth-century Welsh political
history. Voting power was much more fairly distributed to
coincide with the centres of industry and concentration of
population. The actual rise in the electorate was quite considerable — about 50 per cent in the counties and 250 per cent in
the boroughs. But only in those centres where the growth of
industry, the creation of new types of communities, and
new leadership patterns had changed the fundamental social
relationships was the 1868 victory complete. Such were the
constituencies of Merthyr and Denbighshire. In these boroughs,
and in the counties, the new electorate, the old disfranchised in
borough and county, sensitized and activized by the years of
intensive education, sprang to life, as if to claim their new-found

freedom. The outstanding feature of the election was the way in which the new working-class voters organized themselves in distinct, independent, political movements.

In the 1868 general election Wales returned twenty-three Liberals and ten Tories, as compared with eighteen Liberals and fourteen Tories in the previous election. The election results must not, however, be distorted. Only three Members of Parliament were Nonconformists, and the remaining thirty were Anglicans. Ten Tories were returned, and most of the twenty-three Liberals were Whig in character. But some of the victories over the old order were dramatic, and the election did represent a cracking of the ice. The 1868 election signalled profound changes in Welsh political life, and these are perhaps best illustrated in microcosm.

The Merthyr Election of 1868

Merthyr Tydfil was the largest borough constituency in Wales and, as a result of the Reform Act of 1867, its population was estimated to be 105,000. It embraced two of the most heavily industrialized and densely populated valleys in the country, which were separated by a mountain ridge: the eastern half included the great industrial centres of Merthyr Tydfil and Dowlais; and in the western half lay the industrial conurbation of Aberdare. The Reform Act of 1867 increased the numbers of voters in this borough from 1,387 in 1866 to 14,577 in 1868. The skilled and unskilled labourers in the ironworks and mines were enfranchised, and the old middle-class electorate was swamped. The borough had been a safe seat for the ironmasters, successfully controlled by the Guest interest. H.A. Bruce, a local man, and a senior trustee of the Dowlais Ironworks, had represented the constituency since 1852. Over a period of sixteen years Bruce had risen to a position of eminence in the Liberal Party, and he would soon become Home Secretary in Gladstone's first administration.

As soon as it was known that Merthyr would be granted an additional member, election fever began. One of the most formidable candidates was Richard Fothergill, a local iron-master who ranked next to the Guests and the Crawshays. Most of his support came from the middle and commercial classes, but one leading member of Fothergill's Election Committee was the

Revd Dr Thomas Price, the editor of the Baptist monthly, *Seren Cymru*, and the leading Baptist in the area. His chapel and home at Aberdare were the centre of an influence which permeated the two valleys. Price had been an enthusiastic supporter of the Liberation Society, and in 1867 he had been instrumental in forming a Representation Society in the area. He supported Fothergill and Bruce, and he believed that the new voters would rally behind his lead.

The Representation Society eventually decided not to follow Price's lead, and chose a candidate whom it believed would be acceptable to the eighty-one Nonconformist congregations of the two valleys which were allied to the Society. The Aberdare Nonconformists also supported the decision, and Henry Richard, secretary of the Peace Society, was invited to contest the election. Richard was reluctant at first to rush into the election: he was not a rich man, his experience of electioneering was limited, and he had no connections with the constituency. His caution and detachment endeared him to his supporters and soon the Representation Society called itself the, 'Henry Richard or Nonconformist Committee'.

Soon it became clear that Richard's arrival on the scene would challenge the position of the senior, and sitting member, H.A. Bruce. Richard's appeal to the new voter made it certain by October 1867 that the contest for the second seat would not be fought between Richard and Fothergill, but between Fothergill and Bruce. The power of Nonconformity, and, in particular, the work of the Liberation Society, in educating the working-class voter and paving the way for a more informed public opinion, was one factor in Bruce's eventual downfall. The other factor was the growth of a movement which had developed side by side with Nonconformist influence, and sometimes antipathetically to it, the robust tradition of working-class Radicalism.

Bruce's refusal to vote for the secret ballot, his conditional acceptance of Nonconformist views on education, his 'traditional' views on the relation of Church and State, and his denial of the existence of any 'Welsh' problems, estranged him from the electorate. But there were also industrial reasons for his rejection. The colliers argued that Bruce was unsympathetic to them, and they noted that he had denounced them during the last great strike in the coalfield in the winter of 1857–8. The election of 1868 was fought at a time when there was a slump in the coal and iron trades, and a depression was affecting both industries. Bruce was unable to communicate effectively with the working-class voters and he underestimated the tradition of working-class politics which had survived since the 1830s and 1840s. The newspapers which opposed him were the radical *Merthyr Telegraph* and the Chartist *Merthyr Star*. The colliers further attacked him on the vexed question of safety in the mines, and they accused him of being in favour of those masters who were agitating for the statutory establishment of a double-shift system in the valleys. Working-class issues were gradually pushing to the forefront and, as they did so, Bruce's support began to dissipate.

Henry Richard was returned at the top of the poll, with an overwhelming majority over both of the other candidates, and Richard Fothergill captured the second seat. H.A. Bruce, the sitting tenant for sixteen years, was ousted, and not only by the force of Nonconformity, but for industrial reasons as well. A new working-class electorate had voiced its opinions clearly, and echoes would soon be heard in other parts of the country, and in other elections.

The Denbighshire 1868 Elections

The year 1868 was a miraculous one in many constituencies: in Carmarthenshire, E.J. Sartoris, a landowner of Radical leanings, topped the poll; in Carmarthen district, a Whig gained a seat for the Liberals; in Cardiganshire, a Nonconformist-industrialist, E.M. Richards, ousted the Vaughans of Trawscoed; David Williams of Penrhyndeudraeth was returned unopposed in Merioneth; and in Merthyr itself, Henry Richard's triumph symbolized the alliance of working-class Radicalism and organized Nonconformity.

In the borough and county elections in Denbighshire there were some notable changes: the Liberal Watkin Williams, a prosperous barrister, defeated the Tory landowner, Townsend Mainwaring, in the boroughs; and the Radical, George Osborne Morgan, another successful barrister, replaced the Whig, Colonel Biddulph of Chirk Castle. In Denbighshire, as in Merthyr, the important forces at work seem to have been industrial and religio-political. In the industrial areas there were deep underlying grievances in the coalfield, as strikes and attempts to form a union revealed. In 1862 Bryan Smith, a local man, started to organize the north Wales unions into a trade union, and this body flourished in 1863 and 1864. In the iron trades there was a severe depression and a wage reduction, and, at the time of the general election in November 1868 the men of Rhiwabon were on strike. The old Chartist political traditions were restless in the 1850s and 1860s in industrial Denbighshire, and lectures delivered by old Chartist warhorses such as Henry Vincent were well attended in the 1850s.

The Nonconformists were strong in Denbighshire, as the 1851 census on religion reveals. The Nonconformist chapels provided seating for 56 per cent of the population, while the Established Church could accommodate only 31 per cent. The rural areas were particularly well endowed with chapels: in Llanrwst and the surrounding rural area there were forty-one Nonconformist chapels compared with fifteen Anglican churches. These forty-one chapels provided seating for 66.5 per cent of the people. The Liberation Society had also been most active in the county, and had specially selected the area for a concerted campaign. Denbigh was, like Aberdare, Merthyr, Swansea and Caernarfon, one of the provincial capitals of the Principality; and they had achieved this status by virtue of their presses and their impact on public opinion.

Political dissent, advancing working-class Radicalism, and an extension of the franchise, combined to effect significant changes in Denbighshire. The crucial issue in the ensuing general election was which party would capture the new voters. The Liberals did so, and for a variety of reasons: the seeds of working-class Liberalism had been present in the Denbigh boroughs at least as early as the 1852 general election; the Liberals were far better organized than the Conservatives in the 1868 election; the influence of that great Nonconformist propagandist, Thomas Gee, the enthusiastic editor of *Baner ac Amserau Cymru*, was crucial — he was a leading supporter of the Denbigh Reform Association and he devoted considerable space in his paper to political issues; and the Liberation Society had paid particular attention to the north Wales counties in 1863–4 and in 1867–8.

The eventual results of the general election showed that, in the county, Osborne Morgan was elected in second place to Sir Watkin Williams Wynn. Morgan secured 31 per cent of the vote to Sir Watkin Williams Wynn's 39.5 per cent. Though it was a clear Liberal victory, the fact that Sir Watkin Williams Wynn headed the poll, and that Colonel Biddulph lost by only a small margin, suggests that many electors were still quite traditionalist. Despite the attacks by Thomas Gee on Sir Watkin Williams Wynn, he was widely recognized as a supportive landlord by many people in north Wales. The real significance of the election, as in Merthyr Tydfil, is that the old and the new traditions continued side by side. The year 1868 was only partly a year of miracles: the millennium would commence in the 1880s.

The Aftermath of the Election

The politics of the 1860s in Wales is characterized by the emergence of what is often called a 'national' view of Welsh affairs, with a consequent breakdown of the ancient particularism of the counties. The eminent historian, Dr K.O. Morgan, has described the period from 1868 to 1886 as a transition from Radicalism to Nationalism. The sequel to the 1868 election was as significant as the results themselves. Tenants were evicted throughout Wales for voting contrary to the wishes of the landed interest, and the evictions were especially severe in Caernarfonshire, Carmarthenshire and Cardiganshire. The newly-elected member for Merthyr, Henry Richard, soon took up the issue at Westminster, and the resulting furore helped towards the appointment of the Hartington Committee on Parliamentary and Municipal Elections. The weight of evidence produced convinced many Liberals of the need for voter protection, and the Nonconformists gave stout support. Wales played a distinct role in attaining the secret ballot in 1872.

With the exception of the ballot, little was achieved in the way of electoral reform in the period from 1867 to 1880. Yet they were years when pent-up enthusiasm found expression in such associations as the Land and Labour League, and the National Education League. There was also the obscure, and rather eccentric Magna Carta Association. This originated with the claim to the Tichborne estates by a man professing to be Roger Tichborne, eldest son of the family, supposed drowned in 1859. The main aims of the movement, which began in 1866 and lasted until the 1870s, were justice for the under-privileged and the restitution of Magna Carta and the Bill of Rights, a free and honest press, triennial parliaments, the payment of MPs, and the ever-popular abolition of income tax. In the period 1875–6 branches were set up at Merthyr, Aberdare, Hirwaun, Mountain Ash, Dowlais, Swansea, and Ystalyfera. During its existence, the movement captured the popular imagination and fascinated the press.

After the 1868 election Welsh Nonconformists readily identified with the seemingly similar Irish campaign for disestablishment, and the enactment of disestablishment in Ireland in the summer of 1869 led to similar demands from Wales. On 5 August 1869, Watkin Williams, the newly-returned member for the Denbigh borough, gave notice of a motion calling for the termination of the establishment of the Church in Wales. Williams acted wholly independently of his colleagues and the Liberation Society, and a rift emerged among the Welsh Liberals; sixteen Welsh members, including eight Conservatives and eight Liberals, voted against his motion. The Liberation Society had urged its Welsh members to allow the ballot to be settled first and to wait for the appropriate moment to introduce the issue before the Houses of Parliament.

One other result of the 1868 election was the growth of a new cohesion among the Welsh members at Westminster; and a sense that there should be separate laws for Wales. The debate on political evictions in Wales in July 1869 was one example, as was the campaign for a secret ballot. In 1872 the attention of Welsh members focused on the longstanding grievance of the appointment of English judges to Welsh-speaking areas. Osborne Morgan, the elected member for Denbighshire, and a distinguished barrister to boot, quoted Gladstone's appointment of Bishop Joshua Hughes to St Asaph in 1870 as a parallel. The grievance remained and Osborne Morgan again referred to the matter in the new Parliament of 1874. The years from 1874 to 1880 were uneventful ones for Wales at Westminster, and the Liberals lost some ground in the Principality at the 1874 election. Nineteen Liberals and fourteen Conservatives were returned in Wales, with a net loss of four seats to the Liberals. The election results were not without some consolation for the Liberal Party: the Whig element was gradually being eroded, and three more Nonconformists were returned for the displaced Whigs.

In the field of education, also, there was a new vitality in Welsh public life after 1868. It was specifically in the realm of higher education that a Welsh question emerged, which evoked a sympathetic response from both sides of the political spectrum. H. Hussey Vivian, the Swansea copper king, rose in the House of Commons on 1 July 1879, to highlight the deficiencies of higher education in Wales. He showed that, while Ireland had 1,634 university students (1:3,121 of the population), and Scotland could claim a total of 4,000 (1:840), the total number of Welsh students enjoying higher education of any kind, at Jesus College, Oxford, at Lampeter College, and at Aberystwyth College, amounted to a mere 189. The future of higher education, and of the struggling Aberystwyth College in particular, were made more precarious by the absence of any organized schooling above the elementary level. This debate on Welsh higher education was extremely important for it became a political issue for the first time, and when Gladstone returned to power he set up a committee of inquiry into higher education in Wales, with Lord Aberdare as chairman. Its Report recommended the creation of a system of intermediate schools, and it led to the establishment of two new colleges at Cardiff and Bangor.

From the 1860s onwards, therefore, national political ideologies and techniques gradually penetrated the constituencies and there emerged a 'national' view of politics. A number of factors probably produced this transition from Radicalism to Nationalism: the extension of the franchise and the subsequent growth of democracy at both a national and local level had promoted the latent Nationalism in popular Radicalism; the campaign for public education had given Nationalism its cultural ideal; the agricultural depression from the late 1870s had provided the catalyst of economic hardship; the passing of the Sunday Closing Act in 1881, and other public gestures had afforded a precedent for Welsh legislation; and disestablishment was affectionately worn as the badge of national recognition. The 'Welsh question' was fast becoming a political reality.

SUGGESTED READING

G.E. Jones, *Modern Wales* (Cambridge, 1984).
I.G. Jones, *Explorations and Explanations* (Llandysul, 1981).
I.G. Jones, *Communities* (Llandysul, 1987).
W. Jones, *Thomas Edward Ellis, 1859–1899* (Cardiff, 1986).
K.O. Morgan, *Wales in British Politics, 1868–1922* (Cardiff, 1970).
P. Morgan and D. Thomas, *Wales: The Shaping of a Nation* (London, 1984).

Articles:
D.J.V. Jones, 'The Merthyr Riots of 1831', *W.H.R.*, 3 (1966–7).
D.J.V. Jones, 'The Carmarthen Riots of 1831', *W.H.R.*, 4 (1968–9).
I.G. Jones, 'Merthyr Tydfil: The Politics of Survival', *Llafur*, 2, no. 1 (1976).
I.G. Jones, 'Politics in Merthyr Tydfil', *Glamorgan Historian*, 10 (1974).
R.T. Jones, 'The Origins of the Nonconformist Dis-establishment Campaign', *J.H.S. Ch.in W.*, XX (1970).
Jane Morgan, 'Denbighshire's Annus Mirabilis: the Borough and County Elections of 1868', *W.H.R.*, 7 (1974–5).
R.D. Rees, 'Electioneering Ideals Current in South Wales, 1790–1832', *W.H.R.*, 2 (1964–5).
D.A. Wager, 'Welsh Politics and Parliamentary Reform, 1780–1832', *W.H.R.*, 7 (1974–5).

13. The Welsh Nation 1880–1906

Industrial and Economic Growth

BY the 1880s the contrast between industrial and rural Wales was most striking. The census of 1881 showed that there were 1,577,000 inhabitants in Wales, an increase of 150,000 since 1871. But the growth was largely confined to the industrial areas: much of the increase was in Glamorgan, whose population had expanded from 405,798 to 518,383, a rise of 27 per cent, and the third largest recorded in any county in Britain. The urban areas, in particular, exhibited some startling growth-rates; while the upland regions showed a decline — Merthyr Tydfil and Aberdare had experienced a fall in population between 1871 and 1881. In rural Wales — in Breconshire, Radnorshire, and Montgomery in mid Wales, and in Pembrokeshire and Cardiganshire in the west — there was also a considerable drop in the population in the last quarter of the century.

Industrial Wales, and especially the mining valleys of south Wales, was swept along in a period of growth and expansion from 1880 to 1914. It would seem that only the Ruhr in Germany and the industrial sections of the USA could rival south Wales as centres of heavy industry. The chief reason for this growth was the extraordinary expansion of the Welsh coal industry. The production of coal of different types leapt up from 16 million tons in the early 1870s to 30 million tons in 1891, and to 56.8 million in 1913. In that year south Wales was responsible for one-fifth of the entire coal production of British mines, and, with nearly 30 of its 56 million tons going for export, it supplied almost one-third of the entire world exports in coal of all types. Welsh collieries numbered 485 in 1913, and 323 of these were located in Glamorgan. The labour force in Welsh mines totalled well over 250,000 men.

One of the most important growth-points was the Rhondda valleys, where major new collieries were opened in the years from 1891 to 1914. Manpower in the Rhondda mines increased from 25,000 in 1885 to 41,000 in 1913. In the anthracite areas of the Swansea Valley and east Carmarthenshire there was also unprecedented expansion. The output of Welsh anthracite coal grew almost threefold, from 1,676,128 tons in 1895 to 4,778,114 tons in 1913. Small villages suddenly grew into sizeable industrial centres, and places like Pontardawe, Brynamman, Ammanford, and Gowerton rose to prominence on the industrial landscape.

The tin-plate industry also thrived in the last quarter of the century. One expansionary period was from 1876 to 1882, when eighteen new works were established in Glamorgan and Carmarthenshire. The second wave of expansion lapped the industrial zones of the counties in the years 1886 to 1891, when ten new works were built. The last few years of the 1880s are regarded as one of the most prosperous eras in the history of the trade.

The 1880s proved to be the turning-point in the steel industry, for it was then that Welsh tin-plate manufacturers turned over to the making of steel. Many new steelworks emerged on the coastal belt in south-west Wales. In the eastern parts, also, there was a gradual move away from the old upland regions to new coastal sites. Dowlais opened its new plant at the East Moors site, in the Cardiff dockland, and steel production commenced there in 1895. In 1885 a continuous steel-making plant, with the first Siemens open-hearth steel furnace in Britain, was built at Brymbo, near Wrexham; and a major steel industry grew up in north-east Wales also. Shotton and Brymbo were to be important centres of steel production down to the 1970s.

Industry, Culture and Language

It has been forcefully argued, notably by Professor Brinley Thomas, that the population explosion in Wales in the second half of the nineteenth century was a blessing to the Welsh language. The Welsh-speaking people who left the countryside were not forced to emigrate to England or overseas; they were able to migrate to the rapidly growing industrial districts of Wales. The 1891 census showed that nearly 900,000 people were Welsh speaking in Wales (excluding Monmouthshire), and 90 per cent of them were living in the five counties most affected by industrialization — Glamorgan, Carmarthenshire, Denbighshire, Flintshire, and Caernarfonshire. That would seem to suggest that industrialization actually helped to preserve the Welsh language in the nineteenth century.

In 1851 the parish of Ystradyfodwg (which later comprised a large part of the Rhondda) had a population of only 950. By 1871, after the opening of twenty steam-coal pits and the Taff Vale Railway, the population of the parish had risen from 950 to 17,000. From 1871 to 1911 the population of the Rhondda valleys grew from 24,000 to 153,000 as a result of the expansion of the steam-coal trade. In this heavily industrialized region, the growth of the Welsh-speaking population was dependent upon the constant inflow of native Welsh-speakers from the Welsh rural counties. But the number of Welsh-speakers was also determined by the natural increase (that is, the excess of births over deaths) in the industrial areas. Each wave of in-migrants, consisted of marriageable young men: the marriage-rate in the industrial communities was high, and the birth-rate in the colliery districts was the highest in Britain. In the four decades after 1861, the population of Glamorgan rose by more than half a million: less than a third of this (167,000) was due to net inward migration, and over two-thirds (367,000) was the result of an excess of births over deaths.

The history of the Welsh language in Monmouthshire throws light on the impact of industrialization in that sensitive border county. As the iron industry expanded from the 1780s to the 1830s thousands of young Welsh-speaking people moved into Monmouthshire from the rural counties of Montgomeryshire, Brecknockshire, Carmarthenshire, and Cardiganshire. There was a massive in-migration of Welsh-speakers which radically altered the linguistic balance in favour of Welsh. A recent researcher has shown that of a population of 45,568 in Monmouthshire in 1801, 80 per cent (36,000) were Welsh-speakers. The vast majority of the population spoke Welsh to each other, and the language of protest movements, such as the Scotch Cattle and Chartism, was Welsh. The mass of the population had turned away from the Established Church and affiliated themselves to Nonconformity partly because the church services were conducted in the language of the upper-class English minority. But the decade 1861–71 brought problems for the language, as the old iron towns declined and the coal regions attracted people away from the Monmouthshire valleys. Anglicization was the main result of migration after 1861 in Monmouthshire: bilingualism became much more widespread; English chapels were set up; and there was the impact of the new educational institutions, with their emphasis on English as the key to commercial, social and academic success. The result of the changing pattern of migration, with an increasing flow of English migrants into the industrial areas of Monmouthshire, was a decline in the number of Welsh-speakers; as the figures in Table 13.1 indicate.

Table 13.1

	1801	*1861*	*1871*	*1891*	*1901*
Population of Monmouthshire	45,568	174,633	195,448	260,033	274,415
Percentage of Welsh-speakers	80	40	28.9	15.2	13.0
Number of Welsh-speakers	36,000	70,000	56,500	39,559	35,690

The Anglicization of Monmouthshire was caused, therefore, by the substantial English immigration, accompanied by the out-migration of many thousands of Welsh people from the declining iron districts to the expanding coal communities in the Rhondda and Aberdare valleys.

The language survived reasonably well until the 1890s, when English immigration became a predominant force. In the first decade of the new century over 100,000 immigrants crossed the border into the Welsh valleys. Even in the Rhondda the status of Welsh was threatened, and the proportion of Welsh-speakers in the population of Wales fell from 49.9 per cent in 1901 to 43.5 per cent in 1911. The decline continued so that the Welsh-speaking proportion reached 20.8 per cent in 1971 and 18.9 per cent in 1981. If Wales had remained an agricultural country, her population of 350,000 in the mid eighteenth century might have grown to about 700,000 by the mid-Victorian period. The effect of agricultural depression from the 1880s onwards would probably have reduced that figure to 500,000 in 1901. Even if the Welsh-speaking proportion had been as high as 70 per cent, the number speaking Welsh at the beginning of this century would have been only 350,000, instead of over a million as it actually was. On the other hand, the 350,000 Welsh-speakers would have been spread more evenly and would probably have been less exposed to the powerful force of Anglicization.

Industrialization and the concomitant demographic and economic forces were important in preserving and promoting the Welsh language in the nineteenth century. The other vitally significant factor was the close connection that had developed between the Welsh language and organized religion since the Protestant Reformation of the sixteenth century. Religious leaders in the last century were unanimous in believing that there were special features belonging to these religious organizations: one belief was that Wales was the most religious part of Britain; secondly, they held that the appeal of religion in Wales by mid-century was universal, and certainly not determined by class considerations; thirdly, that religion in Wales was equally successful in town and country; and, fourthly, that the purity of the Protestant faith was nowhere more secure than in Wales. Language was an essential component in the religious experience and the Victorians claimed that they had succeeded in bringing to fruition what governments had attempted at the time of the Reformation, but which their instrument for this purpose, the Established Church, had failed to do.

There were some strange and ominous indications of an increasingly uneasy relationship between language and religion in nineteenth-century Wales. One ambiguous element in the relationship was the growing admiration of ministers for the English culture; and so many aspirants to the ministry made strenuous efforts to learn English. English was accepted as a prestige-giving and status-conferring language. Another factor was the emergence of the movement to build chapels for the English immigrants in the Welsh towns. The campaign had commenced in the 1850s and it attracted many of Nonconformity's celebrities. By mid-century, English was commonly accepted as the language of science, business, commerce, philosophy, and the arts; while Welsh was the language of religion. This trend had some serious implications: religion was being degraded in comparison with other mental and social activities; it was being defined in exclusive terms; and English was featuring as the language of ambition, of well-being, and of progress.

The common people clung to the Welsh language, because it was *their* language. It was their language in the sense that it was incorporated into their own institutions, the chapels, Sunday schools, temperance societies, choral unions and their eisteddfodau. The Welsh language had become a way of expressing social differences, for it marked them off from the English and the Anglicizing middle classes. The language also expressed national differences and embodied a separate and heroic past. It was the precious possession of workers in the face of the inhuman and brutalizing forces of industrialism: above all, it inspired confidence and pride in one's heritage, history and culture.

With the gradual collapse of the Welsh economy after the First World War the class war in the coalfields intensified, and Welshmen turned not to Methodism but to Marx. Economic and demographic factors, therefore, played a vital role in contracting the linguistic frontier. Severe unemployment followed and a steady stream of emigration contributed to the decline in the fortunes of language. At the beginning of the century Welshmen had turned yet again to the chapels for guidance and leadership, and the 1904 revival was possibly the last great expression of that unique relationship between language, culture, and religion. Ordinary Welshmen had tried to make religion what it had once been — popular, non-clerical, unsophisticated, organic, and Welsh-language based. When that revival failed to answer their prayers, a new gospel and a new medium of communication penetrated the coalfields: the language of Socialism, namely, English.

Political Changes

By the 1880s there was increasing agitation for parliamentary reform emanating partly from the activities of reform associations in the 1870s. The National Agricultural Labourers' Union took up the banner of reform, as did the National Reform Union at its annual conference of 1883. In July of that year a rally of 12,000 miners in the Rhondda Valley called for parliamentary reform, and when the Lords had rejected the Franchise Bill, protest meetings were held in all parts of Wales. At Tredegar, Llandysul, Llangefni, and in scores of other places agricultural workers objected to the Lords' denial of their just claims. As in 1831–2, strong feelings against the Lords mounted steadily, and the reform campaign climaxed in Wales with the appearances of Joseph Chamberlain at Newtown and Denbigh in October 1884.

When the 1884 Reform Act was passed, it increased the United Kingdom electorate from two-and-a-half million to five million. In Wales thousands of miners, tin-platers, and steel-workers became voters, as well as workers in rural areas. Glamorgan was transformed from a two-member constituency with 12,785 voters in 1880 into five new county divisions with a combined electorate of 43,449. In the rural areas there were some major changes: Caernarfonshire, a two-member constituency with 6,361 voters in 1880, was divided into two constituencies, with a total electorate of 18,114; an increase of almost 200 per cent in the number of voters. The Welsh county electorate actually increased from 74,936 to 200,373.

The Redistribution Act of 1885 destroyed the old distinction between borough and county, and created constituencies of more equal size. Wales favoured under the new scheme, with one member for 45,342 voters, while the ratio for England was one member for 54,000. After 1885 Wales had thirty-four seats. Yet, although the 1884–5 Acts had some far-reaching effects on Wales and the whole of Britain, by 1911 only 63 per cent of all adult males were on the electoral roll. The 1884 Act left about 12 per cent of all the adult male population disfranchised. The five Glamorgan divisions had a total population of 1,120,910, of which 104,099 were voters. At Merthyr Tydfil there were 23,518 voters out of a population of 143,849. The 1884–5 Acts were an important step towards democracy, but the effects should not be overemphasized.

At the ensuing 1885 election the Liberals won thirty seats, and fourteen of the Liberal MPs were Nonconformists. Alfred Thomas, president of the Baptist Union, was elected for East

Glamorgan; and John Thomas, chairman of the Methodist Association of North Wales, captured Flint district. In a spectacular contest in East Denbighshire, Osborne Morgan ousted Sir Watkin Williams Wynn, whose family had held the county seat since 1715. In the July election of 1886 the Liberals maintained their hold, seizing twenty-five of the Welsh seats, with Osborne Morgan clinging on to East Denbighshire. In the next couple of years the Welsh Liberals went from strength to strength: their opinions carried greater weight in the Liberal Party; and their policies of land reform, education, temperance, and disestablishment made spectacular progress in the Party. Welsh disestablishment took second place on the Liberals' Newcastle programme of 1891. At the election of July 1892 the Welsh Liberals captured all but three of the thirty-four seats, and most won with huge majorities. It seemed that, in theory at least, the Welsh Liberals held the balance in Gladstone's administration, with its majority of only forty.

After 1894, however, Liberal fortunes began to decline as the new Rosebery administration tottered. There was open dissension between the new Liberal premier, Rosebery, and his colleagues, as the Party became increasingly divided over its priorities: Irish home rule had failed yet again in its parliamentary passage; the *Cymru Fydd* nationalist campaign was rupturing the Welsh party; agricultural depression reigned in the rural areas; and there was hardship in some of the industrial districts, and particularly in the tin-plate sector which was reeling from the effects of the McKinley tariff. It came as no surprise, therefore, that, at the July 1895 election, the Unionist vote should rise in Wales. The Conservatives won nine seats, their best performance in any Welsh general election in the period 1880 to 1924. At the 1900 'Khaki' election the Liberals gained three seats to restore their overall total to twenty-eight; and in January 1906 they swept the electoral board to take thirty-four seats in Wales.

It is widely recognized that the years after 1886 ushered in a new era of political activity. There were new men, new issues, and new protests in Welsh society. The new generation of young politicians replaced figures like Henry Richard, Hussey Vivian and Lewis Llewelyn Dillwyn. One promising Liberal was Tom Ellis, elected for Merioneth in 1886, and later to become the Party's chief whip in 1894. D.A. Thomas, elected for Merthyr

Tydfil from 1888 to 1910, a coalowner and proprietor of the Cambrian Collieries, was another ascending star in the Liberal constellation. Perhaps the most dynamic and luminous was David Lloyd George, who was returned for the Caernarfon boroughs in April 1890, at the age of twenty-seven. He took the lead in pressing for radical reforms in the years after 1892 and helped make Wales a political reality. These young leaders were the products of decades of Liberal achievement in the constituencies for, by the 1880s, there were Liberal associations peppered all over Wales; and in 1886–7 the Liberal federations of north and south Wales had been set up at Wrexham and Merthyr Tydfil.

The new issues that dominated Welsh politics in the post-1886 period were temperance, education, tithes, land reform, home rule, and disestablishment. The temperance campaigners could claim one startling victory in 1881, the Welsh Sunday Closing Act. This is recognized as being the first distinctively Welsh Act of Parliament: it testified to the existence of a Welsh political identity. Welsh education also took some remarkable strides in this period, notably with the passing of the Welsh Intermediate Education Act of 1889, which was discussed in Chapter II. The land question reappeared in the period after 1886, probably as a response to the agricultural depression and the agitation of the new populists, such as T.E. Ellis. A Welsh Land League was set up at Rhyl in 1886 under the leadership of that stormy petrel, Thomas Gee of Denbigh. It campaigned for a massive reduction in rents, security of tenure, and a land court to adjudicate on rents. In 1888 and 1892 Tom Ellis launched two parliamentary debates on the Welsh land question, and Gladstone appointed a Royal Commission to investigate the land problems in 1892. The Commission operated from 1893 to 1895 and produced its report in 1896. This report was in fact a combination of two opposed reports: one reflected the views of the six Liberal members; the other manifested the pro-landlord stance of the three Unionists. The Commission had little positive impact: its importance was that it exhibited the essential nature of Welsh Liberalism at this time, as a revolt against a static, hierarchical social order.

The land issue and the question of education took second place to the vital matter of disestablishment. After 1886 this was demanded for the sake of religious equality, but it was urged largely for national reasons. Disestablishment assumed a new importance after 1886, for a variety of reasons: the Welsh MPs felt that they had been given a specific mandate for disestablishment at the polls; the growing importance of the Celtic nations within the Liberal Party helped the cause; at the Nottingham conference in 1887, the National Liberal Federation had formally adopted the issue as a major item on its programme; leading Liberals, like Morley and Rosebery, had embraced the principle; and Gladstone, an ardent Anglican, had nevertheless pledged his support. When he became Prime Minister in 1892 Welshmen expected that he would soon tackle the matter. Alas, their hopes were to be dashed, and only some half-hearted shuffling took place. When Rosebery succeeded Gladstone as Prime Minister, a Welsh Disestablishment Bill followed, introduced by H.H. Asquith as Home Secretary. This bill was lost in a whirlpool of work in the 1894 parliamentary session. A successor passed its second reading in the House of Commons by forty-four votes on 1 April 1895. Unfortunately, when the Liberals fell from office in June, the bill was still locked in committee stage. During the next ten years of Tory rule, there was no action on Welsh disestablishment. The 1894 bill did, however, provide a model for later bills introduced in 1909 and 1912–14. Welsh disestablishment was not finally achieved until 1920.

Liberalism, despite some social and industrial challenges, retained its dominance of Welsh affairs in the years from 1886 to 1906. Welsh Liberalism, for the most part, was firmly based on that self-contained, small-town, middle-class élite which had emerged in the preceding decades and was now flexing its muscles and stretching out for political power. Liberal associations had been formed in all parts of Wales by this class of shopkeepers, doctors, journalists, solicitors, merchants and Nonconformist ministers. The thirty-seven Liberal members on the first Cardiganshire County Council formed in 1889 included thirteen tenant farmers, eleven small businessmen and shopkeepers, four ministers, two surgeons, and one stonemason. These people bridged the worlds of municipal politics, local government, chapel affairs, and social leadership in organic, democratic communities.

Local government was a crucial component of Liberalism, and the newly-formed county councils in 1888–9 displayed the transmogrification from the old, hierarchical, traditional system of political activity to the new, more democratic model. In north Wales, in the local government elections of January 1889, 175 Liberal councillors were returned out of 260; while in south Wales there were 215 Liberal councillors out of 330. The Liberal control of local councils was securely maintained for almost thirty years, and its ideological platform sustained the essential issues of social equality and civic libertarianism. On economic questions the Liberals had little new to say, and on industrial matters they were judiciously silent. The Liberals assumed that all classes would work together harmoniously, and that the middle and working classes would co-operate in the production of goods and services. In Wales there seemed no need, as yet, to construct an economic or social philosophy, and the associations remained blissfully ignorant of the surging undercurrents of conflict and protest. Liberal associations offered few opportunities for working men to be selected as electoral candidates, and always reluctantly accepted them. The labour movement and its local representatives, such as D.J. Rees, editor of the *Llais Llafur* newspaper, or Mabon, the miners' leader, were prepared to remain within the Liberal community. Indeed, for these people the call of community was of greater importance than the pull of class.

Social Protest and Industrial Conflict

Rural Protest

By the 1880s rural Wales was already beginning to display the symptoms of declining opportunity and low investment. In the ten years up to 1881, Breconshire, Radnorshire, and Montgomeryshire in mid Wales, and Pembrokeshire and Cardiganshire in the west, were showing a fall in population. Decline and depression were setting in and, in the years 1881–91, population fell in eight out of thirteen Welsh counties. The fall in prices hit the relatively important corn-growing areas of Flintshire, Denbighshire, the Vale of Glamorgan, and south Pembrokeshire. The downward trend began in 1874–5 in wheat and barley prices, and a year later in oats, and it continued to

1896. From 1861 to 1871, and 1894 to 1898 wheat prices fell by 51 per cent, barley by 42 per cent, and oats by 37 per cent. Corn farmers were not alone in suffering from foreign competition in the last quarter of the century. The perfecting of refrigeration techniques led to the importation of frozen and chilled meat from the 1880s onwards. Dairy farmers also experienced growing competition from imported butter, cheese, and eggs from Europe, and cheese from America. The depression in Welsh livestock and dairy farming only really began in the mid-1880s and lasted through to 1896. Growing imports of wool and a spell of bad weather combined to lower wool prices by 45 per cent in the years 1872–4 and 1891–2.

The improvement in economic conditions in mid-century and the advent of a railway system had pushed up the rental values of properties in Wales. It is estimated that rent increases ranged from 5 to 30 per cent, depending on such factors as land elevation, previous rental, fertility, land hunger, and the proximity to railways. In addition to money rents there were other duties and services in kind to be paid to the landowners. Food rents and service rents could be charged to the tenants. Another grievance was the payment of tithes. Since the Tithe Commutation Act of 1836 this particular levy had been paid in cash; and, in times of agricultural depression and cash shortage, it could be a particularly irksome and onerous charge. It was the tithe charge which succeeded in coalescing the tenants' dislike of the landowners with their resentment at the Anglican Church. Agricultural depression, a falling population, the exorbitant rentals, social hardship on the land, the impact of Non-conformist radicalism in the area, and the memories of political evictions all combined to fuel the attack on the tithes. Organized protests were conducted in north-east Wales from 1886 to 1891. The first agitation occurred in January 1886 in Denbighshire, and the Anti-Tithe League was formed at a farmers' meeting at Rhuthin in early September 1886. The initial aim of the League was to support the farmers in their attempts to achieve tithe rebates. There had been a drastic fall in the prices of stock in 1885–6, and this made the burden of the tithe payment seem that much harsher. Some landlords had responded sympathetically to the plight of their tenants and lowered rents. A leading light in the campaign was Thomas Gee, who used his paper,

Baner ac Amserau Cymru, to focus opposition to the tithe and to direct the movement.

In the autumn and early winter of 1886 protests spread through the Vale of Clwyd and north-west Flintshire. In June 1887 a serious disturbance occurred at Mochdre, when the Riot Act was read and eighty-four people were injured, including thirty-four policemen. Those who refused to pay tithes often found that their property was confiscated and sold at auction; and policemen usually had to accompany the auctioneer as he went about his business. The tithe disturbances spread from the north-east across into the neighbouring counties of Caernarfonshire and Montgomeryshire. In 1889 there were even incidents in the citadel of the old Rebeccaites in Cardiganshire and Pembrokeshire. Protests continued throughout 1889 and 1890, and petered out in 1891 once the Tithe Rent Charge Act was passed. This measure stipulated that tithes should be paid to the Church by the landlords rather than by the tenant farmers. Although the Nonconformists no longer had to pay to an 'alien church', the landlords now increased tenants' rents to cover the tithe payment. Henceforth, the 'land question' was targeted at the landlords, and Gee and his supporters began to argue that their religious objection to tithes could only be settled once the Church had been disestablished. The Land League, after 1888, increasingly turned its attentions to the disestablishment campaign.

Unionism, Industrial Conflict and Labour Representation

The creation of an industrial society in south Wales had produced some acute social problems, made worse by the enormous influx of population into the mining valleys. By 1891, the population of the Rhondda was already over 127,000; while Cardiff's population stood at 182,259 in 1911. Up to the 1890s most of the immigrants had come from rural Wales, and they brought their cultural apparatus with them: chapels, Sunday schools, eisteddfodau, singing festivals, and denominational journals. After the 1890s the flood of immigrants came from outside Wales, from the contiguous English counties. Urban overcrowding, poverty and ill-health reigned among the inhabitants of the straggling and sprawling valley communities. Welsh local authorities built only 776 dwellings in the period

1890 to 1909. The figures for infant mortality were appalling: in 1911 the five major boroughs of south Wales recorded a death-rate of 380 children per 1,000 born.

The working men and their unions seemed almost powerless in the face of such intractable forces. In the mid and late 1870s the trade union movement was hit by a depression in trade, and membership of the TUC declined sharply. The south Wales miners reverted to district unions in this period and, by the late 1870s, there was evidence of union activity in Wales. Branches of the large amalgamated English unions — carpenters, iron moulders, tailors, bricklayers, stonemasons, plasterers, engineers, and blacksmiths — now existed in a large number of Welsh towns. Unions also sprang up in the tin-plate and iron industries — a poorly administered tin-plate association operated in west Glamorgan and Carmarthenshire in the early 1870s, while iron and steel unions functioned in south Wales after 1872.

The most startling early success story was when the North Wales Quarrymen's Union was launched in the Queen's Hotel, Caernarfon, in April 1874. Apart from a few months in 1878, when the union organized some 8 to 16,000 quarrymen in the slate mines of north-west Wales, its history was one of weakness, ineffectiveness and defeat. Its membership declined constantly from an average of 7,667 members for the period 1875–80 to an average of 4,376 in the years 1880–5, 3,469 in the 1890s, and 2,995 for the first decade of the twentieth century. When it affiliated to the General Federation of Trade Unions in 1899 it had fewer than 1,000 members. The reasons for its failure are not difficult to find: the depression in the industry in the 1880s and through the 1890s was an important factor; the nature of the industry, with its wide distribution of quarries, and the huge variation in scale between the different enterprises, was a debilitating feature; there was lack of decisive leadership, and a tendency to adhere to the rules of a market economy and to defer to the employers. It was not until the late 1890s that the NWQU secured the services of an able and energetic leader, W.H. Williams of Bethesda, who developed a united industrial policy and broke with the *laissez-faire* liberalism of the *ancien régime*. The union's moderate, conciliatory and deferential policies up to the 1890s had crippled effective industrial action.

By the early 1880s individual trade unions were displaying an increased interest in political activity. The NWQU was itself taking a more active political role. Union political involvement was stimulated by the agitation for the extension of the franchise, and in Wales it was the colliers who assumed the most active and prominent part in this franchise agitation. In the Rhondda, for example, the battle for the vote emanated not from the Liberal associations, but from the miners' associations. Miners held demonstrations in favour of the reform agitation at Pontypool, Ystalyfera, and many other industrial townships. In west Wales the South Wales Miners' Association took up the cause and held a massive demonstration of miners, tin-plate workers and agricultural labourers at Carmarthen in August 1884.

No general union had existed among the south Wales colliers from 1879 to 1883, and certainly there had been no effective organization in the coalfield as a whole before 1898. Yet, it was in these years that the foundations were laid; and the period after 1875 witnessed the growth of several district unions which were eventually to merge and form the South Wales Miners' Federation. It was in December 1875 that the first sliding-scale agreement was signed, whereby miners would accept a drop of $7\frac{1}{2}$ per cent in wages for each alteration of 1s. in prices. The sliding scale lasted for over twenty-five years and soured industrial relations in the intervening period. A steady fall in wage-rates from November 1891 to June 1893 led to an intensification of the campaign against the scale, but to no avail. Wage-rates continued their steady decline from 1894 to 1899. By 1896 a majority of over 30,000 men were serving notice to terminate the sliding scale. Even Mabon, lay preacher and moderate miners' leader, was edging slowly towards a modification of the scale. By January 1898 Mabon, William Brace, the Monmouthshire miners' leader, and others, were still prepared to negotiate a new agreement provided that the terms were modified in favour of the miners. The miners demanded a 10 per cent wage increase and a basic wage. The coalowners retaliated and suspended negotiations in February. By March 1898, 100,000 miners were out of work in a lock-out which lasted six months.

The strike was a complete victory for the coalowners; and during the stoppage whole villages and valleys were thrown into an abyss of depression and hardship. Soup kitchens and emergency feeding schemes were organized to try to alleviate the human suffering. The miners' defeat could largely be attributed to their financial and organizational weaknesses. But 1898 was a year deeply engrained in the miners' psyche and certain hard-learned lessons would not be forgotten. By October 1898, the South Wales Miners' Federation was formed and, in January 1899, the miners of south Wales had agreed to affiliate to the Miners' Federation of Great Britain. In December 1898 the new federation had attracted the support of 60,000 miners. By the end of 1899, 104,212 miners had joined the union. The old fabric of peace and industrial co-operation was disintegrating and in 1900 and 1901 the Federation led a series of 'stop-days', in which the miners were ordered to stop work for twenty-four hours. In December 1902 the Miners' Federation challenged the sliding scale, and it was soon replaced by a new system governed by a joint conciliation board. The new agreement also collapsed in 1905, and a further settlement was signed. By 1906 the Miners' Federation in south Wales could boast a membership of 120,000; and, as a result of augmenting wage-rates and a revival in trade, the number of miners affiliated to the union had reached 144,579 by 1908.

The miners were not alone in intensifying their union activities from the 1880s onwards. South Wales shared in the great expansion in trade unionism from 1889 to 1892. The success of the 'new unions' among the London dockers in 1889 boosted morale in the industrial valleys of south Wales and encouraged unions, such as the Amalgamated Society of Railway Servants (ASRS), to extend their activities. From 1887 onwards there was a distinct revival in unionism, and the South Wales and Monmouthshire Clerks' Association was formed in that year. Evangelical unionism soon spread to embrace other groups, such as tramway workers, riggers, boatmen, blacksmiths, bakers, and flour-mill workers. Even more significant was the growth of unions among unskilled workers. The Railway Workers' Union was formed to rival the ASRS, and the Dockers' Union set up branches in Cardiff, Newport and Swansea. It seemed as if the contagion of industrial unrest was unstoppable and it even infected schoolchildren in Swansea in October 1889. Teachers were assaulted and several boys were fined. These new unions spearheaded the new working-class militancy which appeared in the years after 1914. It was in south Wales that the actual struggle for the unions' defence of the right to strike without financial penalties took place in the celebrated Taff Vale Railway strike of 1900. The railwaymen were forced to pay £23,000 damages to the company and their right to strike was questioned by the judiciary. But the incident merely spurred the railwaymen into further militant activity after 1906.

In the 1870s and 1880s the idea of direct labour representation began to grow in importance. Working men, especially after the franchise reform of 1884 and the local government changes of 1888, were flexing their political muscles and claiming a voice in determining political representation. In north Wales the quarrymen of Caernarfonshire had contributed to the Liberal triumph of 1868 and the recapture of the seat in 1880; while the workers of Blaenau Ffestiniog had demonstrated their political radicalism by putting up their own Independent Liberal candidate in the 1885 by-election. In Rhondda the miners returned Mabon in 1885, when he appeared as a Lib-Lab candidate against the official Liberal. There were tensions also between the official Liberals and the working class in Carmarthenshire, Caernarfonshire, and Merthyr; and the crux of the matter was the lack of working-class representation in local Liberal associations. In some ways the Liberal Government of 1880–85 presented a second chance for the party to realize the expectations of the labouring classes. At the 1885 election, however, only thirteen working men went to the polls in England and Wales, eleven of whom were successful. The following year fifteen stood as candidates, and ten were successful. In the meantime, the idea of labour representation was making slow but steady progress in Wales, as in Britain as a whole.

Indeed, there was only one real challenge to the Liberals in this period, and that was the growth of the Labour movement. 'Mabonism', with its essential props of class harmony and co-operation, gave way to class conflict after the débâcle of 1898. Socialist ideas gradually penetrated the coalfields and tightened their hold on the working classes. The political and ideological upheaval was accelerated by a variety of factors: first, there was the growth of the Independent Labour Party in south Wales from 1898 to 1905, and in the north-east, at Wrexham and Rhos. The ILP claimed ninety-five branches in the south and nine in the north by 1910. It had infiltrated the slate-quarrying districts of Caernarfonshire and Merioneth, as well as the industrial heartland of south Wales. There were ILP strongholds from Llanelli to Newport, with particularly energetic branches at Briton Ferry and Aberdare. Secondly, the increased militancy of the South Wales Miners' Federation now turned to political matters and acted as the principal promoter of the Labour Party. New miners' agents like Charles Stanton in Aberdare, David Watts Morgan in Rhondda, and Vernon Hartshorn in Maesteg challenged the old order of Mabonism and urged the workers to commit themselves to the Labour movement. In 1908, when the Miners' Federation of Great Britain voted in favour of affiliating to the Labour Party, the Welsh miners voted with the majority.

Thirdly, the ILP and the tutorial classes of the Central Labour College after 1909, owed much to the democratic and educational traditions of Welsh Nonconformity and, in particular, to the Nonconformist academies, the Sunday schools. The new union activists often spoke warmly of their experiences in these pantheons of learning, and many were deeply moved by the 1904 revival. Some regarded it as yet another visitation, an apocalyptic symbol of imminent change and transformation.

Finally, the influx of new immigrants from the 1890s onwards brought an ethnic and generational change to the coalfield. Young men were moving in from the English counties and many of them were quite impatient of the sterile and tortoise-like procedures of Mabonism. These young activists challenged the political and industrial framework of the south Wales coalfield and, by 1906, a new industrial ethos prevailed in south Wales. Socialism and unionism gradually became the new religion of the working classes, and the language of the new creed was English. The rejection of Welsh was a symbolic gesture, combining both the rejection of the political philosophy of Lib-Labism and the affirmation of new solidarities, a novel idealistic posture.

The Welsh Nation

A National Revival

Nationhood is probably as old as the Welsh themselves. The Venerable Bede cited the difference between the Welsh and the Anglo-Saxons as early as 597. At the turn of the last century two forces contributed to the rise of Nationalism in Wales. The first was the coming of industry. Industrialization led to an increase in the number of Welsh-speakers and it provided jobs for them. It produced also some towns of sizeable proportions around which national institutions emerged — colleges, museums, presses, and churches. The other factor of supreme importance was the growth of Nonconformity as the religion of Wales. The chapels nurtured a feeling of Welshness, and Nonconformity almost became synonymous with Welshness. The Nonconformists protected the language and the history of Wales; what they could not achieve was the creation of political and administrative unity. There was no focus for national life and no specifically Welsh administrative institutions.

There were some voices, even among the respectable ranks of Victorian Nonconformity, who felt that the cries of cultural nationalism were not sufficient to protect the soul of nationhood. Michael D. Jones was one such figure. He went much further than most of his contemporaries in arguing for the existence of Wales as a political community. He sensed that a nation's future depended on her will to survive, and that the fate of a language rested on the will and moral choice of her people. He appreciated also that the fate of the Welsh language was a political matter and that official status was an essential prerequisite for the safety of the language. Above all, he politicized the whole concept of nationalism and rejected the half-hearted measure of disestablishment. He felt that the Liberals were committing a grievous error in putting dis-establishment as an important plank in their programme. He would accept nothing short of home rule for Wales; and the experiment to establish a colony in Patagonia was, in some sense, an attempt to realize that dream.

Someone who took up this theme was Robert Ambrose Jones, or Emrys ap Iwan (1851–1906), a Methodist minister from the Vale of Clwyd. He was a lonely, sometimes eccentric, and often vilified figure. A well-travelled and gifted linguist, he criticized his typical countryman for being a hypocrite, a philistine, a parochial and un-European figure, who had been led astray by an ignorant bourgeoisie. Like Michael D. Jones, he firmly believed that the individual Welshman would determine the fate of his nation, and that the nation's destiny rested on the existence of the Welsh language. He argued that the language was the only defence against annihilation: imperialism, capitalism and utilitarianism were the enemies of Wales. He advocated Europe as the sphere in which Wales should find contentment and growth. From 1876 to 1903 he was a frequent contributor to the press and the lengthy letter became his standard literary form. His political writings concentrated on four basic themes: the fate of Welsh and its teaching in schools and at home; the attack on imperialism; his defence of Ireland and support for the Irish question; and his constant appeal for home rule for Wales. In April 1892 he wrote to *Y Geninen* urging his countrymen to establish a Welsh National Party at the next general election.

From the 1880s onwards there emerged a more robust, vital, and evangelical national confidence. A combination of factors coalesced to produce a national renaissance: first, there was the effect of nationalist sentiments which had swept through Europe since 1848 and had produced a sense of national consciousness and identity in many European countries. Secondly, the growth of political democracy and franchise reform was enabling Welshmen to challenge the fortresses of civic and social inequalities. Thirdly, economic expansion brought new prosperity and confidence to the Principality, and provided Wales with a wealthy professional and mercantile class who would assume the mantle of political and social leadership.

Of paramount importance was a fourth factor, a cultural renaissance in the last quarter of the century. This had many characteristics: in 1885 a Society was founded by Beriah Gwynfe Evans for the Utilization of the Welsh Language, whose aim was to promote the use of the composition, grammar and translation of Welsh in schools; after 1880 the National Eisteddfod assumed a new status, which was given national recognition when W.E. Gladstone, the Prime Minister, visited the Wrexham Eisteddfod in 1888; at Oxford intelligent young Welshmen of the calibre of John Morris-Jones, O.M. Edwards and Daniel Lleufer Thomas, were forming a new society of Welsh-speaking undergraduates, Cymdeithas Dafydd ap Gwilym, in 1886; the writing of Welsh history was pioneered by John Edward Lloyd, who produced his history of Wales before the Edwardian conquest in 1913; there was a new interest in the language, its structure and technical aspects, and the pioneer in this field was John Morris-Jones, whose major contribution *Welsh Grammar: Phonology and Accidence*, appeared also in 1913.

Perhaps the most obvious political manifestation of this cultural awakening was the emergence of the *Cymru Fydd* movement in the 1880s. The *Cymru Fydd* League was formed in 1886, and the first branch established in London. This was followed by a second branch at Liverpool in 1887. The first branch in Wales was set up in Barry in 1891. The initial emphasis in these early branches was almost entirely cultural and literary; but from 1888 onwards there was a new note in *Cymru Fydd* circles as those sympathizers in Liberal ranks began calling for Welsh home rule. T.E. Ellis, a rising star in the Liberal party, delivered a famous speech at Bala in September 1890 in which he appealed for a Welsh parliament. In April 1890 David Lloyd George was elected for the Caernarfon boroughs, and he soon began pushing for this more political version of a *Cymru Fydd* vision. Ellis and others slowly found themselves being relegated to the sidelines as the angry young Radicals tried to make home rule the central plank of the Welsh Liberal Party's programme.

After the 1892 parliamentary election, the Liberals were returned with a slender majority of forty which rested on the balance of thirty-one Welsh Liberals. The fortunes of the *Cymru Fydd* supporters were given a sudden, distinct fillip. In August 1894 a national *Cymru Fydd* League was formed at Llandrindod Wells and in January 1895 a new magazine called *Young Wales* was launched. In April 1895 the *Cymru Fydd* League merged with the North Wales Liberal Federation and the scene was set for a dialogue with the South Wales Liberal Federation and its chairman, D.A. Thomas, MP, the opulent coalowner. Although Thomas had pioneered the *Cymru Fydd* cause, he and his followers were now unsure of the implications of a merger with the North; and the bone of discontent was the secularization of church property. The South felt that Glamorgan and Monmouthshire would lose out to the rapacious men of the North and negotiations eventually crumbled over the proposed council for allocating church endowments. At the famous Newport meeting of January 1896 the aspirations of *Cymru Fydd* and nationalistic hopes of Lloyd George were shattered. A crucial motion to merge the South Wales Federation with the *Cymru Fydd* League was lost by 133 votes to 70, and Lloyd George, who had addressed the assembly, fled for his life as the meeting erupted into a cacophony of abuse and protest.

It was a sad ending to the home rule episode and little would be heard of the issue until E.T. John campaigned for self-government in the years after 1910. The failure of *Cymru Fydd* revealed some underlying divisions in Welsh political and social life, echoes of which would reverberate through the years: there was a distinct split between North and South which militated against political unity; the movement displayed a lack of nationalist sentiment among the populace; thirdly, there appeared to be a cleavage between those who promoted a cultural and literary form of Nationalism, and the political protagonists; fourthly, a schism had emerged between the Welsh hinterland, and the industrial and coastal parts of Wales; and finally, *Cymru Fydd* was clearly undermined by divisions within the Liberal associations in Wales, as Liberal voters opted not for the apparent impotence of separation but for the expected fruits of British Liberal imperialism.

SUGGESTED READING

E.W. Evans, *The Miners of South Wales* (Cardiff, 1961).

R. Brinley Jones (ed.), *The Anatomy of Wales* (Glamorgan, 1972).

K.O. Morgan, *Wales in British Politics, 1868–1922* (Cardiff, 1970).

K.O. Morgan, *The Rebirth of a Nation, Wales 1880–1980* (Oxford, 1981).

C. Parry, *The Radical Tradition in Welsh Politics* (Hull, 1970).

D. Smith (ed.), *A People and a Proletariat: Wales, 1780–1980* (London, 1980).

G. Williams, *Religion, Language and Nationality in Wales* (Cardiff, 1979).

G.A. Williams, *When was Wales?* (London, 1985).

Articles:

R.M. Jones, 'A Trade Union in Nineteenth-Century Gwynedd: The North Wales Quarrymen's Union, 1874–1900', *Trans. Caer Hist. Soc.*, 35 (1974).

W.R. Lambert, 'The Welsh Sunday Closing Act, 1881', *W.H.R.*, 6 (1972–3).

K.O. Morgan, 'Cardiganshire Politics: The Liberal Ascendancy, 1885–1923', *Ceredigion*, 5 (1964–7).

B. Thomas, 'A Cauldron of Rebirth: Population and the Welsh Language in the Nineteenth Century', *W.H.R.*, 13 (1987).

L.J. Williams, 'The New Unionism in South Wales, 1889–92', *W.H.R.*, 1 (1960–3).

Conclusion

JUST over 200 years ago a period of unprecedented industrialization opened in the history of Wales. In the second half of the eighteenth century an iron industry was established by immigrant ironmasters, subsidized by English capital, on the northern rim of the south Wales coalfield. They transformed south Wales into the most important sector of the British iron industry until about 1850. The second phase of industrialization arched the period 1850 to 1914, when the Welsh coalfield supplied steam and anthracite coals to markets all over the world. During this era most of the capital was local, and a considerable proportion of the coalowners were Welsh. By 1891 Welsh coal output was 30 million tons, and by 1913 it had risen to 56 million tons. In that year alone, shipments overseas accounted for 38.7 million tons. Exports dominated the trade of the south Wales ports in the years before the First World War, and in 1913 they accounted for 89 per cent of the total trade. In the last quarter of the nineteenth century and in the early years of the new century south Wales had become a boom economy, based on a flourishing export trade and fuelled by a massive immigration.

These were the years in which the fortunes of the Welsh language were determined, and recent scholarship has shown that the 1890s were the watershed years. In the decades before then the forces of assimilation were stronger over most of Wales than was the wave of English immigration. The growth of the Welsh-speaking population was the result not only of in-migration from the Welsh rural areas but also of the natural increase in the industrial zones. In the first decade of the new century, however, over 100,000 immigrants from outside Wales streamed into the industrial valleys. The proportion of Welsh-speakers in the population of Wales fell from 49.9 per cent in 1901 to 43.5 per cent in 1911. This triggered off a steady slide so

319

that by 1981 the proportion of Welsh-speakers had fallen to 18.9 per cent of the population.

The 1851 census of religious worship showed that Wales was fast becoming a Nonconformist nation. In 1851 there were 2,770 Welsh Nonconformist chapels in Wales capable of accommodating 611,000 people, or 70 per cent of all church accommodation. After mid-century a religious culture developed in Wales: it was strongly and robustly Nonconformist in character, and it determined, to a large extent, the political and social developments thereafter. It seems an inescapable conclusion that religion, language and nationality were once more inextricably linked, and that the period from 1850 to 1914 encompassed the golden years of Welsh Nonconformity.

The new society forged by industrialization produced a very different brand of politics. A distinction between the closed, exclusive society of the rural communities and the relatively open and receptive industrial regions seems to have developed in the years after 1815. The national reform societies and radical organizations of various commitments fastened on to the industrial towns as the places of most likely success. After 1840 industrialization and Nonconformity were the pillars which upheld political consciousness.

Despite the fact that Welsh agriculture was relatively poor and under-capitalized throughout most of the nineteenth century, the undeniable conclusion to be drawn about most of Welsh economic and social life in the years between 1815 and 1914 is that it was overwhelmingly successful and thriving. The social structure responded to this commercial success; and Cardiff, the capital city of Wales, began to look like a metropolis by 1914. There was economic affluence, professional advancement, social confidence, a religious optimism, and a distinct cultural vitality. The Edwardian years from 1905 onwards were, in comparative terms, a halcyon period for Wales and Welshmen. But there was also a distinct undercurrent of unrest, unease and conflict, both at home and abroad. Shadows lurked in the peaceful quarters of Edwardian Wales; and few Welshmen would have believed that the country would soon be plunged into a world war, and into the despair of economic stagnation, industrial conflict and mass unemployment.

Index

326 *Index*

Llanarmon Dyffryn Ceiriog British
  school, 101
Llanbedr National school, 109
Llandaff Diocesan Board of
  Education, 250
Llandaff Diocesan Church Extension
  Society, 230–1, 234, 236–7, 250
Llandaff National school, 109
Llandovery National school, 106,
  107
Llandygái National schools, 117, 258
Llandysilio National school, 109
Llanelli copper industry, 17
Llanelli Copperworks' school, 115,
  252, 254–5, 258, 263
Llanerch-yr-Aur lead mine, 21
Llanfachreth British school, 101
Llanfawr British school, 101
Llangefni National school, 106
Llangeler, population 1851–1901,
  175
Llangollen British school, 101
Llangyfelach Church school, 116
Llanllwchaearn National school, 109
Llanover, Lady (Augusta Hall), 79,
  227
Llansamlet National colliery school,
  256
Llansantffraid National school, 109
Llantrisant British school, 101
Llantwit Major National school, 108
*Llawlyfr ar Hanes y Diwygiadau
  Crefyddol yng Nghymru*, 89–90
Llewelyn, J.T.D., Penllergaer, 56
Llewelyn, John, Penllergaer, 157
Llewelyns, Penllergaer, 116
Lloyd, John Edward, 316
Llwynypia school, 257
Llyfr Tonau Cynulleidfaol, 222
local government, 276–8, 305–6
  Act 1872, 275
  Act 1888, 269
  Act 1894, 55
Locket's Merthyr Collieries Ltd., 189

Mabers, G.W., 235
Mabon (*see* Abraham, William)
Mabon's Day, 190
Macadam, 34
Machynlleth National school, 107
Mackworth, Sir Humphrey, 111, 114
Madocks, William Alexander, 99
Maerdy collieries, 188–9

Maesteg Ironworks, 27
magistrates, 136–7, 141, 235
Magna Carta Association, 292–3
Mainwaring, Townsend, 290
Mansels, Glamorgan, 32
Margam National school, 105
Margam Tinworks, 181
  school, 115
Marsh, Herbert, Bishop of Llandaff,
  83–4
Marsh, T.E., Llanidloes magistrate,
  147–8
Martin, E.P., 185
Martin, Edward, Swansea, 32
Mathias, Revd T.D., Merthyr, 286
Maynooth College, 173
McKinley tariff, 58, 63, 182, 183, 303
Melincrythan Tinworks' school, 256
Melingriffith forge, 15
Melingriffith Tinworks, 98, 115
  school, 98, 115
Menelaus, William, 184
Merllyn lead mine, 20
Merthyr Guardian, 74, 222
Merthyr Reform League, 281
Merthyr Star, 290
Merthyr Telegraph, 290
Merthyr Tydfil, 11, 12
  condition in 1850, 44–5
  crime in 1850, 70, 71–4, 86
  election 1868, 284, 288–90, 292
  population increase, 75–6
  riots 1831, 68, 123, 163–5
Miall, Edward, 282
Mid Wales Railway, 192
Miers, John, 182
militia, 138–9
Mills, Revd J., 103
Mimosa, vessel, 64
Miner and Workman's Advocate, 286
Moggridge, John, 157
Monmouthshire Canal, 36, 37, 38
Montgomeryshire Agricultural
  Society, 197–8
Morewood, E., and Co., 182, 186
Morfa Tinplate Works, 255
Morgan, Sir Charles, Tredegar, 6,
  100, 156, 158
Morgan, David Watts, Rhondda,
  313
Morgan, Edward, 135–6
Morgan, George Osborne, 290, 292,
  293, 303